Early Childhood Mathematics

Susan Sperry Smith
Cardinal Stritch College

Allyn and Bacon
Boston   London   Toronto   Sydney   Tokyo   Singapore

Series Editor: Frances Helland
Editorial Assistant: Kate Wagstaffe
Editorial-Production Administrator: Joe Sweeney
Editorial-Production Service: Walsh Associates
Composition Buyer: Linda Cox
Manufacturing Buyer: Suzanne Lareau
Cover Administrator: Suzanne Harbison

Library of Congress Cataloging-in-Publication Data

Sperry Smith, Susan.
    Early childhood mathematics / Susan Sperry Smith.
        p.   cm.
    Includes bibliographical references and index.
    ISBN 0-205-16757-8
        1. Mathematics—Study and teaching (Early childhood)   I. Title.
QA135.5.S579   1996
372.7'044—dc20   96-22759
                                                                            CIP

Printed in the United States of America
10 9 8 7 6 5 4 3 2 1   00 99 98 97 96

For Dickson and Tracy

Contents

Preface

This book is intended as a preservice mathematics methods textbook for prospective teachers of children ages 3 to 8 years old. It also gives in-service early childhood educators a helpful resource for their classroom activities.

The contents of this book highlight the essential mathematical ideas that form the foundation for a comprehensive early childhood mathematics curriculum. With this in mind, the trio of national standards textbooks published by the National Council of Teacher of Mathematics (1989, 1991, & 1995) guide the selection of specific mathematics content. These authoritative guides are referenced throughout the chapters.

The contents of this book encourage the teacher to create an active learning environment that fosters curiosity, confidence, and persistence. The knowledge of important mathematical relationships, number sense, and the ability to solve problems are three key ingredients to successful acquisition of the discipline of mathematics in the early years.

A textbook that meets the needs of adult learners must address their real fears and anxiety about mathematics. These students bring their own past experiences to the college classroom or workshop setting. Chapter 1 addresses these fears as well as myths about the study of mathematics perhaps gleaned from their own educational background. Chapter 2 highlights the general relationship between the English language and the language of math. It affords teachers of young children an overview of the concepts developed during the critical language learning years, especially as they relate to mathematics.

The majority of this book (Chapters 3–11) addresses the way in which children develop knowledge about specific mathematics content. Efforts were made to make the material interesting and accessible for today's student, without sacrificing the need for a solid research base that serves as the foundation for best practice. Most references are from current sources, although some older sources are still of importance to our understanding of how children think about mathematical ideas. Each of these chapters contains the following unique features:

- An overview of key mathematical principles.
- A wealth of ideas on how informal and formal learning occurs around a particular mathematical strand.
- Specific references to a great many nursery rhymes, children's songs, and children's literature can be found within the chapter as an integral part of exploration of each content area.
- A specific set of activity cards to help beginning teachers get started. These are found in the section Ready-Set-Math.

- A section on ways adult learners can extend their own experiences of a particular topic, Activities and Study Questions. These activities attempt to link mathematics to an adult's view of mathematics and everyday life and to promote critical thinking about mathematics.
- A collection of sources of interesting ideas and classroom activities that deserve greater study. Many of these articles provide an excellent springboard for classroom teachers, and can be an inspiration to beginning teachers. These resources are found in the section called Further Reading.
- A listing of classroom equipment that may help the beginning teacher prepare a stimulating environment.

The unique learning needs of children from diverse cultures and of children who are disabled are discussed in several sections of the book. Of particular interest is the information on the learning characteristics of these children, found in Chapter 1, the information on planning for instruction found in Chapter 13, and methods of alternative assessment, found in Chapter 12. Prospective teachers need many opportunities to study methods of instruction and opportunities to practice meeting the needs of the underserved in *actual* classroom settings. These important experiences must be a part of all teacher training programs.

Finally, the integration of technology, such as calculators and computers, is addressed in many places in this textbook. Many schools face severe budget constraints and have not tapped into this rich source to extend mathematical learning. A list of excellent software choices for the early childhood classroom, or for use at home, can be found in Appendix A.

In summary, there was a need to bring together the emerging research base on how young children approach the study of mathematical relationships with the reality of daily life in an early childhood classroom. The final chapter illustrates a thematic approach that could be developed from curricular webs on topics of interest to young children. These activities are not meant to be rigid or unyielding. Rather, they might be sources of ideas that trigger creativity in all of us.

Young children are the greatest resource for curricular planning. They have the imagination and zest for life so many older children and adults have lost. Our work is always a joy when they benefit from our careful attention to their vision.

Acknowledgments

I wish to thank many people who helped me during the preparation of this book. Their advice, encouragement, and support meant so much to me throughout the process. I appreciate the help of Sr. Gabrielle Kowalski and Dr. Robert Pavlik, who reviewed the contents of this book. A number of people contributed to the preparation of the manuscript: Joanne Froelich, Mark Gilroy, Pat Gilroy, Mary Lou Glasl, Joyce Schaefer, Dickson Smith, Betty Wyatt, Mei-Hua Charity Yang, and especially my secretary, Mary Graf. I am eternally grateful to each of them for their willingness to help. Finally, I want to thank my editor at Allyn & Bacon, Nancy Forsyth, and her editorial assistant, Kate Wagstaffe, for their unwavering support and helpful advice. Their enthusiasm and constructive ideas made the writing of this work much easier than I had originally thought possible.

I would also like to acknowledge the following reviewers: Anne Dorsey, University of Cincinnati; Claire Graham, Framingham State College; Susan Johnson, Northwestern College; Janice D. Kinard; Nancy Lutz, Clark State Community College; and Meghan Twiest, Indiana University of Pennsylvania.

1 Mathematics and You

THE KINDERGARTEN CHILDREN in Mrs. Martz's class sit in a circle, eagerly waiting for story time to begin. Today's story, *Miss Spider's Tea Party*, is new to everyone. A lonely spider wants to welcome guests for tea. Groups of bugs arrive in sets of one to nine, but quickly depart before they become "lunch" for the spider. They misunderstand her intentions, and finally a moth encourages eleven guests to stay. Everyone has a wonderful time, including the class.

The children enjoy naming the bugs and counting the pictures. They like to retell the sequence and act out the story. They add new characters to the narrative. On a warm spring the children decide to go outside and have a tea party. The children have been exploring the natural world of insects and spiders. Mathematics becomes a part of the daily life of the classroom in both planned and spontaneous activities. One goal of this book is to help you see how mathematics evolves in the early childhood curriculum. Before studying mathematics as a scholarly discipline, it is helpful to take a closer look at mathematics and you.

How You Were Taught: Then and Now

"One, two, buckle my shoe. . . ." Math is child's play. Children enjoy math and often play math games for fun. They pick math-related activities for free time and indoor recess. When you were young, you may have felt the same way.

But something happens to many people as they move from enjoyable informal math to school math. Perhaps you were subjected to repetition of already learned material, year after year. Then new topics were rushed or skipped altogether. You tried to catch on to superficial rules, key words, or tricks in pursuit of the one right answer.

When you asked the teacher for help, you may have heard the same explanation that didn't make sense the first time. In summary, for many of you school math was an exasperating experience. As you progressed through middle school and high school, each new course brought more difficult material seemingly divorced from any common sense meaning.

That was "then"—you are part of "now." The philosophy, focus, curriculum, learning strategies, and methods are changing. Young people deserve a strong foundation in math. For all children to succeed you will need to teach differently from the way most of you were taught. This is an enormous challenge. It is easy to revert back to the old comfortable way you saw your math teachers use every day for many years. To help you prepare for the future, this chapter examines a number of overriding issues. Pay careful attention to how you feel as well as what you know about these possible barriers to success.

Math Anxiety—You Can Handle It

Math anxiety is real. A mild case of uneasiness may occur when you are asked to divide up the restaurant check or fill out the short form (1040EZ) for your taxes. You avoid required math classes until the last possible moment.

Or you could have a full-blown case in which you get sweaty palms, feel physically sick and feel faint, and are racked with overriding feelings of dread. You have a panic attack and cannot perform on a test or in the classroom. You seek out tutors, but they may or may not be able to help you. Just learning the lesson is not what you need. Feelings of panic paralyze you. Strong emotions put a serious barrier between you and your success. Your career goals are often in jeopardy.

Perhaps you have been told that you may have a learning disability in math. To find out for sure you need a professional assessment. Very few people have a real math disability (Bender, 1995). Most likely you need help of a different nature.

If you suffer from a mild case of math anxiety, realize that you are not alone. Some experts say that a majority of Americans feel the way you do. Math may not be your favorite subject, but you can do it well if you take the time and have a patient teacher who uses multiple examples and manipulatives to teach the concept. Perhaps you can work with a partner both inside and outside of class. You have a right to ask for extra help. Asking for another way of looking at the problem is the bright thing to do. Having questions doesn't mean you are stupid. Go to the library and find books such as *Mind Over Math* (Kogelman & Warren, 1978) for a fresh approach to your problem.

If you suffer from a severe case of math anxiety, you may need a trained counselor to help you overcome your fears. Counselors can use methods such as the ones employed with people who have high anxiety or phobias (such as fear of heights or snakes). Your fear is a learned behavior and as such can be unlearned. Positive self-talk is key. Say to yourself, "I can succeed in math if I work hard." While you are struggling with your own problem, please do not pass on your negative feelings to your students or (if you are a parent) to your own children. Avoid telling young children statements like, "I can't help you, I was never any good at math in school," or "Ask your dad" (without even trying to read the problem), or "I hate math." If you are teaching and come to a confusing section of your math textbook, avoid making uncomplimentary remarks such as, "Most of math doesn't make any sense, and here's another example. I'm not sure what you pupils are supposed to learn from this unit." A positive approach might be to skip the textbook explanation and ask another professional for a better way to teach the material. Math anxiety can be overcome, and every student needs confidence that math will be a positive experience.

Ten Myths About Teaching Mathematics to All Children

Many people grow up with false ideas or misinformation about how children learn math. If you believe these myths or pass them on to other people, it may impede your chances to teach math well. The classroom examples in this section of the book often refer to the traditional educational practices in the primary grades. During those formative years you formed your first impressions of mathematics as a discipline.

1. "Some people are good at math and some people aren't."
Perhaps you believe that boys are better at math than girls. In fact there are very few differences in mathematics performance until about seventh grade.

Many cultural practices can explain the difference rather than lack of mathematical talent (Meyer & Fennema, 1988). Think about alternative reasons for this occurrence and how society's view of women's roles is changing.

You may have heard that Asian students are better at math than American students. Research shows that whatever differences occur in later years are not the result of a head start or innate ability. At the preschool and kindergarten level, American and Asian children generally perform at the same level. A challenging math curriculum and a strong motivation to work hard on school subjects account for the later differences (Song & Ginsberg, 1987; Shigematsu & Sowder, 1994).

Sometimes people think that speed or quickness with the basic facts has something to do with being good at math. In first or second grade a child looks around the room and sees that everyone has finished a worksheet. The fastest students on a three-minute timed test are put into the top math group. Those students are seen as good at math while the slower student is not. In fact, speed has very little to do with mathematical ability. Speed emphasizes a powerful memory over understanding the concept, and it is not how mathematicians work. A mathematician may spend days, weeks, months, or years on a problem. The problem can be set aside, or mulled over.

Doing math is more like doing a 1,000-piece jigsaw puzzle, where you are finished except for the blue sky. You try a piece, then another. Perhaps you line up the remaining pieces a certain way. You work at it and then stop for a while. Persistence and intuition are as important as speed. Taking more time to solve a math problem doesn't mean that you are less capable than someone else.

2. "Mathematics is the same as arithmetic."
A granddaughter was overheard telling her grandma, "We don't have arithmetic, we have math." She is right. Arithmetic refers to a narrow view of the subject. The emphasis is on learning the basic facts, memorizing how to compute, and applying these number skills to consumer needs such as a checkbook or figuring miles-per-gallon. Mathematics holds a broader view. It contains a number of interrelated strands, including measurement, geometry, statistics, and probability. Besides paper and pencil computation, a variety of skills using mental math are taught.

The National Council of Teachers of Mathematics (NCTM) *Curriculum and Evaluation Standards* (1989) give teachers an excellent guide for developing a comprehensive math curriculum. Some students may have more immediate success with some strands, such as geometry, over number work. But all students can master the essential concepts in all strands.

3. "You need a textbook to really teach math."

School district personnel adopt a textbook series as a way to help implement the written math curriculum. A textbook series can create a sense of uniformity across grades, impart a philosophy to teachers new to the district, and stimulate change among the experienced personnel. Recent editions of textbook series claim to follow the guidelines as set forth in the National Standards (NCTM, 1989). But there is no substitute for excellent teacher preparation about the mathematical strands that are appropriate for each child's developmental level. The living curriculum exists in the teacher's head and is created to fit the needs of a particular group of students. Students' interests and prior knowledge differ from year to year. The best textbook is of little help to a poor teacher.

The fact is that many good teachers do not want or need a student textbook in the lower grades. Instead, math is created from everyday activities (i.e., shopping at a store), thematic units (i.e., dinosaurs), or children's literature (i.e., *The Tale of Peter Rabbit*). Good teachers do not fear that they will stray too far from the general math objectives for their grades or not cover enough material without a book. They have a sense of confidence that is contagious. Their students think about math, experiment, record the results, and reflect on their learning.

4. "Calculators will rot children's brains."

Many parents and school board members believe that access to calculators undermines mastering of basic facts and procedures. They feel widespread usage will result in a generation of adults who can't add. Also, in the past, students in special education classes were taught to use a calculator as a last resort. It seemed like the easy way out when years of drill had failed. It will take a long time to undo this powerful myth.

The fact is that over 80 research studies consistently show that using calculators for instruction and testing results in superior math achievement and high levels of student self-confidence (Hembree & Dessart, 1992).

To use a calculator accurately, the student must be able to estimate and/or round-off the approximate answer. The human brain knows how to find a correct answer, not the machine.

The calculator is more than a number cruncher. In the early grades the calculator can illustrate number patterns. Repeated adding of the same number shows a form of early multiplication. Repeated subtracting of the same number from a larger number shows a way of thinking about division. More examples of how to use calculators creatively are found throughout the book.

Most important, using a calculator saves valuable time for problem solving. It frees us from the mundane tasks that we could do longhand, for more meaningful exploration of a math topic. The rule of thumb is, "What would an adult do in everyday life?" An adult would add up a long string of numbers on a calculator. Once the basic concept of adding has been mastered, it makes sense for the young child to do the same thing.

5. "Computation means figuring with paper and pencil."

That is what most adults learned in school. Little emphasis was placed on the variety of computational skills needed in the real world. The four ways people use numbers are:

1. Mental math with estimating
2. Mental math for accuracy
3. Paper and pencil math with estimating
4. Paper and pencil math for accuracy

Mental math with estimating happens often in everyday life. For example, you are at the grocery checkout counter, look in your cart, and calculate the approximate amount of groceries you've gathered. Then you make a decision, "Do I have enough cash, or do I want to write a check?" At the restaurant the meal is over, and it's time to pay the bill. You look at the total and calculate the tip. In either example you came close enough by estimating the numbers in order to make a decision.

Mental math for accuracy happens when someone asks you to "add 89 cents and 89 cents in your head." Most of you round up to 90 cents and subtract the two pennies. Some of you start with the ones place and add "9 + 9." Then you regroup and add the tens column. This method is similar to paper and pencil math. Neither approach is wrong. They are two different ways of solving the same problem. Mental math generally relies on calculating using the fives, the tens, and the doubles. There is no need to write the numbers down on paper.

Paper and pencil math with estimating happens when you decide to buy wallpaper. It is impractical to go to the store and say, "I'll take four rolls." Instead you use paper and pencil and a tape measure to calculate the number of rolls you'll need. But you cannot get your final sum down to the square inch. There are windows, doors, and fixtures to consider. The pattern repeats at certain intervals. Besides, wallpaper is sold by the roll. So at some point you must decide whether your estimate is close enough.

Many professionals use paper and pencil math with estimating. Media polls on the likely outcome of an election report the results with the degree of error present in the survey. Executives review data on the buying habits of consumers to decide whether to continue offering a product, increase production, or discontinue manufacturing the item. Every 10 years the census is taken. It is impossible to count every person in the country. Efforts are made to get the count within a small margin of error. Paper and pencil data are collected and analyzed by millions of computers around the world. The data are full of errors and never complete. Yet adults make their living from their best judgments about what it all means. The study of statistics and probability aids in making more informed decisions.

Paper and pencil math for accuracy happens when you balance your checkbook. You add and subtract on paper. Surveys show that approximately 80 to 90% of elementary school math is spent on figuring out the answers to worksheets or textbook problems in the basic areas of addition, subtraction, multiplication, division, fractions, decimals, and percent. Because students have had so much drill in these skills, they score much better on this kind of basic math than they do on solving story problems. Unfortunately, in some textbook series, basic algorithms are repeated at every grade level. The material is redundant, so the wise teacher pretests for mastery. Then valuable time can be spent on more challenging math units.

6. "Manipulatives teach mathematics."

By themselves manipulatives do not teach anything. In fact, studies show that students can acquire a rote meaning for major concepts by using manipulatives as well as by the traditional verbal approaches. In one study, students moved Base 10 blocks across place value mats, without understanding this fundamental property of our number system (Ross, 1986).

A good manipulative bridges the gap between informal math and formal school math. To accomplish this objective, the manipulative must fit the developmental level of the child. For example, young children prefer "discrete" or individual counters when figuring out a problem. They want to count three beans and four beans in order to get seven beans. A "continuous" material like colored wooden rods, where a green rod represents three and a purple rod represents four, would be hard to use (Baroody, 1986).

Proportional materials such as beansticks are more appropriate for second graders. The abacus is nonproportional and helpful in displaying larger numbers for third graders. American money is a nonproportional system. A dime is not twice the size of a nickel, nor is a quarter five times the size of a nickel. The lack of a relationship between size and amount may explain why learning coin equivalencies is so difficult for young children.

A teacher can listen to the child's explanation of the math concept as taught with the manipulative. In many places in this book, and especially in Chapter 12, you will find many approaches to assessment. Having children communicate their own thinking about a particular problem provides one of your best clues to math success.

7. "You can learn math by listening and with plenty of drill."

In the past students spent much of their math class listening and watching the teacher explain a procedure. Perhaps some better students would come to the blackboard and solve the problem. Then a homework page was assigned, and the teacher circulated around the classroom giving extra help to a few puzzled pupils. The next day the homework was corrected by calling on individual students to respond with an answer. If your answer was correct, you were relieved, even if you didn't know why you got it right. If the answer was wrong, there was little time to figure out the cause of the error.

In today's classroom, the teaching/learning process is changed. Students actively think about a problem, attempt to solve it, and justify their approach. Lively discussion occurs in small groups, large groups, or with the teacher. The emphasis is on "doing math." The more you do it the better you'll become. It is no different than learning to dance or play basketball. Practice improves your skills. Drill takes on a new meaning. Timed tests are de-emphasized in the National Council of Teachers of Mathematics' Curriculum and Evaluation Standards for School Mathematics (1989) while increasing efficiency is encouraged by using games and appropriate computer software. Mastery of certain facts occurs at each grade level, but with an emphasis on meaning and with a longer time period for completion.

The professionals in each school district need to establish credible benchmarks to document learning and to hold teachers accountable for student progress. Otherwise, the early childhood curriculum can degenerate into a situation of fun and play with beans and sticks. Under the worst circumstances, students enter fourth grade with little or no knowledge of math. The benchmark assessment tools must use a wide variety of real life measures and be based on research about how young children really learn math. A set of recycled behavioral math objectives from previous decades is not adequate.

8. "You need to divide the class into three math groups."

In the past, many teachers assigned students to small groups for math instruction. There were "the redbirds, the bluebirds, and the buzzards." These groupings were often decided on the basis of arbitrary achievements, such as speed in reciting the basic facts. At times they were formed in first grade and remained fairly stable throughout the elementary school years. In the upper grades the top group attended a class in pre-algebra while the other groups took more arithmetic.

Teachers in the upper grades and in high school often used whole group instruction exclusively. This arrangement resulted in more time spent on a math topic and with less attention paid to individual student responses.

Now grouping is done in a more flexible manner. Certain groups emerge at every level. One group with special needs is the gifted. These children can be identified as early as age three. At each grade level, developmental benchmarks occur that separate students by ability. In kindergarten/first grade, some students can "conserve numbers" as measured by Piaget's Tests of Conservation and some cannot. In first grade, some students can solve complex story problems while other students cannot. In second/third grade, some students readily exhibit a basic understanding of place value system, while others are still forming a way to think about the concept. By the spring of a school year many differences between students may be apparent. (Occasionally a large group of students is very homogeneous, so no sharp contrasts appear.) The key to a decision about grouping is whether each pupil is receiving a *challenging* math experience.

The curricular topic also affects grouping. Pattern activities are generally done alone. Other activities, such as dramatic play in "The Little Store" are done with cooperative groups. Classroom examples found in each chapter will suggest the grouping options other teachers have used with success.

However, many times during the school year children should be given the opportunity to solve a problem or a piece of a problem individually. All students need time to think and formulate an answer. Then they can share their ideas with a partner or contribute them to a group. It can be easy to sit back quietly and wait for someone else to do all the work. But math is learned by doing, not just by listening.

9. "There isn't enough time to do assessment in a real classroom."

Good teachers recognize that "there never seems to be enough time to get everything done that I planned." Organizing materials, changing from one activity to another, even getting ready for recess, takes time. Experienced teachers handle routine chores such as taking attendance or collecting field trip permission slips efficiently. Precious moments are saved for instruction and learning. Some teachers naturally develop systems for staying ahead of complex tasks. Other teachers struggle with being "organizationally impaired."

Ongoing assessment is one key to effective teaching. Professionals constantly use their eyes and ears to judge the classroom climate and children's learning. Just as doctors and nurses chart a patient's progress several times a day, the teacher keeps a clipboard or notebook handy to record the day's events.

Notes and charts of pupil progress help plan tomorrow's activities. They become part of a wide variety of tools, including a review of student work, a collection of student products as found in a portfolio, and records of student interviews and teacher observations about a student's level of confidence, curiosity, and inventiveness.

Two criteria help make the assessment process manageable. First, the tools and tasks chosen should have "high utility" (Adelman & Taylor, 1982). High utility refers to choosing methods that will give the most accurate picture of what the child knows and feels about math. Newer methods favor work samples, student writing, interviews, and observation over standardized testing.

Second, the tools and tasks should pass the test of "economy" (Adelman & Taylor, 1982). Economy refers to whether there are resources of time, money, and expertise to carry out the plan. Some districts mandate elaborate, expensive, and time-consuming assessment procedures that do not fit the reality of the classroom as it exists. Extensive training may be needed to use the "rubric" (criteria for judging success) on an instrument. Money may be needed for substitute teachers to free up the time of the classroom teacher to conduct individual interviews. Field testing of any plan before school-wide or district-wide implementation will help refine a system that is workable and yields meaningful results.

10. "If you wait long enough, this 'new' curriculum will go away."

Veteran teachers have seen many reform movements come and go. In math they may have been asked to teach the "new math" or set theory. Recently, movements such as computer-assisted instruction, which promised to transform classroom learning, have yet to materialize. Perhaps they feel these latest efforts at math reform will dissipate too.

These efforts will not fail because first of all the NCTM Standards (1989, 1991, & 1995) and other position papers have widespread support among many professionals, including organizations that represent principals and school board members. The guidelines from these documents have been used to rewrite major commercial textbook series and are helping to reform assessment practices at the state and national levels.

Second, the heart and soul of the new curriculum is problem solving, especially as it relates to everyday life. The emphasis is on connecting meaning to math symbols, interrelating the various strands of math (the way many professionals do math), and solving interesting problems. Manipulatives are used to bridge the gap between informal learning and abstract ideas. These elements appeal to children, teachers, and parents.

The NCTM Standards set the direction but are not a grade level curriculum. This flexibility allows teachers and local curriculum specialists to design units and instructional plans suited to a particular school district. Professionals acknowledge that it will take 10 years or longer to see significant progress across the country.

Finally, the new math curriculum is accessible to students with a variety of learning styles and motivational interests. Units such as "popcorn math," "balloon math," or "baseball math" reach students from many backgrounds and abilities. All the elements are present for this reform movement to last and ultimately succeed.

Success for Every Child

Reaching underserved groups

It has been commonly acknowledged that the field of mathematics has been dominated by Anglo and Asian males (Sells, 1980). In 1991, the NCTM Board of Directors promulgated this statement:

> As a professional organization and as individuals within that organization, the Board of Directors sees the comprehensive mathematics education of every child as its most compelling goal.

By "every child" we mean specifically—

- students who have been denied access in any way to educational opportunities as well as those who have not;
- students who are African-American, Hispanic, American Indian, and other minorities as well as those who are considered to be a part of the majority;
- students who are female as well as those who are male
- students who have not been successful in school and in mathematics as well as those who have been successful[*] (p. 4)

Every student, regardless of race, gender or language, should participate in mathematics to the fullest extent possible. Access to college or technical training, to civil service positions, to many military careers or careers in general commerce, are available only to those individuals with knowledge of advanced mathematics. Tracking minority and special education students into remedial consumer math classes may contribute to lack of success in later life. These decisions are often made by well-meaning individuals who know little math themselves. Some units in consumer math, such as calculating interest on long-term loans, are as difficult as many algebra or geometry units. There can be a tendency to give up on formal education too soon, with the notion that the students are getting too old to gain a thorough understanding of math concepts. Rote seems quicker, but it is a bandage approach.

Students with limited English proficiency (LEP) need special consideration. LEP students benefit from instruction in both languages and incorporation of information from the student's culture into the content of the lessons (Tikunoff,

[*]Reprinted with permission from the *Professional Standards for Teaching Mathematics* (1991) by the National Council of Teachers of Mathematics.

1985). All students, regardless of native tongue, need instruction in the meaning of terms such as area and perimeter. And many students need additional time to process the teacher's words and to absorb their meaning.

The Seven Intelligences

Perhaps we can increase the probability that all children will succeed by offering a curriculum based on a wide variety of natural human abilities. Gardner and Hatch (1989) identified seven distinctive intelligences that are not necessarily assessed by IQ tests. In addition to the commonly assessed areas of logical/mathematical thinking and linguistic proficiency, these researchers added the following intelligences: musical, spatial, bodily/kinesthetic, interpersonal, and intrapersonal. Their research indicated that all children are "smart" in one or more ways and that these patterns emerge early in life. These areas of strengths may be avenues for reaching many students who do not easily learn by traditional methods.

How do these abilities relate to math instruction? In early childhood education, most teachers incorporate the seven areas naturally across the curriculum. Musical/rhythmic intelligence is used to discover and analyze pattern. Also, music and bodily/kinesthetic intelligence or movement often form the basis for counting games. Spatial intelligence helps students use geometry to create house plans, simple gardens, and pattern block "animals."

Interpersonal intelligence aids group leaders to guide their classmates in solving complex math problems. Intrapersonal abilities come into play as students talk or write about how they approached a math topic. It also affects whether students feel confident and curious about math.

Other researchers have studied this approach in depth. Maker, Nielson, and Rogers (1994) wrote an extensive article that illustrated how combining the research on multiple intelligences and the research on creativity/problem solving could result in exciting K–2 curricular activities. Their goal was to reach all children and to bring out the giftedness in children attending a large, multicultural school district. Several examples using mathematics as a base show how the research works in a practical way. A reflective teacher may wish to pursue further study about these promising psychological theories.

The Child Who Is Gifted

It is possible for a child prodigy in music, math, and chess to be discovered around the age of three. These children use very sophisticated strategies to solve problems and appear capable of solving far more complex mathematical tasks than other children. According to researchers, mathematically talented children were adept at the following problem solving tasks (Pendarvis, Howley, & Howley, 1990):

1. Organizing material
2. Recognizing patterns or rules
3. Changing the representation of the problem and recognizing patterns and rules in the new representation
4. Comprehending very complex structures and working within these structures
5. Reversing processes
6. Finding (constructing) related problems (p. 256)

Mathematically gifted children deserve special attention so that their unique needs are met. It is not enough to give them next year's textbook as enrichment. They will need to attend class with students at upper levels and often finish high school at an early age. They tend to choose careers as engineers, doctors, or scientists. While in grade school it may be necessary to match the student with a community mentor or have the student attend university level math courses. Every effort should be made to encourage these children to pursue their talents and enjoy the challenge of mathematics.

The Child with Learning Disabilities

Children with learning disabilities have great difficulty in processing information that they hear or read. Very few students have a disability in the area of math. It is not known how many students actually have such a learning disability because many students are mislabeled as having a problem, when in reality they were victims of poor teaching (Bender, 1995). Those students who have an authentic disability will be given specially designed instruction by their special education teacher.

For the majority of students with learning disabilities who attend regular math class, the teacher must be alert to three important aspects of the teaching/learning process. First, when giving directions or explaining a math concept, it will be important to realize that the student with learning disabilities will have difficulty following your words after listening to them only one time. It may be necessary to repeat your directions or ask the student to tell you what he or she just heard so that you are sure the student followed the whole message. When it comes time for the student to respond, it may take quite a bit longer for the student to formulate an answer and to explain verbally what he or she is thinking. More patience and more time is necessary if the student is to actually have a chance to participate in the math lesson.

Second, if there is any reading involved in a particular lesson, the student will have great difficulty with the task and perhaps show signs of frustration and embarrassment at his or her inability to perform. Finally, an overstimulating classroom in which there are many materials and supplies, colorful wall charts and posters, or a great deal of noise may cause a student to be off-task. These distractions compete with his attention to the lesson.

For a greater understanding of each individual student, it will be necessary to consult with the special education teacher, who has drawn a profile of each student's strengths and weaknesses. Since most children's disabilities are not in mathematics, there should be no reason that they cannot learn and enjoy the full spectrum of all of the strands in the curriculum. Many of the most interesting math activities do not rely heavily on memory, but involve creative thinking, planning, and discussions with peers. With the proper support and patient understanding by all teachers, the student with learning disabilities can have a successful math experience.

The Child Who Is Cognitively Disabled (Children with Mental Retardation)

Children who have cognitive disability (mental retardation) have significantly below average intelligence and significantly below average adaptive behavior. That is to say, they are developmentally behind their peer group in both their cognitive abilities and their interests and skills. They often act like younger-aged children. In today's classrooms more and more children with cognitive disability are mainstreamed or included in the regular pre-school or elementary classroom. There is not a separate curriculum for these children that is entirely different from the regular math curriculum. Instead, they benefit from exposure and repeated practice in activities found in the regular education math curriculum, but at a developmentally appropriate level. If needed, the special education teacher will design specific educational services for each child.

As the regular class teacher you will need to practice getting their attention before you begin to talk. Special education teachers often use more prompts than are needed with a regular child. Once the teacher has the child's attention and the child is focused on the material with the right kind of prompt, it is possible to deliver the material in a way that the child can understand. Naturally more practice will be involved so that the child retains the material for a long period of time.

At the upper grade levels, children with cognitive disability do not take classes in algebra and geometry as is expected for most students. Instead they focus their education on vocationally oriented math skills. But in the early years they can achieve success in early counting skills, early pattern work, and simple addition and subtraction story problems. Later in their school career, they will focus on money, time, and measurement. It is possible for these children to join in with their regular classmates and participate to some extent in the regular math program.

Where We Are Going—The NCTM Standards

In 1989, the NCTM published its *Curriculum and Evaluation Standards for School Mathematics*. The Standards proposed a vision of school mathematics for each of three grade ranges: kindergarten through grade 4, grades 5 through 8, and grades 9 through 12. In order to prepare today's students for the twenty-first century, it is necessary to provide a wide variety of opportunities for each child to experience a challenging math curriculum. To implement this vision of reform, the NCTM established five general student goals related to mathematics:

1. Learn to value mathematics
2 Become confident in the ability to do mathematics
3. Become mathematical problem solvers
4. Learn to communicate mathematically
5. Learn to reason mathematically[*] (p. 5–6)

The emphasis is on developing student abilities in the areas of problem solving, thinking about math, and talking about math. Every opportunity is taken to link the study of mathematics to other disciplines. The curriculum has a broad base with many strands. Here is a list of the NCTM Standards for elementary school mathematics, K-4:

Estimation
Number sense and numeration
Concepts of whole number operations
Whole number computation
Geometry and spatial sense
Measurement
Statistics and probability
Fractions and decimals
Patterns and relationships[*] (p. 15)

The dimensions of these strands as they relate to the early childhood curriculum form the basis for much of this book. Important concepts will be explained and defined. Informal classroom and home activities will be illustrated by example. Classroom activities and games that enhance children's learning will illustrate how teachers weave math into the daily life of the classroom.

Developmentally Appropriate Education: Creating the Best Learning Environment

Any curriculum designed for young children should be "developmentally appropriate." The National Association for the Education of Young Children (NAYEC, 1986) used two dimensions to describe good practice: age appropriateness and individual appropriateness. First, teachers must have a thorough knowledge of the physical, emotional, and cognitive development of each age

---

[*]Reprinted with the permission from the *Curriculum and Evaluation Standards for School Mathematics* (1989) by the National Council of Teachers of Mathematics.

span. A six-month old infant cannot run a foot race. Age appropriateness gives teachers these broad parameters. Second, each child has special interests, abilities, and prior knowledge from home and culture. Therefore, individual appropriateness means that a good match is made between an individual child and the curriculum.

Most experts believe that children's play is the key to mental growth. Time to play and a wide variety of concrete materials are essential. Children should not be rushed to finish a project or hurried from one activity to another. Active exploration and interaction with other people takes time. Likewise, a room containing only paper and pencil or coloring activities is not appropriate. For example, building with wooden blocks is an excellent math experience in geometry as well as in dramatic play and storytelling. This experience cannot be replaced by coloring a picture of a house.

Piaget, Vygotsky, and Bruner

The writings of three famous cognitive psychologists give teachers additional information on developmentally appropriate education. Piaget, Vygotsky, and Bruner have influenced education throughout this century and have made significant contributions to the way teachers of mathematics approach the process of teaching and learning. Their ideas form the basis for constructivism, a theory that views the child as creating knowledge by acting on experience gained from the world and then finding meaning in it. Children recreate or reinvent mathematics as they interact with concrete materials, math symbols, and story problems.

Jean Piaget (1896–1980) proposed a four-stage theory of cognitive development. In stage 2, preoperational thinking (ages 2–7 years), children rapidly acquire language and the ability to use symbols to represent real objects. However, many math tasks, such as conservation of numbers, volume, or capacity are not achieved until the next stage, the concrete stage, ages 7 to 11. Piaget's view that maturation precedes learning and that certain tasks are fixed benchmarks has come under scrutiny. Teachers have found that many children who have had an extensive preschool education and parental teaching can perform a variety of tasks at earlier ages. Nevertheless, Piaget's general conception of learning has much validity for today's classroom. The strengths of the Piagetian approach include a focus on the child's thinking, or the process, not just the answer; self-initiated, active involvement in a rich environment; avoiding pushing the child to be adult like, and viewing the role of the teacher as a guide or resource person.

Lev Semenovich Vygotsky (1896–1934) was a famous Russian psychologist who lived in the early part of this century. His work was not translated until the 1970s, and his ideas have only recently become influential in North America. Vygotsky espouses two kinds of development, natural and cultural. Natural development influences learning as the result of maturation. Cultural development results from the child's interaction with other members of the culture and is enhanced by the use of language.

Learning happens when children are working within their "zone of proximal development." This zone encompasses tasks that the child cannot yet do alone, but that can be accomplished with help from classmates or adults. As children learn, they guide their thinking by talking to themselves—"private speech." Adults use private speech when they mentally compose a list of what they need to accomplish during the day and talk themselves through it. In a cooperative learning group, children hear other people's thoughts and assimilate their ideas into their own private speech.

Vygotsky feels that children in the early stages of learning need a great deal of support or "scaffolding" in order to grasp a task. Later this guidance or set of prompts is gradually reduced so the child can master the skill independently. Teachers can encourage "talking aloud" about how a student got the answer and encourage listening skills while other students explain their solutions.

Typical standardized and classroom tests assess only what a child already knows or the lower level of the zone of proximal development. Another type of assessment such as a one-to-one interview, in which the teacher uses suitable prompts, can elicit the higher zone of proximal development.

For example, a first grade student is asked to count three yellow buttons and four blue buttons. "How many buttons do we have?" The child starts with the number one and touches each button. Can the child count on from the three yellow buttons? The teacher prompts the child, "Let's see. We have three yellow buttons. Can we say . . . three . . . and count 4-5-6-7?" After a few examples the child sees the pattern and can accomplish this "counting on" task. Therefore this skill is in the child's zone of proximal development. If the child persists in starting over each time with number one, then the task is not developmentally appropriate. At times peers can give the right kind of hints or prompts to each other, while not overwhelming their classmates' self-confidence.

Jerome Bruner (b. 1915) also influenced education over this past century. He describes intellectual development as proceeding from an enactive mode to an iconic mode and then finally into a symbolic mode. In the first stage, infants and toddlers can only act and react to the physical world. The young child sees a shiny button on an adult's jacket and grabs for it. Around age two or three a variety of sensory images are formed. In the iconic mode, the child can realize an adult is absent and recall a visual, auditory or tactile image of the person. If a box of cookies are put on a shelf, the child can think about the cookies after eating just one and ask for "more."

About the age of five or six the child can use a symbolic mode such as oral language, picture story drawing, or number writing to represent thinking. Bruner's three modes are found in today's math instruction: physically doing math with manipulatives; doing mental math by thinking in terms of memories of visual, auditory or kinesthetic clues; and finally being able to use number symbols with meaning. In the symbolic mode a six-year-old might solve an addition problem of "six plus seven" by saying, "I took the 7, and I knew it was 6 + 1, so I added the 6 to the other 6, and then I put the 1 back on and got 13."

Summary

With knowledge of the theories, visions, and research presented in this chapter, today's teacher can approach the challenge of planning an exciting, developmentally appropriate curriculum for all children. When our expectations are high, children will reach the goal where everyone enjoys math and can use it as a language and a tool for future success. Children cannot teach themselves math without your guidance and support.

As you reflect on your own mathematics education and the myths surrounding the discipline, you will gain insight into your own misconceptions and attitudes about your role. Professional organizations such as the National Council of Teachers of Mathematics and the National Association for the Education of Young Children set high standards to help you become a knowledgeable, responsive educator. A dedicated professional takes on the responsibility of becoming a lifelong learner. This book is one tool to help you begin this journey.

Activities and Study Questions

1. Review the information on math anxiety and the myths surrounding mathematics education. Reflect on your own experiences and write a journal entry or short paper explaining how these topics shaped your viewpoint on math.

2. Research the statistics on the current status of women and minorities employed in math- or science-related careers. What implication might you draw from the data? Be prepared to share your findings with the class.

3. Interview an early childhood teacher about the role that the standards of professional organizations such as the NCTM and the NAEYC play in the development of the local curriculum. What changes have occurred over the past decade? Write a brief report of your discussion.

4. Read the article (cited in Further Reading) by Maker, Nielson, and Rogers (1994) and develop a continuum of activities based upon their research. The goal of the continuum is to build curricular activities around the strengths of diverse learners.

5. Examine a teacher's manual from an elementary mathematics textbook series. Compare the content of a particular grade to the mathematical strands suggested by the NCTM Standards. What areas seem to have the most coverage?

Further Reading

Bohan, H. J., & Shawaker, P. B. (1994). Using manipulatives effectively: A drive down the rounding road. *Arithmetic Teacher*, 41, 246–248.

The concrete, bridging, and abstract stages of using manipulatives are illustrated by lessons from the primary classroom. This approach gives teachers a way to think about the role of materials in lesson planning and instruction.

Maker, C. J., Nielson, A. B., & Rogers, J. A. (1994). Giftedness, diversity, and problem solving. *Teaching Exceptional Children, 26,* 4–21. *The authors use the theory of multiple intelligences and research on giftedness to create assessment and curricular tools that reach diverse groups of students. Practical suggestions in mathematics make their approach especially useful.*

National Association for the Education of Young Children. (1994). NAEYC position statement: A conceptual framework for early childhood professional development. *Young Children, 49,* Washington, D.C.: Author. *The National Association for the Education of Young Children has developed a conceptual framework for the effective professional development of early childhood professionals. Guidelines are given for a unifying framework and for the education of preservice teachers. Their principles are worthy of review by students preparing to enter this arena.*

Reys, B. J., & Long, V. M. (1995). Implementing the professional standards for teaching mathematics: Teacher as architect of mathematical tasks. *Teaching Children Mathematics,* 1, 296–299. *The authors explore criteria to judge the usefulness of mathematical tasks. Successful endeavors involve one or more of their essential ideas. Their guidelines expand upon the NCTM Standards in a meaningful way.*

Sameroff, A., & McDonough, S. C. (1994). Educational implications of developmental transitions: Revisiting the 5- to 7-year shift. *Phi Delta Kappan, 76,* 188–193. *The authors chronicle the debate over whether substantial shifts in memory and cognition take place between the ages of 5 and 7 years. The role that cultural factors play in these mental relationships is explored. One major achievement of this age period may be the ability to enjoy learning for its own sake.*

References

Adelman, H. S., & Taylor, L. (1983). *Learning disabilities in perspective.* Glenview, IL: Scott, Foresman and Company.

Baroody, A. (1989). Manipulatives don't come with guarantees. *Arithmetic Teacher, 36,* 4–5.

Bender, W. N. (1995). *Learning disabilities: Characteristics, identification, and teaching strategies.* Boston: Allyn & Bacon.

Gardner, H., & Hatch, T. (1989). Multiple intelligences go to school. *Educational Leadership, 18* (8), 4–10.

Hembree, R., & Dessart, D. (1992). Research on calculators in mathematics education. In J. T. Fey (Ed.) *1992 yearbook: Calculators in mathematics education,* (p. 30). Reston, VA: National Council of Teachers of Mathematics.

Kirk, D. (1994). *Miss Spider's tea party.* NY: Scholastic Inc.

Kogelman, S., & Warren, J. (1978). *Mind over math.* New York: McGraw-Hill.

Maker, C. J., Nielson, A. B., & Rogers, J. A. (1994). Giftedness, diversity, and problem solving. *Teaching Exceptional Children, 26,* 4–21.

Meyer, M. R., & Fennema, E. (1988). Girls, boys and mathematics. In T. R. Post (Ed.). *Teaching mathematics in grades K-8* (pp. 406–425). Boston: Allyn & Bacon.

National Association for the Education of Young Children (1986). *Developmentally appropriate practice* (pp. 2–5). Washington, D.C.: Author.

National Council of Teachers of Mathematics (1989). *Curriculum and evaluation standards for school mathematics.* Reston, VA: Author.

National Council of Teachers of Mathematics (1991). *Professional standards for teaching mathematics.* Reston, VA: Author.

National Council of Teachers of Mathematics (1995). *Assessment standards for school mathematics.* Reston, VA: Author.

Pendarvis, E. D., Howley, A. A., & Howley, C. B. (1990). *The abilities of gifted children.* Englewood Cliffs, N. J.: Prentice-Hall.

Ross, S. H. (1986). The development of children's place-value numeration concepts in grades two through five. Paper presented at the annual meeting of the *American Educational Research Association.* San Francisco.

Sells, L. W. (1980). The mathematics filter and the

education of women and minorities. In L. H. Fox, L. Brody, & D. Tobin (Eds.) *Women and the mathematical mystique* (p. 68). Baltimore: John Hopkins University Press.

Shigematsu, K. & Sowder, L. (1994). Drawings for story problems: Practices in Japan and the United States. *Arithmetic Teacher, 41*, 9, 544–547.

Song, M. J. & Ginsberg, H. P. (1987). The development of informal and formal mathematical thinking in Korean and American children. *Child Development, 58*, 1286–1296.

Tikunoff, W. J. (1985). *Applying significant bilingual instructional features in the classroom.* National Clearinghouse for Bilingual Education, 34.

2 The Language of Math

AROUND THE WORLD people of all ages speak math. How does this language develop? What can an early childhood educator do to enhance this process? In infancy and toddlerhood, children begin to acquire many language concepts. School experiences extend and enrich language learning. While some children come to school with an extensive ability to communicate, others need help in developing a rich repertoire of shared meanings. The language of mathematics is embedded in the development of many verbal communication skills. When mastered, mathematics concepts as expressed in English become an aid to thinking.

Young children enjoy listening and talking in natural settings. Dramatic play is an important activity that encourages spontaneous conversation and role-play about the adult world. The lyrics of familiar songs and nursery rhymes give children the opportunity to repeat familiar words and phrases in a joyful way. And many picture books and children's stories focus on language learning, using interesting themes and pictures.

Developing Math Language Using Song and Verse

Many traditional songs and nursery rhymes contain themes that encourage language learning in mathematics. For the "Three Little Kittens" *lose* their mittens and *find* their mittens. Children enjoy matching sets of mittens hidden in the room. Here are some additional examples. An excellent songbook, *Where Is Thumbkin?* (Schiller & Moore, 1993), provides a valuable resource for musical material. Children learn naturally while enjoying a wonderful medium.

Math Language	*Traditional Songs*
Up and down	"Eensy Weensy Spider"
Over the mountain The other side	"The Bear Went Over the Mountain"
On the back of the crocodile Inside the crocodile	"The Crocodile Song"
Cold–hot Low–high Soft–hard	"The Three Bears" (to the tune of "Twinkle, Twinkle Little Star")
Jumping on the bed Falling off the bed	"Three Little Monkeys"
Young–old	"Billy Boy"
Up–down–halfway Up	"The Grand Old Duke of York"

Developing Math Language Through Children's Literature

There are many excellent resources that reference the world of mathematics to specific titles of children's literature. The book, *How to Use Children's Literature to Teach Mathematics* (Welchman-Tischler, 1992) shows teachers how to connect mathematics, literature, and critical thinking skills. Instructional strategies and follow-up activities are identified by grade level. New titles arrive at libraries and bookstores daily. A children's librarian will help you find the best selections for your classroom.

Here are four examples that illustrate how the language of math is directly or indirectly taught using appealing picture books and stories.

"More, More, More," said the Baby (Williams, 1990)

This picture book shows babies from diverse cultures having fun and enjoying "more and more" activities with their caregivers. Language concepts such as "middle" (a belly button), as well as everyday experiences such as counting toes and being tossed gently in the air, are beautifully illustrated. This book is suitable for toddlers.

Fast–Slow, High–Low (Spier, 1972)

The author highlights pairs of opposites in an upper corner and surrounds the words with many separate examples. The wealth of ideas and excellent artwork provide a beginning for wonderful conversation about the concepts. This book is suitable for preschoolers.

All About Opposites (Thomson, 1987)

Bella and Rosy Rabbit go through the city pushing a big package on wheels. Many pairs of opposites, such as empty–full, are illustrated. The package holds lots of toys for Rosy, with opportunities for children to spot many opposites. This book is suitable for preschoolers.

Big Mama's (Crew, 1991)

The grandchildren take a journey to visit their grandparent's farm in the south. They take the train, ride to the farm, take off their socks and shoes, drink from the well, go fishing, and visit the barn. Many positional words are illustrated. The sequential nature of taking a trip lends itself to the ordering of events and the retelling of the story. Children can create their own tale of a journey and share it with the class. This book appeals to preschool through primary age children.

These brief synopses from children's literature give the early childhood educator a glimpse of the rich sources of language learning available at the library or bookstore. With careful planning and imagination, the teacher can use books to enrich the lives of generations of children.

Math Language and Older Children

Older children benefit from a clear understanding of a wide variety of technical terms, symbols, and ways of describing procedures in order to help them appreciate the logic of a math sentence. It takes careful explanation, listening, and practice to acquire this language accurately. Otherwise, even the best students think of solving equations as paying attention to the latest "trick" the teacher demonstrated on the board. They feel they need to memorize it just long enough to pass the test, then it's on to the next "trick." A curriculum that helps children acquire this language will enable them to enjoy its beauty, pattern, and versatility, which can benefit them in everyday life.

Let's take the example of subtraction. Young children commonly use the phrase "take away." This is natural, and there is no need to "correct" the child. However, "take away" is only one of three common forms of story problems that can be solved using subtraction. In a more formal way, subtraction is used when you know the whole (sum) and one part (addend) and are looking for the other part. This definition allows for a more accurate view of the procedure.

Here is a better example of subtraction language in a story problem: "Jason has a pizza cut into six pieces. He eats two pieces. How many pieces could his sister Sarah eat?" The teacher says: "How many pieces were in the *whole* pizza? How many pieces are eaten? And what pieces are still on the plate?" Careful attention to the way a problem is phrased helps the young child understand the process of subtraction in many ways. This approach guides the child away from relying on rote phrases or key words to solve problems.

The language of math can be a challenge to many children when there are English meanings and math meanings. For example, is a "plane" an airplane or a two-dimensional set of points? Is an "operation" a trip to the hospital or a procedure like addition or subtraction? Because some concepts are rarely heard in activities outside of school, it is extremely important that enough time is taken in the classroom to make the meaning of the math language clear to the children (Caps & Pickreign, 1993). By doing this you are well on your way to implementing the Standard on Communication (NCTM, 1989).

Math Concepts Found in the Early Childhood Curriculum

A wide variety of words comprise a good math vocabulary. Teachers are often surprised to learn about these words. They don't realize that everyday words such as "over" and "under" are a part of the math curriculum. In this section you will find specific listings of key words by category: comparing, positional, directional, sequence, time, shape, and number. The words are listed along with general suggestions on how they may be woven into the daily activities of the early childhood classroom. Many teachers find it helpful to see the whole list in one section of the book.

In later chapters these foundational concepts become the basis for an in-depth discussion of each mathematical strand. These chapters also provide suggestions for curricular planning and assessment. The exact mastery ages for many of the words listed here can be found in resources such as the *Learning Accomplishment Profile, rev. ed.* (1981).

Comparing Words.

The first group of words are "the comparing" words. In comparing, the child gains confidence in observing differences in a variety of characteristics such as size, temperature, or loudness. A child may compare weight by holding two objects or using a pan scale to weigh them. Here is a list of the common comparing words that form a strong foundation for an early childhood program:

Big–Little	Toy animals, dolls, people, cars, and trucks
Large–Small	Beach balls and tennis balls, toy dishes and real dishes, purses and luggage
Tall–Short	People, trees, skyscrapers, and houses
Fast–Slow	Songs played at different speeds, cars, children's actions
Heavy–Light	Rocks, empty and full milk cartons, feathers and blocks
Hot–Cold	Food, drinks, and the weather
Young–Old	Babies and grown-ups, trees
Loud–Soft	People's voices, musical instruments, recordings
High–Low	Playground equipment, airplanes and cars, people on balconies, musical instruments
Near–Far	People and things in different positions

In Figure 2–1, a child discovers which fruit weighs the most by using dinosaur counters.

Positional Words.

Positional words help the child grasp many concepts about space that will be important in later learning. As children play in the block corner or in the housekeeping corner, they have many opportunities to use these words. When they stack objects they can talk about the one on top, the one in the middle, and the one on the bottom. When they play with the doll house, they can talk about going inside the house to take a nap or coming back outside to play with their friends.

The most difficult words in the positional group refer to the concept of left and right. Some adults have trouble with these two concepts and rely on crutches such as looking at a ring finger to find out which direction is which. This is normal since it demands that we be able to differentiate ourselves into two components in relation to the midline. For example, a friend might say: "Look at the cardinal in the tree! Where? On the left!" You may not turn in the direction of the bird quickly enough to catch a glimpse. You may have trouble with right and left orientation, especially if you must first assume the orientation of your friend.

Figure 2–1   A child using a balance scale to weigh fruit with dinosaur counters

---

Examples

Playing with a doll house   Stacking objects
or a parking garage

in   top
out   bottom
inside   middle
outside   together
apart
over
under

Examples

Discussing dishes and the placement of food on the table:

"Your cup is on the right."
right-left

Directional Words.

Directional words involve movement. In order to experience these words, children can perform actions either in the form of a musical game or an interesting gym activity. In addition, these words are common when children are playing with toys that have the capacity to move, for example, small cars and trucks.

Examples

Using a musical activity or gym game or using cars and trucks:

forward	backward
up	down
toward	away from
around	
to the right	to the left

Sequence Words.

Sequence words are very important because they develop a sense of order, which will help the child later when more complex problems are found in our number systems. Children can experience these words firsthand when they line up for an activity or when they put a group of toys (such as farm animals) in a row. It is possible to talk about where each animal is in relation to the other animals. When lining up, it is possible to recognize that a child may be first in line. Children will have more difficulty differentiating the other sequence words when they do not have an opportunity to see the entire line from a distance. For example, the class forms a line to go outside for recess. A child who is "fourth" in line may have trouble telling you the ordinal name for his position.

Examples

Making a line of zoo animals where each animal is totally different from its neighbor:

first	last
beginning	end
before	after
in front of	in back of
ahead of	behind
middle	
next to	

The Language of Time.

A number of words comprise the language of time. Time words are acquired over a series of many years. According to Piaget, the acquisition of this concept begins in early childhood but it is not until approximately the age of nine that children can really grasp time concepts (Copeland, 1984). In the very early years, children start to understand the idea that something good may be coming. They can think about the idea that tomorrow is their birthday or that tomorrow the family is going to take a trip to somewhere such as Disney World. They start to acquire the concepts of morning, afternoon, and night. It is much easier for them to think about things that will be happening in the future than to talk about concepts such as yesterday or last week. Children's time exists in the present. When something is in the past, it may be quickly forgotten unless it was a very traumatic event.

In first grade children learn to tell time using the clock, first to the hour and then to the five minute interval. They begin to learn calendar time, which includes the days of the week, the names of the months, and the concept of a year. Later they grasp the idea of today's date. The actual number or date is a difficult number to remember unless it is a special date such as one's birthday. Finally, there are a number of words having to do with the holidays and the relationship of school days versus weekends.

Examples

Using a classroom chart sequencing daily events, updating a monthly calendar each day, or using commercial and teacher-made clocks to learn to tell time:

General Time Words

morning	evening
night	day
early	late
afternoon	
tonight	
noon	
tomorrow	

Clock Words

long hand	short hand
hour	minutes
watch	alarm clock
seconds	

Calendar Words

days of week	yesterday
tomorrow	name of the month
name of the season	date
holidays	birthday
school day	weekend
vacation	

Shape Words.

The baby's bed has "sides." The nerf ball is round. Cereal comes in a box. We make the bed and tuck in the sheet at the "corners." These informal ways of using shape words help the child describe everyday objects. The following are some of the first words for shape:

Examples

Finding and talking about shapes in the environment:

round	circle
sides	square
corners	triangle
flat	tube
box	stairs
carton	room

Number Words.

A very important group of words describe our number system. Children learn to compare quantity and to recognize relationships such as more or less. For example, "Andy has more candy than I do."

Examples

Talking about quantity at snack time, in the block center, or in the housekeeping center:

more	greater than
less	less than
the same	
many	
fewer	

Children learn to count, "one, two, three." Most children can count up to 100 by the middle of first grade. As a teacher it is helpful to know the difference between the following names for numbers.

Counting numbers	These numbers start with 1, 2, 3, 4, 5 . . .
Whole numbers	These numbers include zero. Example 0, 1, 2, 3, 4, 5 . . .
Cardinal numbers	This number names the total in a set. We match the items in a set to the counting numbers.

0 0 0 0
1 2 3 4

The cardinal number is *4*.

Ordinal numbers   These names give each a position such as first, second, third, fourth, fifth . . .

Ordinal numbers are very difficult for children. It may take them until the age of eight to use the words correctly.

The Symbols of Math

Math does not use the "ABC's" to communicate. Instead, it uses a special group of symbols such as numbers and signs. These symbols are commonly described in four categories:

1. Symbols for ideas (numbers and elements) such as 1, 2, 3, X, Y
2. Symbols for relations (such as =, ≠, >, <)
3. Symbols for operations (such as +, −, ×, ÷)
4. Symbols for punctuation (such as decimal point, comma, parentheses, brackets)

In order to write a complete math thought we must use a minimum of the first two groups. We can write the sentence, "8 > 3." In English the sentence says, "8 is greater than 3." The sentence illustrates using the symbols for numbers and a symbol for relations. In the math sentence "4 + 2 = 6," we use number symbols (4, 2, 6), an operation symbol (the + sign), and a relation symbol (the = sign) (Heddens & Speer, 1992). We use parentheses signs in this sentence, "8 + (3 + 2) = 13." In the early childhood program, we typically do not use the punctuation symbols such as:

brackets $3 \times [1 + (2 + 4)] = 21$

or

braces $(A = \{2, 3, 4\})$

The symbols of math can also be written in the vertical form. These procedures, or *algorithms*, include operations for computing when adding, subtracting, multiplying, or dividing. All adults are familiar with these paper and pencil computations, since the steps in these procedures were taught through rote drill and practice over many years in school. The traditional approach to mathematics stressed mastery of algorithms with little understanding of the reasoning behind the operations. The NCTM Standards (1989) emphasize that children should master basic facts and algorithms, but that mastery should not be expected too soon. Instruction should focus on the "meaningful development of these procedures, not speed of processing" (p. 47). Children should learn when to use paper and pencil calculations, when to do calculations using mental math, and when to do calculations using the tools of a calculator or a computer.

The Number Sentence

A number sentence is written horizontally using the various symbols. For every story problem we can write a number sentence. For example:

1. Charles has 12 apples. He gave 1 apple to Beth. How many apples does Charles have left?

    Math Sentence $12 - 1 = \square$

2. Alita had some apples. She gave 3 to Devon. Now she has 4 apples. How many apples did Alita have to begin with?

    Math Sentence $\square - 3 = 4$

Except for theoretical math, there is a story that could correspond to every math sentence. Even algebra has real life examples that could have brought meaning to those strange equations.

The same number sentence can serve more than one meaning. Let's take the problem, "$6 + 3 = \square$."

"There were 6 dogs and 3 cats in the barn. How many animals lived in the barn?"

or

"There were 6 peaches and 3 pears in the bowl. How many pieces of fruit were in the bowl?"

Finally, a mathematical sentence that has been solved can be judged true or false. We cannot judge whether "$7 + \square = 12$" is true or false. We can say that "$7 + 7 = 12$" is a false statement. We can write $7 + 7 \neq 12$, or "seven plus seven does not equal twelve." Children will develop an understanding of the kinds of symbols and how they are used before they are capable of writing them.

While the preschool child may only understand the concept of numbers such as 1, 2, and 3, the teacher needs to see the big picture of where mathematics education is going. By third grade students should be able to take a story problem and generate several math sentences.

"Melissa had 20 toy dinosaurs. Mary had 14 toy dinosaurs. What can we write about this story?"

$20 + 14 = 34$	Mary and Melissa have 34 dinosaurs in all.
$20 - 14 = 6$	Melissa gave Mary 14 of her dinosaurs. Now she has 6 left.
$20 > 14$	Melissa had more dinosaurs than Mary.
$14 < 20$	Mary has fewer dinosaurs than Melissa.
$14 \neq 20$	Mary and Melissa do not have the same number of dinosaurs.

When teachers at every level assess and plan challenging math classes, students will acquire capabilities beyond what many people were taught in elementary school. The traditional curriculum contained much repetition of material and lots of paper and pencil computation. The new curriculum develops many interesting strands of material to meet the needs of the twenty-first century.

Summary

Children develop a large fund of mathematical knowledge as they grow. Preschoolers learn to ask for "more." When someone is making orange juice, they count along as cans of water are poured into the pitcher "one, two, three." They try to imitate an older brother or sister who can count to 10 or 20. (Slowly they learn to recognize a group of more. For example, this plate has more cookies than that plate. The development of number sense takes many years.)

Some parents and teachers believe that the kindergartner learns to count to 100. Then the first grader masters the basic facts by drill and practice. They also learn to count objects on a page and circle the number in the set. This way of thinking is far removed from the child's natural approach to number and problem solving. Children construct their own knowledge of math, independent of the ways adults think. If we ask an adult, "How much is $7 + 5$?", the person may respond immediately that the answer is "12." A child may think of the problem in a different way. "If 7 is $5 + 2$, and $5 + 5 = 10$, then you can add on the 2 from the 7 to the 10, and get 12."

Children who are allowed to think about a problem and create their own strategy become confident math students. For example, in one kindergarten class each child receives a pea pod that the teacher picked from her garden. One child opens a pod and finds 4 peas on one side and 1 pea on the other. Then a story can be told, "There were 4 peas on one side and 1 pea on the other." The number sentence can be written, $4 + 1 = 5$. "There were 5 peas in my pod."

The challenge to the teacher is to take the powerful tools of the language of math and guide the child to a deeper understanding based on what is already known. In each chapter we will explore a different math strand, and discuss how you can achieve the delicate balance between "guiding learning without overwhelming the child, or subjecting the child to meaningless drill." You are beginning an exciting journey. You can do it!

Ready-Set-Math

Ready-Set-Math

Ring the Bells

Ages 4–5 years

Items needed: A recording of "Are You Sleeping?"
                       A set of bells in different tones

Play the recording, "Are You Sleeping?," and ring the bells to wake up "Brother John." Listen to each bell and decide if it has a high pitch or a low pitch. Try to put the bell sounds in order from low to high.

Ready-Set-Math

Pine Cone Sculptures

Ages 3–4 years

Items needed: Small pine cones
                       White glue
                       Newspaper
                       Paper plates

Have the children design a pine cone sculpture and glue it together. When it dries compare the designs in terms of high–low, or heavy–light. Use a pan scale if needed.

Ready-Set-Math

Old MacDonald's Farm

Ages 5–7 years

Items needed: A recording of "Old MacDonald Had a Farm"
                       A set of animals that appear in the song
                       Word cards for the ordinals from first through seventh

Make ahead: Individual word cards

Listen to the recording of "Old MacDonald Had a Farm" and order the animals according to the sequence presented in the song. Label each animal with a word card indicating its ordinal position, that is, the cow was first, the sheep second, and so on. Practice the sequence from memory without the recording.

◆ **Ready-Set-Math**

Mulberry Bush Days of the Week

Ages: 6–8 years

Items needed:	A recording of "The Mulberry Bush"
	Picture cards depicting the household tasks
	Word cards for the days of the week
Make ahead:	Picture cards
	Word cards

Listen to the recording of "The Mulberry Bush" and order the tasks by the day of the week, that is, wash our clothes, iron our clothes, and so on. Match picture cards of these activities to word cards for the days. Have the class decide on what they do that's special for each day. Have the children draw these pictures and match them to the days of the week. Try to make up a song using their ideas, that is, "This is the way we go to gym, go to gym . . . so early Monday morning."

◆ **Ready-Set-Math**

The More or Less Game

Ages 4–8 years

Items needed:	A stack of comparing cards, one die labeled 1-2-3, 1-2-3, and a pile of counters such as toy bears
Make ahead:	A stack of comparing cards

Take heavy construction paper or cardboard and cut a sheet into playing cards. Draw a picture with a plate of "more" cookies on some cards. Draw a picture of "less" cookies on other cards. Draw two identical plates of cookies on "the same" cards. Shuffle the cards. Print the words (more, less, the same) on the appropriate cards.

To Play: Each player takes 8 counters from the pile in the center of the table. A player shakes the die and picks a card. For example, 3 on the die plus a "more card" means that the child takes 3 more counters. If a child shakes a 2 and turns over a "less card," the child gives back 2 counters. If a child gets "the same" card, the child loses a turn. The child's pile stays the same. The winner is the first person to get enough "less cards" to give back all the counters in the player's pile.

Note: To play the game in less time, start with 5 counters per person.

Activities and Study Questions

1. Choose one category of math language words and create a big book. One source of ideas might be things found in the natural environment of a local classroom.
2. Pick a traditional children's song or nursery rhyme and design an activity that would enhance language learning of a particular math word or words.
3. Read the article by Schwartz and Brown (1995) listed in Further Reading. Interview a preschool child at play and decide which strategies you used to enhance communication. Write a journal entry or short paper on your experience.
4. Interview a kindergarten teacher about how she or he uses the calendar in daily activities. Find out if the teacher feels there is value in teaching by the month. Compare your findings to the discussion found in Schwartz (1994). Be prepared to discuss your interview in class.
5. Conduct an informal assessment of a preschoolers knowledge of one category of math words. For example, use a small car and a garage to see if the child understands directional words such as forward, up, toward, and so on. Write a journal entry or brief paper on your results.

Classroom Equipment

toy animals, dolls, people	doll house
toy cars and trucks	rice, plastic rice
beach balls, tennis balls	colored water
toy dishes, real dishes	stacking toys or objects
records	various jars
rocks	various boxes
feathers	balance scale

Further Reading

Buschman, L. (1995). Communicating in the language of mathematics. *Teaching Children Mathematics*, 1, 324–329. *The author describes a number of approaches to enhance classroom communication. These include the journal, the mathematician's chair, and a family newsletter. Examples are given of several ways to expand on a problem solution, besides having a classroom dialogue.*

Capps, L. R., & Pickreigh, J. (1993). Language connection in mathematics: A critical part of mathematics instruction. *Arithmetic Teacher*, 41, 8–12. *The authors appreciate the challenge of linking language to symbolic representation. They suggest excellent ways to teach the vocabulary and grammar of math as well as the pitfalls of relying on key words to solve problems. Regardless of stu-dents' abilities, the unique language of math must be explicitly taught if learners are to be successful.*

Schwartz, S. L. (1994). Calendar reading: A tradition that begs remodeling. *Teaching Children Mathematics*, 1, 104–109. *The author favors simple, daily schedule charts using pictures over the traditional calendar activities. A weekly calendar may be more appropriate before the monthly calendar is introduced.*

Schwartz, S. L., & Brown, A. B. (1995). Communicating with young children in mathematics: A unique challenge. *Teaching Children Mathematics*, 1, 350–353. *The authors encourage teachers to use three strategies (validating, reviewing, and challenge) to foster language learning without overwhelming the child. Their approach highlights how a developmentally appropriate education takes place everyday in early childhood class-rooms.*

Welchmann-Tischler, R. (1988). Mathematics from children's literature. *Arithmetic Teacher*, 35, 6, 42–47. *The author illustrates classroom activities and games for two popular children's books,* Frog and Toad *and* Caps for Sale. *Her ideas are suitable for preschool age children and provide a wonderful springboard for a teacher's creativity.*

References

Caps, L. and Pickreign, J. (1993). Language connections in mathematics: A critical part of mathematics instruction. *Arithmetic Teacher,* 41, 1, 8–12.

Copeland, R. W. (1984). *How children learn mathematics: Teaching implications of Piaget's research.* New York: Macmillan.

Crew, D. (1991). *Big mama's.* New York: The Trumpet Club.

Heddens, J., & Speer, W. (1992). *Today's Mathematics*, 7th ed., New York: Macmillan.

National Council of Teachers of Mathematics (1989). *Curriculum and evaluation standards for school mathematics.* Reston, VA: Author.

Sanford, A. R., & Zelman, J. G. (1981). *The learning accomplishment profile, rev. ed.* Chapel Hill, NC: Chapel Hill Training–Outreach Project.

Schiller, P., & Moore, T. (1993). *Where is Thumbkin?* Mt. Rainer, MD: Gryphon House.

Spier, P. (1972). *Fast–slow, high–low.* Garden City, NY: Doubleday & Company.

Thomson, R. (1987). *All about opposites.* Milwaukee, WI: Garth Stevens Publishing.

Welchmann-Tischler, R. (1992). *How to use children's literature to teach mathematics.* Reston, VA: National Council of Teachers of Mathematics.

Williams, V. B. (1990). *"More, more, more," said the baby.* New York: Greenwillow Books.

3 Early Math Concepts: Matching, Classification, Comparing, and Ordering or Seriation

THE YOUNG CHILD is a curious being. The infant feels its bottle for size, shape, and weight. Is it too big to grasp or too heavy to hold? The toddler dresses its doll for the day's play or for a night's rest. Time and sequence are explored. Farm animals are lined up and fed cereal, showing an ability to match.

According to Piaget, *physical knowledge* about color, size, shape, and texture can be used to construct *logico-mathematical* knowledge. Logico-mathematical knowledge is concerned with important relationships that create the early foundations of mathematical thinking (Copeland, 1984). Teachers of young children study the mathematical relationships of matching, classification, comparing, and ordering or seriation in order to guide their pupils' learning in an appropriate way. Teachers who understand the foundations of early math develop a curriculum created around challenging problem-solving activities at the children's levels. Lack of knowledge of these early math concepts may result in "rushing the child" through rote learning skills, such as counting, writing numerals, and finding the number of objects in a set. Furthermore, since most children accomplish these tasks during the preschool and primary grade years, the lack of development of these areas of logical thinking may indicate a lag in a child's development. These children may require additional assessments and may need help from a specialist.

Matching

Matching is the concept of one-to-one correspondence. When a child hands out cupcakes, each friend gets one treat. Perhaps there are just enough cupcakes or there may be "extra." When counting pennies, each penny is counted once. Matching forms the basis for our number system.

One of the earliest words a toddler says is "more." When the glass of apple juice is gone, the cry goes out, "More—more?" Children as young as two grasp the intuitive notion of things being added or taken away. Research studies have shown that when children (ages 2–4 years) are shown a set of three objects and the set is altered by covering it and adding another object, they easily see that it is no longer the same. When asked "how to fix it," they remove the new piece (Gellman & Gallistel, 1978; Brush, 1972). These ways of thinking develop the concepts of "more–less–the same."

When a child can remember or create "the same," then it is possible to match two sets. For example, the child is asked to match chickens and eggs. Each chicken gets the same amount, or one egg. There may be more eggs in the basket. These are the "extra eggs." Matching is a prerequisite skill for the more difficult tasks of conservation. Piaget's tests of conservation are used to assess children's development at a later age and are described in Chapter 7.

When assessing matching tasks, four dimensions are considered:

1. Are the items identical or different?
2. Are there many items to match, or just a few?
3. Is there the same number in each set?
4. Are the sets "joined or not joined?"

1. Are the items identical or different?
   Different items are easier to match.
   a. Easier.

Figure 3–1

   b. Harder.

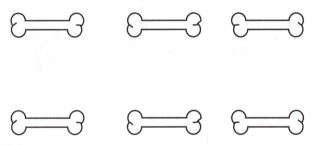

Figure 3–2

The example of dogs and bowls is easier because the child has the visual advantage of two different objects to match. When given both a line of bones and a pile of identical bones, a child has more trouble making sure each bone has a mate.

2. Are there many items to match, or just a few?
   a. Easier (five or fewer items).

Figure 3–3

b. Harder (more than five items).

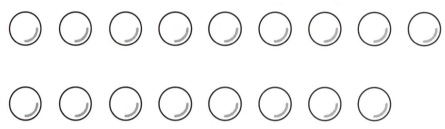

Figure 3–4

The more items that need to be matched, the harder the task. The line can seem to waiver, and it may be more difficult to be certain that no item was skipped.

3. Is there the same number in each set?
   a. Easier (even sets).

Figure 3–5

b. Harder (not enough, or too many in one set).

Figure 3–6

Most children like to match sets so they end up even. When some bears do not get a cherry, it seems like the job is not done until more cherries are found.

4. Are the sets "joined or not joined?"
   a. Joined is easier.

Figure 3–7   Joined sets—people on chairs.

   b. Not joined is harder.

Figure 3–8   Unjoined sets—do we have enough chairs?

It is easier to check if matching is successful when sets are joined. In the example of people and chairs, the child can tell right away if there are enough seats because of the physical proximity of the person and the objects.

Matching: Informal Learning Around Home and School

Everyday routines provide many opportunities for matching. Getting dressed involves one sock on each foot and then one shoe. Each buttonhole gets a button. At the breakfast table there is one bowl of cereal with one spoon and a glass of juice. It's time to go to school so one mitten goes on each hand and one boot on each foot. Everyone gets on the bus, and it's time to find a seat for every passenger.

At school each child has one locker or one hook for a coat and perhaps one mailbox for notes. Everyone needs a magazine, a bottle of glue, and a box of crayons for art. In the toy corner each car holds a driver, and the bus has one seat for each passenger.

Many toys lend themselves to matching. One rider can fit on each horse or in each plane. Dolls wear shoes, and pots and pans can have a certain spot on the shelf. In some families each person's towel goes on a particular hook. Parents and teachers can aid in matching when helping the child with table setting, treat distribution, or giving out balloons and favors at a birthday party. A single dandelion can go into each glass to decorate the table at a barbecue.

By the age of four most children are able to match objects. Children with cognitive developmental delays will have difficulty with the activities described in this section. Therefore, assessment of early matching abilities may help a teacher identify whether a certain child needs special attention.

When using concrete objects, it is helpful to show the child how to match items in a sequence from the child's left to right. For example, here the teacher helps the child match rabbits and carrots (Figure 3–9):

Figure 3–9

This method of lining up objects in horizontal rows shows the problem clearly and will help the child solve certain kinds of word problems in later years. For example, here is a typical first grade story problem:

There were five clowns and three balloons. How many clowns do not get a balloon? (Figure 3–10)

Figure 3–10

In addition, objects matched in horizontal lines will help in graphing activities in which rows are displayed. If pictures of clowns and balloons are graphed, the teacher might ask:

"How many more clowns are there than balloons?"

   or

"How many fewer balloons are there than clowns?"

Matching is one of the earliest mathematical concepts to develop. It forms the foundation for the development of many kinds of logical thinking.

Assessment of Matching Abilities

Assessment is an integral part of the planning, teaching, and review process. Each day you can observe and interview your students. As you move about the classroom or work with a small group at a table, you can see and hear how each child approaches matching activities. Here are some ways you might evaluate each child's progress:

Observe

How does the child spend time lining up the toys and putting together matches? Does the child report that more items are needed, that is, "I don't have enough cups for the table."

Interview

Ask the child to tell you a story about matched items and the problem of not having enough or having too many. How did the child decide this outcome? What could be done to remedy the situation?

When passing out items at school, for example, scissors to each person, ask "What can you do to pass out the scissors so everyone gets one? Where do you want to start?"

Performance Assessment—Identical Sets

Ages 4–5 years

Items needed: Identical items such as 36 green counting bears, lima beans or Cheerios, toothpicks.

1. Identical matching:
   Make a row of 8 green bears and have 8 more available. Ask the child to "give each bear a friend."

2. Matching many items:
   Try this task again with a longer row of 18 green bears.

3. Uneven sets:
   Put out 10 bears and give the child 6 lima beans or Cheerios. Ask the child to "give every bear a bean (Cheerio)." Listen to the child's response when he or she notices that there are not enough beans.

4. Joined sets:
   Put out 8 bears and show how to connect each bear with a toothpick and a bean. Ask the child to complete the task, starting from the child's left. (Figure 3–11)

Figure 3–11

Early matching activities are readily accomplished by most young children. If a child cannot perform them, try to have the child match items directly on top of picture cards. Wait several months and return to the basic matching activities. You may wish to ask for advice from your supervisor or math specialist for additional suggestions.

Performance Assessment—Equivalent Sets

Ages 5–7 years
   Items needed: A large number of counters, yarn, or paper plates.

1. Matching or making an equivalent set:
   This task requires the child to count the number of items in one set accurately and to remember the number long enough to create a new set. It also shows understanding of the concept of "the same number."

   Put 14 bears in one pile, perhaps in a circle of yarn, and ask the child to make a group just like it. (Figure 3–12)

Early Classification—Creating Sets

Children learn to put objects in their environment into certain groups or categories with the help of an adult. They see the "*sameness*" that defines the members of the group. For example, first a child learns about the group of animals named "dogs." There is the family dog, a neighbor's dog, and grandma's dog. One day the family takes a car trip on a rural road, and the child spots another "dog." It is a large animal, white with brown spots and a long tail, eating grass in the pasture.

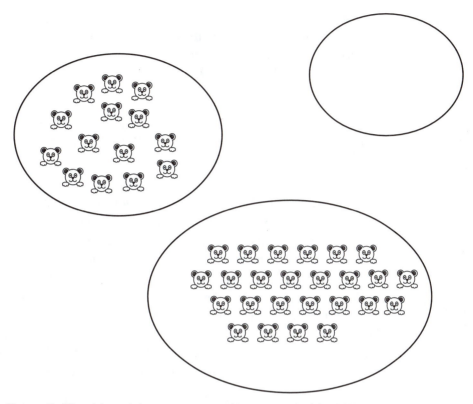

Figure 3–12   Materials to assess making an equivalent set.

"Doggie, doggie," shouts the child. The adult says, "No, it's a cow." So the old notion of "dog" must be revised in the child's mind, and a new group called "cow" must be created. The concept of creating and naming a set begins at an early age and continues throughout life as a way of connecting information and organizing our world.

A set is any well defined group of objects or ideas. A person establishes the characteristics of a set. If the criteria for membership in a set are vague, then it will be hard to decide whether the object or idea belongs to a particular set. For example, let's say we can agree on the group or "set" of cars. What about the set of American cars versus foreign cars? Can we agree on these subsets of the *universal set* of all cars?

We can define the subsets of two-door cars and four-door cars.

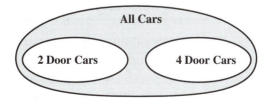

Figure 3–13   Subsets of all cars.

There is the subset of cars under warranty, and the subset of cars in need of major repair (defined as costing over $300). Hopefully, if your car needs repairs, it is also in the set of cars under warranty. This would be the intersection of two sets. (Figure 3–14)

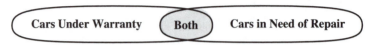

Figure 3–14   The intersection of two sets.

When a certain make of car has a brake defect, the manufacturer can pinpoint the set of owners who need to receive notice of a recall by serial numbers. Every member of this subset must be contacted in order to avoid a tragedy.

A *singular set* contains one member or element, such as a patented prescription drug. The *empty set* contains no elements, such as the set of all live giraffes in the classroom. In math, the number zero is the most famous empty set.

A set need not contain identical objects. Consider the set of dishes: plates, bowls, cups, and saucers. Or the set of golf clubs: woods, irons, and a putter. Sometimes children become confused when they are asked to attach a number to a set in a workbook and all the items are the same. (Figure 3–15)

4   3   5

Circle the correct number of monkeys

Figure 3–15   Workbook example.

A person could try to define a set of ideas, such as the set of American values found in the Declaration of Independence, that is, life, liberty, and the pursuit of happiness. Other disciplines such as history or philosophy look for these kinds of sets.

Children and Sets: Informal Learning Around Home and School

At home and at school children have numerous opportunities to learn about sets. Animals that live on the land . . . animals that live in the water. Pets are distinguished from wild animals. The dolls go in the doll corner, and the blocks are stacked on the block shelf. Teachers can use the term *set* along with the term *group*. Will the set of *all* the children who have their winter jackets on line up?

Some of you are wearing mittens, and *some* are not. *None* of you want to play outside today because it is too cold.

Whenever sorting people by category it is important to be sensitive to the need of most people, especially children, to belong to the popular group. We wouldn't sort groups by tennis shoes if only the rich children had them or by short/tall when everyone wishes to be taller. Of course, no one wants to be in the *singular* set of the last person to be picked for a team.

When children are asked to create sets they usually sort objects first by color and then by other dimensions. Depending on the type of material, children will make up their own groups. For example, when given a box of buttons, they may first start with groups by color, but when asked to sort them a different way, the children may choose the sets of "shiny" and "not shiny." Loops of heavy yarn are provided so the members of the set can be clearly placed in a particular location. Later, yarn will lend itself to creating visual pictures of subsets and intersecting sets. Some children create sets using size (big, little) and shape (round, square) on their own, but many children benefit from guidance from an adult.

Some children follow the teacher's lead by eyeballing or visually matching one object to another. For example, the teacher puts a "0" in the circle and asks the child to find more of these for the group. In this example, the child does not "create" the category of shape but follows the pattern and finds identical "0's".

The best categories come from children's imaginations. One first grader took two rhinestone buttons, a black medium-size button, and a red button and placed them in the circle of yarn. He said it was a "face." (Figure 3–16)

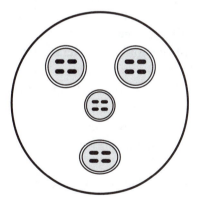

Figure 3–16 A child's set of buttons.

When sorting, many young children create a category of "other" from the items that don't belong in any group. This grouping is normal, especially when working with everyday materials.

In late kindergarten and first grade important work is done when creating all the subsets of a number, that is, $5 = \{5 + 0, 4 + 1, 3 + 2, 2 + 3, 1 + 4, 0 + 5\}$, in joining sets (adding), and separating sets (subtracting). Later chapters discuss these operations in detail.

Classroom Activities Involving Sets

Typically, a classification unit is taught in kindergarten and again in first grade. Other general uses of sets or grouping activities occur often in science class (e.g., desert animals and forest animals), social studies (e.g., city life and farm life), and in number work in math (e.g., joining sets–separating sets).

Students work in small groups based on their ability to explain aloud why they made certain decisions. Talkative children form one group, while shy or quiet children form another group. With three to five children in a small group, the teacher is able to listen to each child.

The teacher prepares for a classification activity by collecting everyday objects such as large buttons. Strings of thick yarn are formed into circles on the desk. White paper is available to make labels or names for the sets. Each child is given a small pile of buttons. The teacher asks an open ended question: "What groups can we make from these buttons?" Hopefully one child contributes a category such as "yellow buttons." If necessary, a yellow marker is used to create a picture card label. The children sort through their piles looking for yellow buttons and discussing what they found.

Perhaps another category is "dark buttons." Any reasonable explanation for inclusion in the set of "dark buttons" is accepted. Several circles are filled. The collection of buttons is returned to the container and redistributed. The objective of the activity is to make as many different groups as possible.

Some groups may need more prompts in order to get started. The teacher could say, "What colors do you find in your pile?" Quiet children need opportunities to justify their choices without being overwhelmed by the talkative members of the group. Talking and labeling the groups may take longer, but the goal is still accomplished. Remember that approximately 8% of males and 4% of females will have trouble with "color blindness." This difficulty usually results in the inability to distinguish the colors red and green.

As students progress they can try to create two categories, that is, pencils with erasers and pencils with no erasers. Finally, they can try to name the two groups without using the negative: For example, pens with caps and pens that retract (pop in). Because students experience very little opportunity to do complex sorting tasks outside the classroom, these activities are one key to later math success.

Assessment of the Relationships Involving Classification

You can learn what your students know about sets in three ways. Informally watch and listen, or interview them for their general progress. At the end of a unit you may wish to conduct a more formal evaluation such as a performance assessment.

Observe

How does the child sort collections of toys such as farm animals? Does the child put all the cows around the trough and the pigs by the fence? Most preschool children make groups from larger sets of objects.

Interview

Ask the child to tell you a story about the play scene or informal sorting activity. How many different dimensions or categories are created? If possible, keep a list of the labels developed by each child.

Performance Assessment

- Ages 4 1/2–6 years
- Items needed: A small collection of everyday objects that vary by at least three dimensions, such as color, size, shape, markings. Sets of buttons, earrings, and jewelry (no sharp objects), shells and stones work well. Thick yarn cut into lengths that can be formed into circles by overlapping the ends. Paper, markers for labels.
- Ask each individual child to create sets and describe them. There are no "right or wrong" answers, or "correct" number of variables. Performance often depends upon prior practice.

Comparing

While early classification has to do with *sameness*, comparing has to do with *difference*. The earliest comparing concepts are opposites that are readily observed and experienced in the preschool years. Ordinarily they do not need to be taught. The common comparing language words are found in Chapter 2.

In addition to comparing two objects or events such as opposites, children may be asked to compare two quantities. When given two piles of beans, the teacher might ask, "Which pile has more? Which pile has less? Are they both the same?" To solve these problems the child will use visual skills, counting, or matching. Finally, comparing is an essential skill for our next concept: order or seriation.

Comparing: Informal Learning Around Home and School

In the preschool–kindergarten years parents can help their child label everyday objects with the comparing words. For example, a pair of words such as "hot–cold" might be highlighted one week. At home and school the child can be encouraged to relate these opposites to immediate experiences. For example, "My soup is too hot to eat," "My milk is cold." While talking about the weather, it may be possible to only use one word, for example, "It's cold outside." It may not be "hot outside" for months. The child needs to say the word aloud, rather than nod affirmatively to an adult's inquiry. Instead of saying, "Is your soup too hot?" you might ask, "Tell me about your soup. . . . " Sometimes adults talk too much when it is the children who need a chance to use new vocabulary words.

Because most preschoolers readily use these words to describe everyday events, there should be little need to incorporate most comparing words into structured activities. Some opposites, such as "heavy–light" will need to be taught while "weighing" a variety of materials on a pan balance scale. Children who lack many comparing language concepts might learn them from children's literature, music, nursery rhymes, or from dramatic play. (See classroom activities for Chapter 2.)

For other opposites, such as "rough–smooth," a shoe box can be filled with items to be sorted: fabrics such as silk, rayon, satin, felt, corduroy, terry cloth, brocade, nubby wool; pieces of kitchen scrubbers, fruit pits; small rocks. Laminated labels of the two categories are stored in the box. Parents and children can contribute to these collections.

Ordering or Seriation

Ordering or seriation involves putting more than two objects, or sets with more than two members, into a sequence. Common ways to order may be by size (little to big), length (short to long), height (short to tall), or width (thin to thick). Later activities involving more complex dimensions such as color (light–dark), texture (rough–smooth), or capacity (less–more liquid) are appropriate.

Ordering is more difficult than comparing because now the child must make several decisions. For example, with three straws of different lengths, the middle straw must be *taller* than the preceding one, but *shorter* than the following one.

Piaget described three stages of growth in ordering (Copeland, 1984). When given a group of sticks of various lengths, the child of three to four years could not order them. The sticks would be placed in *random order*, so that there was no satisfactory pattern. Around the age of five, the child could order the sticks using *trial and error*. The sticks were moved from location to location until the task was accomplished. Finally, the child of six or older could consider all the sticks before moving them, form a plan of operation, and then choose the sticks in a *systematic* fashion.

Young children (ages 2 1/2–5 years) who attend Montessori School often order wooden cylinders by diameter, placing them in self-correcting compartments, or order sets of color tiles by hue. Therefore it would appear that some aspects of ordering tasks improve with practice, and may be accomplished at an earlier age.

Ordering two sets of objects is called *double seriation*. A good example might be the story of "Goldilocks and the Three Bears." Papa Bear gets the big bowl. Mama Bear gets the medium bowl. Baby Bear gets the little bowl. (Figure 3–17)

As long as there is a pattern to the ordering, each set can have it's own system. Papa Bear could get the little bowl because he's on a diet. Mama Bear gets the middle bowl. And Baby Bear is so hungry, he gets the big bowl! In the upper grades, many sets of numbers are ordered so that the relationship between them can be explored.

Figure 3–17   *Example of double seriation.*

Finally, reverse seriation occurs when a previously-decided-upon sequence is used backwards. The most common example would be to count backwards. The sequence is learned one way and then reversed. Counting backwards is a difficult skill to master for many first graders. Some children use it naturally to solve subtraction problems. Others find it tedious. Adults experience reverse seriation when an elevator descends, the temperature falls rapidly, or the remote control flips through the channels in opposite order. Seeing it happen or reading it from an instrument is far easier than memorizing it.

Why is the concept of ordering so important? First, ordering is one foundation of our number system. Two is bigger than one. Three is bigger than two. Second, much confusion exists about the topic and what children should be learning in kindergarten and first grade math. Many parents and teachers do not see the difference between oral counting, which is relatively easy to master, and other counting concepts. These concepts include answering the question "How many?," attaching a numeral to a set (e.g., counting five beach balls and circling, or writing the number five), and labeling a position with an ordinal number (e.g., first). Another difficult concept involves using a number line to measure continuous materials such as an piece of rope.

Ordering or Seration: Informal Learning Around Home and School

Toddlers love to play in the kitchen. Mixing bowls and measuring cups provide nesting experiences as do commercial toys like nesting rings. Daily routines provide sequences according to the time of day, for example, breakfast, lunch, and dinner. Towels may be layered on the rack—bath towel, hand towel, washcloth. The ordinal words, "Who wants to be *first*?" "Are you going to be the *last* one on the bus?" are often heard. Picture books show stages of growth from baby to adult. Children often draw their families in order of age, from little brother to dad. These informal experiences, as well as early counting, involve ordering.

Here are some additional classroom examples. Some ordering materials are available commercially, such as the Montessori nesting cylinders and color tiles, or picture sequence cards of everyday events. In addition, teachers collect boxes containing items such as gloves, mittens, socks, or shoes in various sizes. Plastic jars (from peanut butter) can be filled with different levels of water or rice. Xylophones and pianos have notes arranged from low to high. With a pan balance scale pieces of fruit can be weighed and ordered. For time sequences, the teacher may take photos of daily activities, label them, and put them on the bulletin board.

During science activities, bean plants can be ordered on the windowsill. Forced spring bulbs such as hyacinths, daffodils, tulips, and amaryllis are easy to arrange by height.

Jars of equal size, but filled with different quantities, may help children estimate quantity from visual benchmarks. For example, four separate jars can be filled with 10, 25, 50, and 100 jelly beans. A child scoops some jelly beans from a bowl and decides which jar comes the closest to the quantity scooped.

Beginning in grade one, children learn the ordinal name for the numbers 1 to 10. To make this skill easier, teachers may wish to pair the language words, "number one—first, number two—second, number three—third, and so forth."

Games may be one way to learn about ordering while having fun. The game, "Simon Says," can be played using ordinal commands. For example, Simon Says: "Will the fourth child take a banana step?" When lining up for recess, groups can be called by order. To make a game of it, roll one die, call out the number, for example: "Number 3, the third table gets to be first in line." Whenever this game is played, be sure that the directionality (front to back) of the line is clear so the children can understand their respective positions.

Assessment of Relationships Involving Ordering

You can learn what your students know about order or seriation in three ways. Informally watch or observe, and listen or interview them for their general progress. At the end of a unit you may wish to conduct a performance assessment to see how the children are progressing in their understanding of ordering.

Observe

How does the child accomplish ordering tasks using materials available in the classroom? Can the child order nesting boxes or commercial sets of sequence cards? What about a set of socks in various sizes?

Interview

Ask the child to tell you a story about a family picture. How does the child describe the sizes and ages of each family member?

When given an ordering activity such as a set of straws of various lengths, how does the child approach the activity? Is there a systematic plan for ordering the straws?

Performance Assessment: Ordering

- Ages: 6 1/2 + years
- Items needed: A group of 6 to 8 animals of different heights and a group of toy people.
- Directions: Ask the child to make a line from the animals. The smallest animal goes in front, and then the next animal, until all the animals are in order. Ask the child: "Show me the *fourth* animal." Show me the *second* animal."
  Then make a line of people, and see if the child can name the positions: First, second, . . . eighth. Ask the child: "This person is first. What place does the next person have? . . .?

Summary

Much informal learning about matching, classifying, comparing, and ordering takes place in the preschool years. Teachers recognize the role these important relationships play in the early math curriculum. Careful attention to how children develop language learning, visual–spatial abilities, and logical thinking in each area will help the teacher plan for developmentally appropriate math activities.

Activities and Study Questions

1. Compare and contrast the views of Piaget and Montessori on the development of early math concepts such as comparing, ordering, classification, and counting. Write a journal entry or brief paper describing your conclusions.
2. Collect a set of empty photographic film containers and fill them with everyday materials in various weights. Interview a child of five to six years and watch and listen as the child puts them in order from light to heavy. Begin with three containers and then try five containers.
3. Visit your local library and select a children's book that illustrates sets of objects. Develop a classification activity that could extend the ideas presented in the book. Be prepared to share your book and curricular ideas with the class.
4. Create a Venn diagram on a large piece of paper. Choose characteristics that some members of the class will have and others will not. Have your classmates sign their names in the circles or intersections that apply to them.
5. Develop a set of picture cards of things that go together by association, such as letter carrier (mail box, mail truck, mail bag) or fire fighter (fire truck, hose, hat, boots, and coat, fire hydrant). Ask a preschool child to sort your pictures and identify the items. Decide if the pictures represent people and objects in the child's environment.

Classroom Equipment

toy animals
toy dishes
checkers
lima beans
counters such as small bears
toothpicks
nesting toys
plastic jars of various sizes
balance scale

treasure boxes—
buttons, keys, shells
rocks, bread tags,
bottle caps, earrings
one kind of item per
small checkbook-size box
shoe boxes containing a
variety of mittens or
socks
estimating jar filled with a number of objects
(under 100 items per jar)

Further Reading

Bauch, J. P., & Huei-hsin, J. H. (1988). Montessori: Right or wrong about number concepts? *Arithmetic Teacher*, 36, (6), 8–11. *The authors compare the views of Piaget and Montessori on the way to develop early math concepts such as matching, ordering, and classification. They differ in their approach to the development of number concepts. The article clarifies their thinking in many areas.*

Lewis, C., & Lewis, T. (1995). Math by the month: Dressing up. *Teaching Children Mathematics*, 2, 28 – 29. *The authors use the back-to-school shopping experiences of many families to describe math activities involving clothing. Many ideas relate to ways to classify clothing, including pattern, long–short sleeves, and shoe size.*

Stenmark, J. K., Thompson, V., & Cossey, R. (1986). *Family Math.* Berkeley: University of California.

The authors present a variety of activities and games to develop the concepts of comparing and ordering. The directions are clearly written, and the materials needed are available in most households.

Whitin, D. J., Mills, H., O'Keefe, T., & Thiessen, D. (1994). Links to literature: Exploring subject areas with a counting book. *Teaching Children Mathematics*, 1, 170–174. *Using the classification questions in the children's book,* How Many Snails? A Counting Book, *the authors explore ways to encourage story writing based on the children's unique interests in various attributes. One child wanted to write about animals that live in water and eat bugs. An additional example illustrates the different sets children created for a transportation unit.*

References

Brush, L. R. (1972). Children's conception of addition and subtraction: The relation of formal and informal notions. Unpublished doctoral dissertation, Cornell University.

Copeland, R. W. (1984). *How children learn mathematics: Teaching implications of Piaget's research.* New York: Macmillan.

Gellman, R., & Gallistel, C. R. (1978). *The child's understanding of numbers.* Cambridge: Harvard University Press.

4 Space and Shape

THE DEVELOPMENT OF SPATIAL SENSE is an essential tool for mathematical thinking using geometry. Many adults feel intimidated by tasks such as "counting the number of cubes" in an illustration when only one side view is given. Fortunately, visual imagery and spatial abilities improve with practice (Yackel & Wheatley, 1986; Del Grande, 1990).

The NCTM Standards (1989) define spatial sense in this way:

> Spatial sense is an intuitive feel for one's surroundings and the objects in them. To develop spatial sense, children must have many experiences that focus on geometric relationships: the direction, orientation, and perspectives of objects in space, the relative shape and sizes of figures and objects, and how a change in shape relates to a change in size. (p. 49)

A child's first understanding of geometry occurs as physical knowledge of space. An infant sees a mother's face in one view from below, in another when cuddled in her arms, and yet another view from an infant seat. A face is not a static "photograph" of the person. Instead there are "several faces," depending on the angle of sight.

Adults also perceive shapes differently, depending on the distance. A driver has one view of the last house on the block when driving up the street, and a different view when the car is parked in front. Because adults have developed perspective, they are able to picture the house as a static object.

We orient ourselves and move "in space." The young child reaches for a rattle on the tray, or crawls to the coffee table, and pulls himself up by the rim. Adults walk up a familiar set of stairs without glancing down. But on a novel set of steps leading down to the beach, we watch our feet in order to judge the next movement. A football player throws a pass down field, and the receiver catches it. Two dancers step onto a crowded dance floor and find room to move. A teenager holds up a pair of jeans at the department store and decides whether the size may fit. These activities illustrate some of the ways in which people relate to the space around them.

A second type of judgment about space is made about objects in relation to each other or to their surroundings. How far is it between two trees? Will a hammock fit in the space? Will the toy fit in the shoe box? What is the next color of bead in the pattern created with blue, yellow, and green beads? Here we make decisions based on where things are in relation to each other.

Young children begin their study of geometry with the topic of topology, a special kind of geometry that investigates these kinds of relationships. In topology, materials may be squeezed or stretched to create mathematical investigations. For example, a ball of clay can be turned into a snake and be topologically equivalent. In the geometry of rigid shape (Euclidean geometry), two different shapes—a sphere and a cylinder—are formed.

A geoboard and rubber bands are helpful tools to show many different shapes as created with the same rubber band (see Figure 4–1).

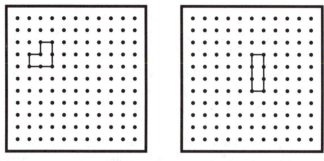

Figure 4–1   *Geoboard shapes.*

Topology is the study of the relationships between objects, places, or events rather than the ability to draw common shapes such as a circle or a square.

In general, children need topological experiences in many sizes of space in order to develop spatial abilities.

Large space   These spaces include playgrounds, fields, or parks with equipment to climb, swing, slide, circle, and run. Gyms can also have enough space for running games, throwing balls, swinging on ropes, or jumping on trampolines.

Medium space   These spaces involve room or floor spaces that allow activities such as block building or housekeeping where children can climb inside the creations, or build a structure taller than themselves.

Small space   These spaces involve tabletop size building such as Legos, Duplos, regular Tinkertoys, and many manipulatives used as part of the math curriculum. The pieces generally fit in a child's hand.

Four topological concepts—proximity, separation, order, and enclosure—form the foundation for preschool/kindergarten experiences in geometry. A few essential ideas are not readily understood until around third grade.

Proximity refers to questions about position, direction, and distance. The topic concerns itself with "Where am I?" or "Where are you?" (in–out, above–below, in front–in back.) "Which way?" (toward–away, around–through, forward–backward), and "Where is it?" (near–far, close to–far from).

Separation refers to the ability to see a whole object as composed of individual parts or pieces. Children draw the human figure as an egg shape with eyes and mouth and sticks for arms/legs. Later a torso, fingers, and toes are added (Sanford & Zelman, 1981). The concept of parts and wholes gradually emerges with experiences in model building, puzzles, and block building. The wheels snap on the toy car. The bear gets a sweater and hat. A garage is built to house the trucks. Later, in the primary grades, the ability to visualize 1,000 little cubes inside a wooden block is needed to use this manipulative as a model of our place value system.

Separation also has to do with recognizing boundaries. A line of yellow tape on the gym floor divides the space. The class stands behind the yellow line until the teacher gives the signal to run. The river separates downtown from the neighborhood. The babysitter says: "Stay on this side of the railroad tracks."

Order refers to the sequence of objects or events. The two common ways to describe order are from "first to last," or backwards, from "last to first." Order can also refer to making a pattern or arranging things in space so that they please the eye. Children learn to sequence a day using picture cards before they can use the vocabulary of first, second, third. Reversing a sequence, such as counting backwards or talking about last week's events is difficult for some first grade students. Pattern activities (Chapter 5) and matching a number to a set (where four counts are matched with the numeral 4, and five counts with the numeral 5) develop a sense of order.

Enclosure refers to being surrounded or boxed in by the surrounding objects. A point on a line can be enclosed by the points on either side. In three-dimensional space, a fence can enclose the animals, or a canister with a lid can enclose the cereal.

While enclosure technically refers to what's inside, there are actually three dimensions pertinent to geometry. For example, in describing a dog house there is the enclosure or space for the dog to live in (cubic yards/meters); the boundary or dimensions of perimeter, wall surface measures, roof measures; and the space outside the house, such as the yard to play in. Young children often confuse area with perimeter. They think the boundary is the same as the enclosure. Activities involving templates help develop these three different spaces. For example, children put the template of a cat on a piece of paper. They trace the outline. Then they can color the cat or the background (Figure 4–2).

Figure 4–2

Space: Informal Learning at Home and School

Developing concepts about space is a natural part of growing up. Opportunities to play in large open areas, on safe playground equipment, and to create objects in medium space are crucial. Children should not be confined to infant seats, playpens, or a small crowded room.

Proximity concepts are developed when teachers and caregivers encourage children to use the special language words for position and direction as described in Chapter 2. "My chair is next to the wall." The beads fell *under* the desk. Board games such as checkers encourage movement and planning about space.

Separation into parts and wholes occurs when children play with dolls and outfits, jigsaw puzzles, Duplos or Legos, paper dolls or models that come apart. Over time children can talk about the various parts of an object. For example, a chair has a seat, legs, and perhaps a back or arms.

Comprehending order is encouraged by reading children's literature such as *Hansel & Gretel*. A sequence of events happens and then is reversed. Many classics for young children, such as *The Very Hungry Caterpillar* (Carle, 1981), use time as a sequence.

Activities that involve the concept of enclosure include building structures with walls, doors, and roofs and housing small animals such as gerbils and birds. Questions asked include: "Is the cage door closed so our bird, Penny, can't fly away?" Collections of animals and fencing also create opportunities for enclosures. Jars with lids and boxes with covers can be filled, closed, and opened at a later time.

Many classroom activities can be created to enhance learning about geometry. An obstacle course can be set up in the gym so that children follow a series of commands using the language of topology. Children climb *under* the sawhorse and crawl through the large box. Commercially produced mats calls "Workmat Math" (Creative Publications) are designed for direct instruction in this math language. These motivating scenes are used at the late kindergarten and first grade levels. Animal-shaped cards (ETA) are covered with pattern blocks. Early cards have the outline of the pieces needed to fill the animal. Later cards can be covered with many different combinations. These cards provide productive seatwork, while teaching about parts and wholes.

Order can be highlighted in a lesson when the teacher puts coins in a piggy bank and asks: "Which coin was last?" Making collages from scraps of fabric, lace, and yarn encourages a sense of balance or interesting arrangements of items on a poster.

Geoboards, rubber bands, and dot recording paper are useful tools to explore changing shapes. Geoboards give exposure to "closed curves" and also help develop visual imagery. A closed curve is made by stopping and starting a figure at the same point. A key ring must be closed in order to hold keys. A hook in the coat closet is open so a jacket can be hung on it.

Bean bag toss is another classroom game that teaches the concept of enclosure. Is the bag inside, outside, or on the square? Finally, block building is an invaluable activity for all students. Block building should be understood as a part of the geometry curriculum that should not be missed by anyone.

Assessment of Spatial Relationships

Observe

Does the child follow directions that use the positional, order, and distance words? Can the child tell when the whole object is present or identify a missing part? Can the child describe the parts of an object? For example, what parts make up your tennis shoe? Can the child build an enclosure with fencing so the animals can't get out? Does the child use the words, "outside–inside" or "between"?

Interview

Ask the child to tell you a story about the classroom activities, such as the obstacle course or model building. With the exception of the words for sequence or order, the concepts and vocabulary highlighted in this chapter should be mastered by age six.

Performance Assessment (Ages 6–7 Years)

- Items needed: A cardboard tube from a paper towel roll or potato chip tube container; cubes or balls of four different colors; pattern blocks, animal shape cards; embedded figure pictures; geoboards, rubber bands, and dot paper.
- Directions: Put three different colored cubes into the tube. "Which one will come out first? (reverse order)
- Have the child find embedded figures, such as birds hidden in the tree.*
- See if the child can cover the animal shape in more than one way.
- Assess whether the child can copy a pattern from the geoboard on dot paper.*

The Art of Block Building

Blocks have been a tradition in kindergarten classrooms since 1914. They are a most useful tool for self-education. When children play with blocks they create their own world and act out scenes important to their lives. Curiosity, imagination, dramatic play, and geometry come together in the block corner.

The teaching techniques used with blocks are simple. First, have enough blocks and have them readily available. Four- and five-year-olds need a variety of shapes, including arches, ramps, cylinders, Y switches, and decorative wooden dowels for elaboration. Store blocks on low shelves or pile them in

---

*Some children with visual perceptual problems will have difficulty with these tasks until the upper grades.

bins. There is no need to label the shapes as a "triangle" or a "cylinder." The whole block construction is key.

When complicated systems for placing blocks back on the shelf are devised, teachers may be reluctant to let children use them. Clean-up seems to take too long, and the essential learning experience is lost. A box of cars, trucks, and people is often stored next to the blocks. However, if children only build highways to race cars, temporarily remove these items and encourage other ideas.

Children may build whatever they like, as long as they do not destroy other people's creations or use a block for a "gun." Children will build what they see in the neighborhood or in the media. Some sessions seem very violent, as they act out their fears. Encourage them to tell a story about their designs. Listen and let the child talk without interruption.

Common early techniques (2–3 year olds) include carrying, stacking, and moving the blocks around. The desire to build a tower as high as it can stand seems universal. Eventually walls and floors emerge.

Sometime after the age of three children solve the problem of bridging or roofing between two walls (Figure 4–3). Walls connect to form enclosures (Figure 4–4).

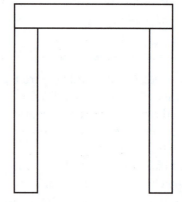

Figure 4–3   Bridging between two walls.

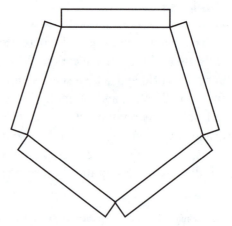

Figure 4–4   Using blocks to make an enclosure.

Older children with emotional problems may build a simple enclosure and crawl in to sleep.

Later techniques (ages four–five years) include dramatic play, naming whole structures, and stair building. Children at one day care center built a "hotel and a McDonald's." They spent the morning going back and forth between the two structures. With adequate time, a variety of blocks and practice, children build very elaborate designs. (Figure 4–5)

Figure 4–5   Kindergarten child and her block building.

Blocks for Girls as Well as Boys

Developing spatial sense takes practice. Many teachers report that girls do not visit the block corner as frequently as boys. Sometimes the boys race to the corner so quickly that the girls abandon their plans to build. Since wooden blocks are expensive, few households can afford to buy them for play at home. Block building teaches so many geometrical concepts that the experience should not be left to chance. Some teachers form small groups and rotate the groups so everyone gets a chance.

Teachers, principals, parent organizations, and school boards need to view block building as an essential part of the curriculum. Block collections need to be purchased and expanded on a regular basis. Many children are enrolled in some form of after-school day care. Block building is a productive way to fill these hours. Also, block building need not be confined to the preschool and kindergarten years. First graders and some second graders would benefit from blocks too.

Shape

Shape is the study of rigid figures, their properties, and their relation to one another. The most common investigations concern the space figures, such as a ball, and the plane figures, such as a circle. An example of a shape relationship concept might be, "Are the two triangles the same (congruent)?" Common three-dimensional or space figures found in the early childhood classroom include the sphere, the cylinder, the cone, the cube, and the rectangular prism (Figure 4–6).

Figure 4–6 *Common space figures.*

Common plane figures include circle, triangle, square, rectangle, rhombus, and ellipse (Figure 4–7).

Figure 4–7 *Common plane figures.*

Children find similarities and differences in forms in the environment. Developing the ability to discriminate one form from another is the instructional goal of the early shape curriculum.

Shape: Informal Learning Around Home and School

Young children learn to tell one shape from another by handling objects. Some are easy to grasp and fit in the mouth. Some roll, and some don't. Some are smooth like a spoon. Others are sharp like a fork. After creating a finger-paint picture or collage, they may "see" a shape—"This looks like my dog."

In the beginning, only an equilateral triangle may be recognized as a triangle.

Other kinds with a variety of angles are rejected. Equilateral triangles are often the only models used in kindergarten. The figures are seen as a whole, without regard to the essential properties of the form.

Space figures are taught first, because these forms can be found in the environment. Often common names such as ball-shaped, or box-shaped describe objects. Cylinder shapes look like tubes or soda cans. Cube shapes look like small blocks or dice. Children invent their own points of reference using everyday experiences.

Informal learning about space figures occurs at home or school when the environment contains many objects to fill, pour from, nest, take apart, and put back together. A kitchen may hold measuring cups that nest, pots and pans with lids to match, and sinks and plastic jars for pouring. A sandbox can have pails and shovels and many forms to fill. Seeing pictures or watching videos, television, or computer screens cannot substitute for hands-on shape experiences. Children must touch and mold shapes as well as recognize them.

Plane figures such as circles and squares are often found in picture books. One beautiful example of shape occurs in Lois Ehlert's book, *Color Zoo* (1989). Many other excellent books can be readily found on library shelves. Parents and relatives often point out the shape name of common household items. The top of a soup can may be an object that lends itself to a lesson in shape: "See, the top is a circle." Many people feel that naming the common shapes is the task of early childhood geometry. Therefore they make an effort to often use the language words such as square or round.

Planning Activities About Shape

Children explore shape in a variety of ways. Four levels of difficulty outline the scope of the process. Generally, children begin with three-dimensional objects and proceed to plane figures.

Level I   *Match* one form to a similar shape. "Put the △ on the picture of a △."

Level II   Sort shapes by similarities. "Put all the △'s in one pile and all the ○'s in another."

Level III   Name the shape: "What shape is this?"

Level IV   Draw the shapes. Copy from a model or draw from memory (difficult).

Most children can draw all the common plane figures, including the rhombus by ages six to seven (Sanford & Zelman, 1981).

Classroom activities at the preschool–kindergarten level should encourage matching and sorting activities. Children can use everyday objects such as fruit to practice matching. One set of real fruit is on the table, while another set of plastic fruit is in the bag: "Put your hand in the bag, and pick a fruit. What do you have?" First the child names the mystery fruit and then removes it. Other kinds of collections can be used, as long as the objects have distinctive features. It would not be fair to put a pencil and a ballpoint pen in the same bag.

Matching is encouraged when a child creates "My book of shapes." Pictures of space figures are cut from magazines and newspapers and glued on paper. An entire book can be devoted to a particular form such as the ball. Or individual pages can be devoted to each form. In the math activity corner, a table can be partitioned and labeled by shape. Children bring objects from home and match them to the right spot on the shape table.

Sorting occurs as part of classification activities. Buttons are sorted by round and square. Shells are sorted by ridges and smooth. Sorting enables children to begin to focus on specific features or on parts of the whole. Later, in the primary grades, these skills will come in handy. Figures will be sorted by the number of corners or kinds of angles.

Children learn to associate a label or name with an object in many ways. It is beneficial to actually mold a shape from clay or play dough. Just tracing a form is not enough. Shapes can be created with toothpicks and marshmallows or gumdrops. Cookie dough can be molded and baked.

The actual drawing of plane figures can be left until first grade. Young children often do not have the fine motor control or the ability to discriminate the unique features of the common shapes. Perspective is needed to draw the space figures. Instead, paper folding of predrawn sections of space figures will aid in recognizing the various sides and corners. The pattern is traced, dotted lines are made for folds, and tape is used to keep the shape intact. Also, simple origami can be an enjoyable art activity as well as a math lesson.

Assessment of Shape

Observe

Does the child use shape to sort and classify? Can common objects be matched to three-dimensional space figures? Using shape picture books, does the child find the shape that goes with the story?

Interview

Ask the child to tell you about a fingerpainting or collage. Are shapes identified? Ask the child to name the basic plane figures and to describe the space figures in everyday terms, for example, oval or ellipse is egg shaped (age 6+ years).

Performance Assessment (Ages 5–6 Years)

- Items needed: Everyday objects such as balls, oatmeal canisters, ice cream cones, boxes, triangles (musical instruments), and the natural classroom environment.
- Ask the child to look around the room and find an example of a particular shape. If needed, show a line drawing of the figure as a prompt.
- Play "The Shape Board Game" as described in the activities section, "Ready-Set-Math."

Geometric Concepts in the Early Grades

Geometric reasoning is a part of many activities at school and in everyday life. Art projects, geography concepts including reading a map, and space exploration use these talents. Understanding form and having good spatial abilities contribute to success in auto design, home decorating, and garden planning. Measuring tools such as rulers and yardsticks, measuring cups, and thermometers rely on spatial sense. Fractional units are taught with pictures. In high school, manipulation of objects in space will aid the understanding of topics in algebra, trigonometry, and calculus. Unfortunately, most adults have had little exposure to geometry in the typical mathematics curriculum. One study of K–4 math textbooks found that, on average, fewer than 7% of the pages were devoted to geometric topics (Fuys, Geddes, and Tichler, 1988). At times, teachers skip these units due to pressure to "cover the rest of the book." Because spatial abilities develop slowly over many years, the NCTM Standards emphasize increased attention in the following areas:

> Standard 9: Geometry and Spatial Sense. In grades K-4, the mathematics curriculum should include two- and three-dimensional geometry so that students can do the following:
>
> - Describe, model, draw, and classify shapes
> - Investigate and predict the results of combining, subdividing, and changing shapes
> - Develop spatial sense
> - Relate geometric ideas to number and measurement ideas
> - Recognize and appreciate geometry in their world[*] (p. 48)

Since so many school subjects, careers and everyday activities depend on geometry, teachers must make a conscious effort to improve geometric instruction in the early years.

One model of geometric understanding was proposed by the Dutch mathematicians, Dina van Hiele-Geldof and her husband, Pierre Marie van Hiele (Crowley, 1987). They wrote that students had trouble with high school geometry because their early training had not allowed them to pass through five developmental stages. Teachers of young children are concerned with stages 0–2, which establish a foundation on which to build in future years.

- Stage 0: Visualization—recognizing and naming figures
- Stage 1: Analysis—describing the attributes
- Stage 2: Informal deduction—classifying and generalizing by attributes
- Stage 3: Deduction—developing proofs using axioms and definitions
- Stage 4: Rigor—working in various geometrical systems (Crowley, 1987)

At stage 0, young children name a figure a "square." They recognize the whole without being able to talk about the parts. At stage 1, children can say:

---

[*]Reprinted with permission from the *Curriculum and Evaluation Standards for School Mathematics* (1989) by the National Council of Teachers of Mathematics.

"There are four corners and four sides. The corners and the sides are the same." At stage 2, they can compare squares to other figures such as a parallelogram. Figures that are squares, can be classified, and information about angles can be used to investigate the forms. Students can organize discoveries about the properties of various figures to create informal definitions of the various classes and subclasses of figures.

To accomplish these three stages, the geometry curriculum in grades 1 to 3 contains these topics:

Recognizing shape
The discovery of the properties of shape
Topological geometry of closed/open curves
Motion geometry (slides, flips, turns)
Lines of symmetry
Mapping, using a grid and early coordinate geometry
Logo—computer software
Area, volume (early concepts)
Angles (early concepts)
Measurement (see Chapter 10)

In the early years, children master shape by molding, matching, creating shape books, and finding and labeling shapes in storybooks and their environments. To discover the properties of shape the teacher starts with the number of "corners" (vertices). These can be colored with a washable marker. Each "face" or side can be marked with a sticky note that shows a picture of a face (Figure 4–8).

Figure 4–8   *Faces mark the sides of a cube.*

Edges can be colored with a different marker. Using the textbooks' visuals is not enough. Real objects and hand-on experiences are needed.

The study of topology continues into the primary grades. Metal templates for the various plane figures are commercially available. An oval can be traced inside the tracing of a square. Children use colored pencils to shade the area not covered by the oval.

The relation of area to perimeter may be explored using an 11-point geoboard. Children think of the geoboard as a piece of farmland. A pig needs a certain amount of land. It is possible to build various sizes of pens using fencing made from the rubber band. A unit of fence stretches from peg to peg. Each new configuration is recorded on geoboard dot paper. If students are allowed only 12 units of fence, the area will change while the perimeter remains the same.

The study of *motion geometry* includes the concepts of "slides" "flips" and "turns." Shapes are moved in space, either by sliding, turning, or rotating (Figure 4–9).

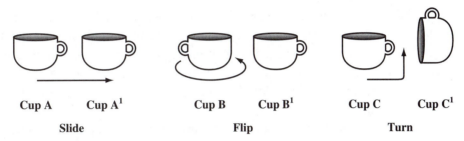

Cup A	Cup A^1		Cup B	Cup B^1		Cup C	Cup C^1
Slide			**Flip**			**Turn**	

Figure 4–9   *Common motions performed on a geometric shape.*

Pattern block activities provide opportunity to experience motion geometry. Blocks are moved, turn, or rotated, and children can create different designs. Units using tangram puzzle pieces and pentomino patterns also study the concepts of motion geometry.

Symmetry adds balance to a design and is pleasing to the eye. Lines of symmetry are found when an object, picture, or design can be separated into two identical halves. In nature, butterflies, some leaves, some flowers, and people have at least one line of symmetry (Figure 4–10). Many quilts have easy to find lines of symmetry. If the quilt pattern isn't too complicated, the cloth can actually be folded along the line. Cut-up fruit such as an orange can show a vertical and a horizontal line.

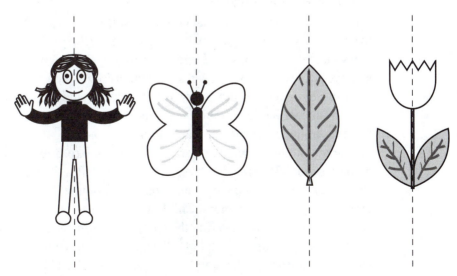

Figure 4–10   Line symmetry.

A natural way to investigate symmetry is by paper folding. In art class, a piece of paper is folded and dabs of colored paint are put on one side. The dry side is pressed over the wet side, and a mirror image appears. Snowflake designs are another possibility. Paper is folded and small triangles are cut. The paper is opened to reveal a symmetrical snowflake.

Another favorite activity involves cutouts of the alphabet. The students attempt to find lines of symmetry. The letters A and M have vertical lines, while B and D have horizontal lines. The letters I and O have both kinds of lines. Some letters, such as H, I, and O can be rotated 180 degrees and stay the same.

Around third grade, students are ready to study lines of symmetry in the various plane figures. The relationship of the number of lines of symmetry to the number of sides is investigated. For example, a square has four lines of symmetry and four sides. The study of symmetry leads to the study of congruence in the upper grades.

Following a "path," "mapping a route," and playing games on a grid develops informal knowledge of *coordinate geometry*. Using a coordinate system it is possible to locate a particular street on a city map. Children learn that when pairs of numbers are given, the first number refers to the horizontal number. The second number is the vertical number. Another way to think about the system is "over and up." One easy game uses a pegboard, two pegs of different colors, and a die marked 1-2-3, 1-2-3. Each play has one peg. The die is tossed. If a 2 comes up, the child reads the numbers and says, "over 2," and moves the peg horizontally. Then the same child shakes again. If the number 1 appears, the child says "up 1," and moves up one hole on the vertical axis. The die is passed to the next player. The winner is the person who gets off the board first.

Numerous companies publish seatwork in which the student finds dots using a coordinate system, such as letters and numbers. The child finds the dots and connects them. A mystery object appears. Students can make up their own puzzles to share with the class.

Logo (Terrapin) is a popular computer software program that allows students to create shapes and angles by moving a cursor (the turtle) on the screen. There are simplified versions of Logo such as Instant Logo to help third graders achieve success and then advance to regular Logo. Active learning experiences with space, including turns, forward, backward, and the concepts of right/left, lead to success on the computer screen. When taught well, Logo enhances the learning of the properties of plane figures and angles.

The geometric concepts of area and volume are often found in the second grade curriculum. Area can be approached as "tiling" with a ceramic tile unit square. The surface is covered and counted. Volume is discussed by filling and emptying various containers. Children guess how many cookies are in the jar and then spill and count to find the answer. Volume is also a major part of measuring, such as cups and quarts. The concept of volume as "what's inside" takes many years to develop. Around third grade, children will see that the amount of water in a glass stays the same when the water is poured into a pitcher. Therefore, early investigations should focus on filling containers with units, such as cookies or cubes, and counting them to find the volume.

Third graders investigate angles as turns. Triangles can be created on the geoboard, transferred to dot paper, and cut out. The various triangles can be sorted by the size of the largest angle, using three sizes—corner size, bigger than a corner, or smaller than a corner. A classroom door can be used to show opening the door to either corner size or less than corner size. Some doors can be opened to wider angles. When investigating the size of angles, a unit measure such as a wedge is helpful (Wilson & Rowland, 1993). A 45-degree unit piece is cut from cardboard. Students describe the measuring of angles by counting wedges (Figure 4–11).

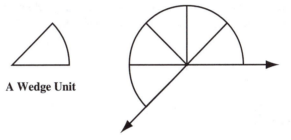

A Wedge Unit

Figure 4–11   An angle measured in wedge units.

Summary

The primary goal of the early geometry curriculum is to begin the process of developing spatial sense. Spatial sense is encouraged and fostered in an atmosphere that helps child experience space and shape in appropriate ways. While many relationships develop naturally, informal learning around home and school may be enhanced by activities such as block building, paper folding, and the use of geoboards. Active learning fosters a good beginning. When teachers build a solid foundation using informal geometric teaching techniques, students experience success in geometry in the upper grades. The teacher cannot rely on the textbook to teach geometry. Therefore, careful study and preparation of teaching activities is the key to student success.

Ready-Set-Math

◆ Ready-Set-Math

Ready-Set-Math:	Rubber Faces
	Ages 3–4 years
Items needed:	Pieces of old rubber gloves
	A permanent marker
Make ahead:	Put faces on the pieces of rubber

The children take turns stretching various pieces of rubber that have faces drawn on them. As they distort a typical face, they tell what happened, for example, "I made a long nose."

◆ Ready-Set-Math

Cookie Dough Shapes

Ages 3–5 years

Items needed:	Cookie dough/play dough
	Oven
	Cookie cutters in various shapes
	Wax paper
	Rolling paper

The teacher prepares the dough and rolls out a piece for each child. The child uses a variety of cookie cutters to create shapes. The cookies are baked. Before they are eaten by the group, the class discusses their attributes, for example, large–small, round–straight edges, corners–sides. Homemade play dough may be substituted for cookie dough.

Ready-Set-Math

The Shape Board Game

Ages 4–5 years

Items needed: A stack of shape cards, one playing board per player

Make ahead: Boards and cards

Take 8 1/2" x 11" cardboard and divide the playing board into nine cells, using a magic marker. Draw a different shape in each cell. Make a set of playing cards to match. Boards are not identical. Add a card with a "frown face," meaning "lose a turn." Include shapes of common objects such as a soda can, a cup, checkers, as well as circle and squares.

To play: Each player picks a card from the stack. If the shape card matches one on the playing board, it is placed on top of the square. If the card is not a match, it is returned to the discard pile.

The winner is the first person to cover all nine shapes.

Ready-Set-Math

The Treasure Chest Game

Ages 5–9 years, depending on the level of clues

Items needed: A small colorful box with a "prize" of candy or box of raisins. A set of clue cards.

Make ahead: Write a series of directions on separate cards. Each card will lead to finding the next card. The final "clue" leads to the treasure box.

Have the children use the cards to draw a path or map of the search, labeling each step in sequence.

Variation: Children write their own clues and exchange them with classmates.

Activities and Study Questions

1. Investigate a traditional quilting pattern and describe how it was created from a geometric perspective. Be prepared to share the history behind the development and popularity of the pattern.
2. Create a list of open and closed curves as they are found in our everyday environment. Write a journal entry or brief paper about your discoveries.
3. Visit a local kindergarten classroom and observe children as they play in the block corner. Do the girls use the blocks as much as the boys? What kinds of imaginary creations are the topic of conversation? How do these themes reflect the children's daily lives? Write a brief paper describing your observation.
4. Review the performance assessments for space and shape. Decide on one area and interview a young child using these tools. Write a short paper about your findings.
5. Review your own personal history concerning the study of geometry. What was your experience in the elementary school years? What happened to you in high school? How has the teaching of geometry changed over the past decades? Write a journal entry or brief report on your reflections.

Classroom Equipment

building blocks
small people, trucks and cars
rubber bands
geoboards
geoboard recording paper
playground equipment
puzzles
models to build, take apart
farm animals and fencing
animal templates to trace and color
children's literature on space,
shape, and sequence
embedded figure pictures
three-dimensional wooden space figures
metal shape templates
finger paint/paper

treasure boxes of items
such as bread tags,
colored pasta, or keys
jars with lids
boxes with covers
pattern blocks
animal shape cards (ETA)
pattern blocks
Workmat kits (Creative
Publications Company)
cardboard tubes from
paper towels
small beads, blocks in
various colors
plastic fruit
toothpicks, marshmallows
clay
cookie dough
origami paper and instructions

Further Reading

Carey, D. A. (1992). The patchwork quilt: A context for problem solving. *Arithmetic Teacher, 40,* 199–203. *The author uses the award-winning book The Patchwork Quilt (Flournoy, 1985) to design a geometry unit involving arrays of square units. Measurement and determination of the size of the units also play an important role. The class may wish to make a simple quilt, and write a story about their squares.*

Claus, A. (1992). Exploring geometry. *Arithmetic Teacher, 40,* 14–17. *The author focuses on some very valuable principles while working in geometry. The school year may begin with lessons such as the ones in triangles described in the article. Geometry develops visual–spatial activities, and provides a rich source of oral and written communication.*

Evered, L. J. (1992). Folded fashions: Symmetry in clothing design. *Arithmetic Teacher, 40,* 204–206. *The author encourages both girls and boys to explore symmetry and pattern making in a fashion design unit. Gowns are constructed from paper napkins, newsprint, or cloth. Illustrations give the teacher a place to begin, so that the students' creations will succeed.*

Lamphere, P. (1994). Investigation: How does it look? *Teaching Children Mathematics, 1,* 222–230. *Students investigate the three-dimensional world with a variety activities, including making a building by paper folding. Students draw patterns for houses, test them, and share them with their peers.*

Smith, J. (1995). Links to literature: Threading mathematics into social studies. *Teaching Children Mathematics, 1,* 438-444. *The author uses several stories from children's literature to stimulate interest in such mathematical concepts as square numbers, tesselations, and analyzing complicated quilting patterns. These traditional patterns tell us much about the history of the United States. The children designed and created their own classroom quilt and hung it in the school hall for everyone to enjoy.*

References

Carle, E. (1981). *The Very Hungry Caterpillar.* New York: Philomel Books.

Crowley, M. L. (1987). The van Hiele model of the development of geometric thought. In M. M. Lindquist & A. P. Schulte, (eds.) *1987 Yearbook: Learning and teaching geometry, K–12.* (pp. 1–16). Reston, VA. National Council of Teachers of Mathematics.

Del Grande, J. J. (1990). Spatial Sense. *Arithmetic Teacher, 37,* (6), 14–20.

Ehlert, L. (1989). *Color Zoo* New York: J. B. Lippincott.

Fuys, D., Geddes, D., & Tichler, R. (1988). The van Hiele model of thinking in geometry among adolescents. *Journal for Research in Mathematics Education, Monograph No. 3.* Reston, VA: National Council of Teachers of Mathematics.

National Council of Teacher of Mathematics (1989). *Curriculum and Evaluation Standards for School Mathematics.* Reston, VA: Author.

Sanford, A. R., & Zelman, J. G. (1981). *Learning accomplishment profile, revised.* Chapel Hill, NC: Chapel Hill Training—Outreach Project.

Wilson, P. S., & Rowland, R. (1993). In R. J. Jensen, (ed.) *Research Ideas for the Classroom: Early Childhood Mathematics.* (pp. 188–189). New York: Macmillan.

Yackel, E., & Wheatley, G. H. (1990). Promoting visual imagery in young people. *Arithmetic Teacher, 37,* (6), 52–58.

5 Pattern

MANY TEACHERS OF YOUNG CHILDREN are surprised to learn that pattern is a major topic in the early math curriculum. Their own early experiences might be confined to figuring out number problems such as 1, 3, 7, 15 . . . on a standardized test. Yet most preschool classrooms own a set of bead pattern cards and a bucket of colored beads to string. Why study pattern beyond "red bead, blue bead, red bead, blue bead . . . ?

The Importance of Pattern

First, number systems have patterns just by the nature of the way they are constructed. Common sequences include the odd and even counting numbers and the perfect squares (1, 4, 9, 16 . . .). In the upper grades students discover the number patterns in Pascal's triangle, and the Fibonacci sequence (1, 1, 2, 3, 5, 8 . . .). In the Fibonacci sequence, after the two 1's, each term is the sum of the two preceding terms. Many patterns in nature, such as the arrangement of sunflower seeds in the cone of the flower, follow this pattern (Sutton, 1992). Adults use patterns such as odd-even to locate a home, by noting which street addresses are found on one side of the street.

Second, looking for patterns is a logical form of problem solving. When a sequence of numbers is involved, or a table of data can be organized into a pattern, then a rule can be generated for making predictions about the solution in general. The rule can be turned into a formula and applied to any similar situation.

Suppose you were given a birthday present of $100 for every calendar date during the year. On June 1st you received $100, June 2nd $200 for a total of $300. A new month began the cycle over. July 1st = $100. About how much is your gift worth in one year? Estimate your answer. Is there a rule or formula to solve this problem?

Pattern plays an important role in the mathematics curriculum. The NCTM *Curriculum and Evaluation Standards for School Mathematics* (1989) highlight patterns and Relationships in Standard 13:

In grades K–4, the mathematics curriculum should include the study of patterns and relationships so that students can

- recognize, describe, extend, and create a wide variety of patterns
- represent and describe mathematical relationships
- explore the use of variables and open sentences to express relationships[*] (p. 60)

[*]Reprinted with permission from the *Curriculum and Evaluation Standards for School Mathematics* (1989) by the National Council of Teachers of Mathematics.

Children enjoy working with patterns, and seem to do extremely well. They readily identify patterns in bulletin board displays and on their own clothing. Even labeling a pattern with an A-B-C code seems easy. A pattern unit can be integrated into the curriculum over several months without running into resistance or boredom. Pattern is one form of problem solving that young children can master using the multiple intelligences of music, art, and movement. Pattern activities become progressively more difficult from preschool through the grade school years. Teachers who understand the developmental sequence of pattern activities can create experiences that will engage the curiosity of all children.

Principles of Pattern

1. Patterns can be numerical (involving numbers) or non-numerical (involving shape, sound, or other attributes such as color or position).

2. Patterns lend themselves to three general types: repeating patterns, growing patterns, and relationship patterns.

In repeating patterns, the core element repeats: 246 246 246.

In growing patterns, the core element is used as a building block to create larger elements: XY XYY XYYY.

In relationship patterns, a connection is made between two sets: one box of crayons has eight crayons. A table can be made from the data, 1 – 8, 2 – 16, 3 – 24 and so on.

A more abstract example might be to create a rule: For any number chosen, the answer is to double the number and add 1. For example, 3 – 7, 8 – 17, 24 – 49. For example: One way to think about the process is to use the concept of a function machine. One number goes "in," another number comes "out." The number 8 goes in, 17 comes out.

3. Children explore pattern on four levels: they *recognize* a pattern; they *describe* a pattern; they *extend* a pattern; and they *create* their own patterns. Young children generally begin with an "ab" core, using color or position (red cube - blue cube, sit - stand). Examples of the four levels, using non- numerical and numerical patterns, are illustrated throughout this chapter.

4. Repeating patterns vary in difficulty when the core element varies by two or more attributes, such as color and number. Easier patterns include AB, AABB, ABC. More difficult patterns include ABB, AAB, ABCC, or other more complex variations.

A pattern can be created with objects such as fruit (apple, pear, apple, pear . . .). The fruit pattern can be translated into a unifix cube train (red, yellow, red, yellow . . .), or an alphabetical code (a, b, a, b,), or notes on an instrument (e.g., the teacher plays a xylophone C-E-C-E) (Figure 5–1).

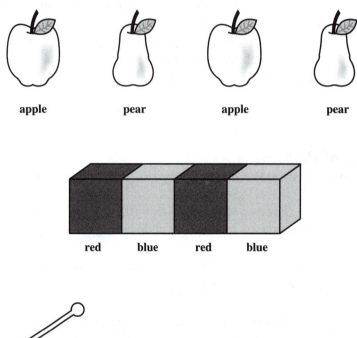

| apple | pear | apple | pear |

| red | blue | red | blue |

Play C - E- C -E

Figure 5–1   Examples of AB repeating patterns.

Recognizing, labeling, and translating patterns are challenging early math experiences.

Early Classroom Activities

In kindergarten and first grade children work with patterns using (1) real objects, (2) themselves, and (3) pattern cards. Children can create their own patterns and share them with the class. In second and third grade, more sophisticated "number" pattern work is done using odd–even, the multiples, and a number chart. Pattern work that combines number and geometry includes recognizing perfect squares and tesselations (Young, 1994). Each kind of pattern activity is described in this chapter.

Real Objects (Kindergarten Level)

Everyday objects such as fruit, nuts, cookies, juice cans\boxes, blocks, or simple toys can be used to create a pattern. A sequence is begun by putting the items in a row in front of a group of children, beginning on the left. Early patterns use two objects, for example, apples and oranges, and keep the number constant—apple, apple, orange, orange (a, a, b, b). More difficult patterns vary the numbers so there are two apples to one orange (apple, apple, orange, apple, apple, orange) or a a b a a b. Adding a third item such as a lemon makes the task more difficult (apple, orange, lemon, apple, orange, lemon). Position also makes a difference. The pattern consisting of apple juice can standing up, apple juice can upside down, orange juice can right side up, apple juice can up, apple juice can down, orange juice can up = a b c, a b c.

Figure 5–2   A positional repeating pattern.

The same general principles for coding a pattern apply to people patterns and pattern cards. Real objects are easy to view from a distance, making it easier to follow the sequence. Children say the pattern aloud as a group to build the rhythm of repetition. Items such as shoes (e.g., tie, no tie) can be used if the characteristic is obvious. Confusion over whether a particular shoe is a member of the set of "tie" shoes muddles the pattern activity.

People Patterns (Kindergarten Level)

In people patterns the children perform various movements or line up to become a physical part of a pattern. A pattern line of boy, girl, boy, girl (a, b, a, b) can be changed daily, for example, girl, girl, boy, girl, girl, boy (a, a, b, a, a, b). Common movement patterns include snap activities or "head, shoulders, knees and toes." Hop, walk, and skip movements offer other possibilities. In each instance it would be helpful if the teacher played an instrument, such as a xylophone, where the notes indicate the pattern sequence. Hearing the pattern repeat reinforces the "whole pattern" occurring over and over. When children are busily engaged in physical activity, they may lose sight of the original intent of the exercise. Unlike objects set in a row on the table, they are "in the pattern" and may miss the critical problem-solving part of creating a pattern, or "what comes next?"

Pattern Cards (Kindergarten–First Grade Level)

In kindergarten and first grade, children are able to follow a card depicting a pattern sequence. These cards are generally made of laminated tag board and are approximately the size of half a sheet of paper. A set of task cards can be created for each kind of everyday object, for example, bottle caps, and kept from year to year.

Teachers generally create their own pattern cards. The following guidelines should result in cards that children can use independently with success.

1. Choose simple objects such as those found in Figure 5–3. Many rocks and shells have features that are too vague to discriminate. Example: Is this a brown rock or a gray rock (Figure 5–3)?

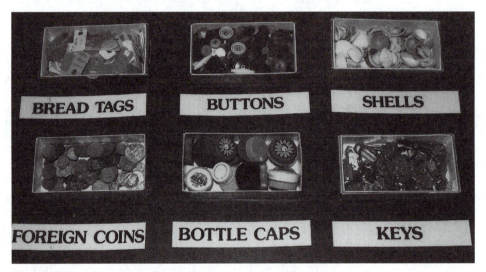

Figure 5–3   Materials for pattern.

2. Be exact. Trace or glue the objects down whenever possible. If color makes a difference in the pattern, then color the card. Choose a shade as close to the original object. Children like precision. Do not color pink buttons when you mean red buttons, or forest green bread tags when you mean light green tags (Figure 5–4).

If the collection is all one color, for example, all silver keys and no gold key, you can leave color out. If there is printing on the object, such as on bread tags, that is a new dimension, and printing needs to appear on the card.

3. Have enough of a particular item if you include it in a pattern. Example: If you only have three red bread tags in the collection, you cannot put a red bread tag into the pattern. The child will not be able to extend the pattern.

4. Vary the level of difficulty of the pattern cards. Make some simple sequences (ab ab), (abc abc), (aa bb aa bb), (aa bb cc aa bb cc) and some more difficult cards (aab aab), (abb abb), (abbc abbc).

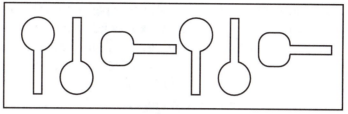

Vague Pattern Card

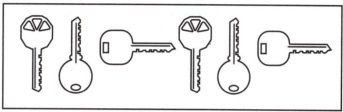

Clear Pattern Card

Figure 5–4

Extending a Pattern

In kindergarten children recognize and describe a pattern. A more difficult challenge would be to extend the pattern by continuing the sequence until a particular item was not available. Large spaces such as the table or the floor provide the room for extension (Figure 5–5).

Figure 5–5   A child extending a pattern wall.

On Their Own

As soon as children grasp the concept of pattern as a sequence that repeats, they can create their own patterns. Four- and five-year-olds enjoy making up their own people patterns and snap-clap patterns. Kindergartners and first graders can create their own patterns and record them on a card. Some teacher assistance may be needed to trace or draw the pattern. Colored paper pieces that match pattern block shapes can be teacher-made or purchased through catalogs.

When glued on black construction paper, these colorful patterns become works of art. Most pattern card work is done individually and quietly, but it is *key* that the teacher asks the child to "read the pattern aloud" as part of the learning experience. For example, Devon has just created a pattern with colored blocks. He says, "red block, red block, yellow block, red block, red block, yellow block." The teacher notes that Devon has created a complex repeating pattern.

Number Patterns for the Primary Grades

Older children, who have experienced a comprehensive pattern curriculum in previous years, are ready for more challenging problems. Two popular units for the second grade include number pattern books and successive squares. in number pattern books each page is devoted to a chart of a particular number sequence. For example, the number sequence 2, 4, 6, 8, 10 . . . is illustrated by pairing each number with a picture of eyes/eyeglasses.

Example: My page of 2's

Pictures of eyeglasses	*#*
O-O	2
O-O, O-O	4
O-O, O-O, O-O	6

The pictures of eyeglasses are cut from magazines or drawn by the child. Other picture pages may include:

Multiples	*Picture Possibilities*
3's	Triangles
	Three-leaf clovers
4's	Squares
	Car wheels
5's	Hands
	Stars
6's	Plastic ring holder from six packs
7's	Weeks from a calendar
8's	Boxes of crayons
	Truck wheels
9's	Players in a baseball field

Number books are an early introduction to the multiplication tables. (For examples of a pattern number book see *Math Their Way*, Baratta-Lorton, 1976, Chapter 12.)

The problem of growing squares involves using wood blocks to build all the possible squares, i.e., 1 block = 1 square, a 4-block square (2 x 2), a 9-block square (3 x 3) and so on. These block designs can be colored on 1-inch graph paper, and a brief description of each construction is written (Van de Walle &

Holbrook, 1987). The early number pattern lays a foundation for concepts of square numbers and square roots. It also forms a background for the concept of "arrays," or describing multiplication problems in terms of rows and columns.

Third grade students investigate the multiples as found on a number chart (0–99). For example, each multiple of four is colored in with a light pencil or crayon (4, 8, 12, 16 . . .). Then the students write stories about what visual patterns emerge, such as diagonals, two spaces over . . . one space down. Thus, the numbers are seen in relationship to the whole grid. For examples of this activity see *Math By All Means* (Burns, 1991).

Pattern in Music and Art

Young children create many pieces of "refrigerator art" in the early years. Both painting and printing activities lend themselves to the expression of pattern. The step-by-step directions for these projects can be found in books such as *Scribble Cookies and Other Independent Creative Art Experiences for Children* (Kohl, 1985). An artistic expression can include pattern by helping the child to repeat the design more than once.

In "silhouette painting," the child fills in the whole stencil with black paint, rather than drawing an outline. The key is to choose distinctive shapes such as sailboats and anchors or hearts and flowers. These patterns can decorate placemats, placecards, wrapping paper, paper bags, bulletin board borders, or the edge of paper plates.

Some of the earliest experiences with pattern are found in the repetitive phrases or rhythms of nursery rhymes and early songs. Three excellent examples are "Twinkle, Twinkle, Little Star"; "Mary Had a Little Lamb"; and "Old McDonald Had a Farm." Rhythm band instruments such as drums, shakers, and sticks emphasize the beat or the refrain. Dried beans can be sealed in a variety of containers to make additional instruments.

Creative movement enhances the pattern of "Duck, Duck, Goose"; "Heads, Shoulders, Knees, and Toes"; or "If You're Happy and You Know It, Clap Your Hands." Young children enjoy acting out the "Bus Song" . . . "The people on the bus go up and down." Music is a natural, enthusiastic way to involve young children in math. These enjoyable activities can be a part of the daily plan for every preschool classroom.

Older children apply fabric paint to stencils on T-shirts, cloth belts, or socks. The design needs to be worked out ahead of application with crayons and paper. Otherwise the pattern might not be complete, or fit in the allotted space.

Printing materials come in many forms. Sponge printing uses cutouts from commercial kitchen sponges or pieces of cosmetic makeup sponges. Sponges are cut into simple shapes such as circles and squares or trees and flowers. Sponges readily absorb watercolor or tempera paint.

In a similar fashion potatoes, carrots, or parsnips are cut in half and the design is scratched, cut, or dug into the vegetable. Any kind of paint will work, and a mix of colors can be done right on the potato.

Ink pads come in a variety of colors. Commercial stamps or such junk items as spools, bottle caps, or checkers may be used with an ink pad. Stamps are available in a variety of sizes and subjects, such as favorite holiday symbols or animals.

Older children can make fingerprint animals or people by pressing a finger-tip onto a stamp pad and then onto a piece of paper. Characters are created by adding felt pen eyes, ears, and hair. Animals such as a rabbit are made from two prints (head, body) with the addition of a penned-in face, ears, whiskers, and tail. One pattern might be "rabbit, carrot, rabbit, carrot . . . ."

Older children can also do paper weaving. The teacher cuts strips of construction paper ahead of time on the paper cutter. Strips of heavy ribbon can also be used. A rectangle is folded and cut so that a series of rows of slits perforate the paper. Using contrasting colors of the construction paper or ribbon, the student "weaves" each strip in and out of the slits. These colorful placemats can be laminated or covered with contact paper. Art activities are a natural use of pattern in our everyday lives.

Summary

The principles of pattern serve as guidelines for teachers who want to develop enjoyable classroom activities. Children never seem to tire of pattern work, and these experiences promote critical thinking and problem solving in unique ways. Early pattern experiences involve accessible activities using color or position. Later work focuses the children's attention on number patterns and the relationship of geometric ideas to number. This chapter has presented a wealth of curricular ideas to help the teacher begin to plan motivating pattern activities.

Ready-Set-Math

Ready-Set-Math

Muffin Pan Pattern

Ages: 3–4 years

Items needed: Muffin pan for one dozen muffins
Paper cupcake holders in various colors
Small objects that vary by color, such as bear counters

The teacher begins a pattern on the top row using two colors of paper cupcake holders. The child continues the pattern in the next rows. Another idea might be to fill the muffin pan with a pattern of blue bear, yellow bear, blue bear, yellow bear. The child continues the pattern, saying the pattern aloud. The song for the day is "Muffin Man."

Ready-Set-Math

Yarn Clothesline

Ages: 3–4 years

Items needed: Several yards of thick yarn
Clothespins
Old socks in various colors

The teacher begins a pattern of socks hanging on the "clothesline," such as brown sock, black sock, brown sock, black sock. The clothesline is strung at the child's eye level so that the child can practice eye–hand coordination as well as patterns.

◆ **Ready-Set-Math**

Necklace Art

Ages: 5–6 years

Items needed: Colorful large tubes or easy to string macaroni
Stiff cord or shoelaces
Masking tape
1" x 9" paper strips
Glue stick

The child decides on a pattern of macaroni for a necklace. The pattern is arranged on a desk and then transferred to the necklace, using a length of cord that has a stiff tip made of masking tape. The ends of cord are tied together to form a necklace.

Pattern necklaces are created by gluing strips of colored paper into rings, attaching a new ring to the previous ring. The child decides on the pattern of color by placing the strips in a row, saying the pattern aloud to the teacher, and then assembling the necklace.

◆ **Ready-Set-Math**

Butterfly Dot Painting

Ages: 5–6 years old

Items needed: Butterfly template to trace and cut
Scissors
Q-tips
Containers of paint in a variety of colors
Heavy construction paper
Old newspaper

The child traces the butterfly shape on a piece of heavy paper, and cuts out the butterfly. (Tracing and cutting are good experiences in the geometry curriculum.) A design is created by dipping a Q-tip into a container of paint, dabbing it on the newspaper to absorb excess liquid, and then on the butterfly. These colorful patterns emerge as a row along the edge of the shape. Additional rows can be added if the child wishes to continue the pattern or create a new one.

Activities and Study Questions

1. Think of a pattern that relates to your life, where two variables are in a relationship, such as the way insurance premiums vary with age. Describe this pattern in a journal entry or brief paper.

2. Investigate the history of a famous numerical pattern such as Pascal's Triangle or the Fibonacci sequence. What applications does the pattern have in everyday life? Write a brief paper on your findings.

3. Solve the problem where you find out how many gifts are received as described in the song, "The Twelve Days of Christmas." Read the article by Woodward (1991) found in the Further Reading section, and compare your approach to other students, ideas in the article, and in your class.

4. Practice one of the card, domino, or calendar magic tricks that are described in the article by Geer (1992). (See Further Reading.) Be prepared to demonstrate your talent to a small group of students and to explain the math behind the magic.

5. Watch a young child create a pattern from everyday objects. How does the child approach the problem? How does the child label the pattern? Write a paragraph or journal entry about your observation.

Classroom Equipment

colored blocks
plastic or real fruit
a xylophone
unifix cubes
juice cans
a box of bread tags
a box of keys
a box of large buttons
a box of bottle caps
crayons
100 chart
tempera paint
watercolor paint
fabric paint
clothespins
large tubes
stiff cord or shoelaces
1" x 9" paper strips
butterfly template
Q-tips
old newspaper

old T-shirts
cloth belts
kitchen sponges
make-up sponges
vegetables such as
potatoes, carrots, parsnips
colored ink pads
strips of construction paper
strips of heavy ribbon
muffin pan for one dozen
muffins
paper cupcake holders
bear counters
several yards of thick yarn
old socks/various colors
macaroni
masking tape
glue stick
scissors
heavy construction paper

Further Reading

Brahier, D. J., Hodapp, S., Speer, W., & Martin, R. (1992). Ideas: Levels 3–4, have a seat. *Arithmetic Teacher, 40,* 30–31. *Third grade students use their own classroom seating arrangements to explore patterns of desk organization. The geometric relationships of 24 desks are modeled with square tiles and recorded on graph paper.*

Burton, G. (1992). *Second grade book.* Reston, VA: NCTM, 1–9. *The text is an excellent source of ideas on early pattern activities for second grade. Units include odd–even, seeing pattern designs from several perspectives, the hundred's chart, and creating introduction to single rules using a "Magic Function Box."*

Geer, C. P. (1992). Exploring patterns, relations, and functions. *Arithmetic Teacher, 39,* 19–21. *Three kinds of magic tricks using dominoes, playing cards, and a calendar are illustrated, along with the mathematical solutions to the problems. Students experience a challenging, entertaining lesson on patterns and relationships. Algebraic formulas connect everyday situations to math.*

Rowan, T. E., & Howden, H. (1989). Patterns, relationships, and function. *Arithmetic Teacher, 37,* 18–24. *The developmental sequence of pattern from kindergarten through grade 8 is traced. Examples of curricular activities are illustrated for each level. Students are encouraged to search the environment for relationships that obey a given rule.*

Van de Walle, J. A., & Holbrook, H. (1987). Patterns, thinking, and problem solving. *Arithmetic Teacher, 34,* 6–12. *The authors write an extensive review of "growing patterns," with the logical transitions to making tables of data and generating pattern formulas for the various constructions. This summary of an eight-week project for third grade can generate exciting curricular activities at this level.*

Woodward, E. (1991). Problem solving in the preservice classroom. *Arithmetic Teacher, 39,* 41–43. *College students in an elementary math methods course are given five homework problems that encourage problem-solving techniques, including pattern. The students' own solutions are illustrated.*

References

Baratta-Lorton, M. (1976). *Math their way.* Menlo Park, CA: Addison-Wesley.

Burns, M. (1991). *Math by all means: Multiplication grade 3.* New Rochelle, NY: Cuisenaire Company.

Kohl, M. (1985). *Scribble cookies and other independent creative art experiences for children.* Bellingham, MA: Bright Ring Publishing.

National Council of Teachers of Mathematics. (1989). *Curriculum and evaluation standards for teaching mathematics.* Reston, VA: Author.

Schiller, P., & Moore, T. (1993). *Where is Thumbkin?* Ranier, MD: Gryphon House.

Sutton, C. (1992). Sunflower spirals obey laws of mathematics. *New Scientist, 134,* 16.

Van de Walle, J. A., & Holbrook, H. (1987). Patterns, thinking, and problem solving. *Arithmetic Teacher, 34,* 6–12.

Young, S. (1994). Tiling, tessellating, and quilting. *Teaching Pre K–8, 24,* 72–74.

6 Graphing

MRS. ROMEREZ CONDUCTS a taste test in her kindergarten of five-year-olds. Each child has three white crackers: one plain cracker, one cracker with creamy peanut butter, and one cracker with chunky peanut butter. The question is: "What cracker do you like best?" The children look at each sample and describe what they see. They talk about how peanut butter can be smooth or lumpy. What makes the lumps? Slowly they take a bite from each cracker. Then each child votes a preference by placing a peanut under the category of choice on a floor mat (see Figure 6–1). Twelve peanuts are found under the jar of creamy peanut butter. Eight children prefer chunky peanut butter. Five children dislike peanut butter. The teacher asks the graphing questions: Which row has more peanuts? Which row has less peanuts? How many more children like creamy peanut butter than chunky peanut butter?

Figure 6–1   *Children using a floor mat.*

At what level of skill development in graphing is Mrs. Romerez's class? What other graphs can be done by these pupils? This chapter outlines the continuum of graphing experiences that lay the foundation for success in later years. Graphing is a motivating way to incorporate a wide variety of problem-solving activities into the everyday life of the classroom.

An Overview of Graphing

The graphing curriculum is part of the curricular strand, Standard II: Statistics and Probability (NCTM, 1989). Here are the guidelines for the K-4 curriculum:

- Collect, organize, and describe data
- Construct, read, and interpret displays of data
- Formulate and solve problems that involve collecting and analyzing data
- Explore concepts of chance[*] (p. 54)

A graph presents numerical information visually. Graphs come in many forms: real objects, pictures, bars, pies or circles, and lines. A graph has a title and names (labels) for each part. Using graphs, children can see and compare similarities, note differences, make judgments, discuss preferences, and count and communicate results. They classify or organize the data, measure, and label the graph. Interpreting a graph uses different abilities than the ones needed to construct a graph. Constructing graphs helps children with the task of reading graphs. They experience how graphs organize information by creating their own from classroom collections, personal characteristics, and daily activities. As children experience a variety of displays, they must learn to choose a display that is the most useful. The various kinds of graphs have advantages and limitations, depending on the kind of data collected.

Topics for Graphing Experiences

The Children Themselves
Hair color—brown, blond, black, red
Shoes—tie, Velcro, slip on
Brothers—sisters
Favorite pets
Favorite foods
Sandwiches—peanut butter, grilled cheese, bologna, ham, turkey, BBQ, hot dogs, hamburgers
Fruit—apples, oranges, bananas

---

[*]Reprinted with permission from the *Curriculum and Evaluation Standards for School Mathematics* (1989) by the National Council of Teachers of Mathematics.

Pizza—cheese, mushroom, sausage, pepperoni
Ice cream—chocolate, vanilla, strawberry
Tooth loss chart—first and second grade
Transportation to school—walk, car, bus

At School
Favorite class—math, reading, art, science, music, gym, recess
Number of children in attendance
Number of pupils in each grade
Number of classrooms on each floor of the building
Number of bulletin boards in each room, perhaps by grade level
Number of permission slips turned in by day of the week

Scoop and Graph
Coins—pennies, nickels, dimes
M & Ms—color
Cookies—a variety of types
Shells—round, long, and thin
Buttons—color, 2 hole/4 hole
Keys—gold, silver

Science
Weather—sunny, cloudy, windy, rain, snow
Air temperature
Number of seeds—apple, orange, grapefruit, a variety of pumpkins
Neighborhoods surveys—for example, kinds of trees on a property (oak, birch, honey locust) or a leaf hunt
Objects that float/sink
Age of newborn classroom pets in days/weeks

Social Studies
Neighborhood surveys
    one-story home/two-story home
    garages—attached, separate, none
    types of stores
    populations of cities, states, countries (third grade)

The Challenge in Reading Graphs

Graphs are a widely used means of presenting information in newspapers, television, and classroom textbooks. However, they can distort information as well. Spatial constancy and the kind of measurement chosen may exaggerate the magnitude of difference.

Graphs pose several challenges for very young children. First, one-to-one correspondence is a key relationship. In the peanut butter survey, one peanut stood for one vote. Second, number conservation also plays a role. For example, the teacher could not "fool" the class into thinking that the five-peanut row was more than the eight-peanut row by spreading out the five peanuts to make it seem like a "longer row" than the eight peanuts. (See Chapter 7 on number conservation.) Third, children need to see the vertical and horizontal axes as stable points of reference.

According to Piaget, children acquire an understanding of the idea of number conservation between the ages of five and seven years. They develop an understanding of horizontal and vertical as constant reference systems at later ages, from six and one-half to as late as twelve years old (Copeland, 1984). Therefore, early graphing experiences rely on simple displays where comparing and counting help children succeed. The teacher creates or purchases graphing strips and mats. Easy-to-fill cells help the child keep objects in one-to-one correspondence. In later years, children grapple with simple circle graphs and line graphs that pose new challenges.

The Graphing Questions

After the graph has been constructed, the teacher models the kinds of questions that children can answer using a graph. When children become familiar with the activity, they can create questions for others to answer. Reading a graph uses two kinds of questions in the early years: comparing questions and counting questions. Upper grade students learn to see sophisticated relationships among the data, extrapolate trends, and predict future events. Comparing questions include:

Which group has more?
Which group has less?

Which group has the greater number?
Which group has the fewer number?

Which group is higher? Lower?
Which group is longer? Shorter?

Which group is biggest? Smallest?
Are there any groups that are the same?

Number questions include:

How many _____ are there?
How many more _____ are there than _____?
How many fewer _____ are there than _____?
How many are there if we put _____ and _____ together?

The word "group" represents the name of the category under discussion. Substitute the actual object, for example in the peanut butter survey, ask

"Which peanut butter was *more* popular?" or "Which kind of peanut butter was chosen by *more* children?"

A successful graphing activity includes active conversation about the visual display. Some teachers keep a copy of these questions on a laminated card so that they are available for easy reference.

Early Experiences with Graphing

Very young children (three–five year olds) spend time comparing, sorting, and classifying everyday objects. Curcio and Folkson (1996) suggested that preschool and kindergarten age children experience many exploratory data-collecting activities, using their own way of organizing information. In one example, the class compared the number of times the word "I" occurred in two of their favorite books. Some children wrote "I" every time they found it. Other children used numerals or tally marks to keep track of the data. The authors felt it was unrealistic for young children to readily grasp the meaning of a rectangular–coordinate grid, such as a graphing floor mat. Children can make a transition from pre-graphing to early graphing by using a ten-strip (Leutzinger, 1990). A ten-strip can be made by taking a 10-inch piece of light colored cardboard and dividing it into 10 sections using a black marker. Use a color that will stand out from a white surface, such as a desk, but not detract from the display of other colors. First, the child scoops a handful of counters, such as wooden blocks, and "guesses" whether there are more or less than the 10 needed to fill the whole strip. Gradually the child learns to fill two ten-strips and to compare the results (Figure 6–2).

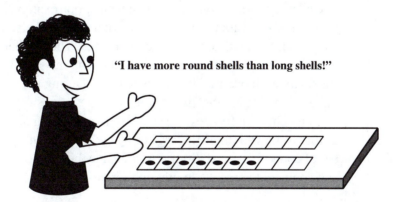

"I have more round shells than long shells!"

Figure 6–2   Child counting and comparing shells using ten-strips.

The ten-strips are labeled: round shells, long shells, and number of shells, with words and pictures. The teacher asks the child some of the graphing questions, such as "How many round shells do you have? Are there more long shells than round shells? Ten-strips can be filled horizontally or vertically to encourage comparisons in both orientations.

Floor Mats Using Real Objects

Many kindergarten teachers make or purchase graphing floor mats (see Figure 6–1). They construct a mat from old window shades or shower curtain liners and colored vinyl tape. Cells are premeasured and marked so that they come out as equal squares. At first, only two rows of cells are needed. Later, up to four rows may be used.

Teachers create a simple two-row graph on one side of the mat. (Commercial products generally are printed with two to four rows.) Floor mats are used in the following sequences (Baratta-Lorton, 1976):

Two real objects
Two picture graphs

Three real objects
Three picture graphs

The teacher labels a row and calls for the children to come forward and place their objects.

Scoop and Graph Objects

Children construct table-size graphs using real objects and a desk-size graphing mat. (Ideas for materials for scoop and graph are found earlier in this chapter.) The teacher prepares a reusable mat of columns and cells, with room to label the parts of the graph. Tablespoons, laundry detergent scoops, or $\frac{1}{4}$ cup measuring cups make good scoops. The teacher puts the objects in a shallow bowl.

Children work individually or in teams. For example, one child "scoops" a small number of items such as coins (pennies, nickels, and dimes). The coins are sorted, counted, and arranged on the mat. The teacher helps label the graph, with coins across the bottom and numbers up the side. Children share their results with each other and with the teacher. During the conversation, the graphing questions guide the discussion.

Older children (grades 1–3) extend their thinking about the coins by writing a story to go with their findings or by creating a math problem using the number of coins on the mat. Some children may be able to add up their total amount and compare the results to other children's results.

Picture Graphs

A picture graph uses pictures of objects rather than the objects themselves. A picture graph is a transition from the real object graph to the symbolic graph. In a taste test of three kinds of fruit (apple, orange, pear), the children could create a floor graph using real fruit. Very young children (4–5 years old) need these concrete experiences with the real world. In late kindergarten and first grade, children are ready to color a picture of their favorite fruit, cut it out, and vote their preference with it. At times they use a laminated photo of themselves, placing it on the graph in the row designated as their favorite fruit.

Some items are not available for graphing. Pictures stand in for favorite pets, favorite television programs, or the way they come to school (walk, bus, car). The teacher can move back and forth between real object graphs and picture graphs as the situation unfolds. There is no need to abandon real object graphs prematurely. First through third graders enjoy working with everyday items that add variety and interest to their school day.

A natural place to find pictures to copy and graph is in children's picture books. Two examples are *Angelina at the Fair* (Holabird, 1985) and *The Berenstain Bears and The Messy Room* (Berenstain & Berenstain, 1983).

Angelina is a mouse who wants to go to the fair with her friends. But her little cousin Henry is visiting. Her parents remind her that she must take Henry along, and to make matters worse, he's a "boy!" At the entrance to the fair is a stand with dozens of brightly colored balloons. The plot proceeds, and eventually these balloons play a role in the outcome.

The balloons come in primary colors and multicolors. The teacher makes a flannel board or construction paper reproductions to match the text. The children sort them into two groups (one color–many colors). A two-column picture graph is created on the flannel board. The children discuss the results, using the graphing questions.

In *The Berenstain Bears and The Messy Room*, Brother and Sister Bear have toys scattered everywhere. The whole family helps organize the mess. Eventually toys are hung in rows on pegboards, sit on benches, or are stored on shelves. A number of pages show familiar objects such as puzzle pieces, dinosaur models, or stuffed animals. Since the pages show four or more kinds of toys, this counting and graphing experience is suited to older children (first–second grade). Pictures of these toys are colored, cut out, and assembled into a graph. Again, the discussion of the results is key. In addition, the children can talk about different ways to store these kinds of playthings. In summary, many children's picture books provide an interesting beginning for picture-graphing activities.

Symbolic Graphs

A symbolic graph uses a block, a tally mark, and an "x" or some other abstract medium to stand for something. For example, the class studies the animals in the farm set. Some are in the barnyard. They can count the toy chickens in the barnyard, or color pictures of chickens that match the number in the barnyard, or cut out squares of paper that equal the number of chickens. These squares are linked together to form a bar graph (Figure 6–3).

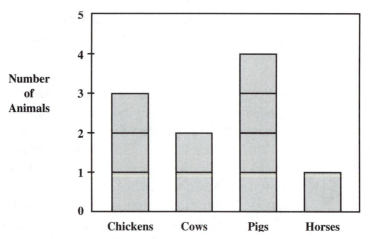

Figure 6–3   Animals in the barnyard.

One teacher has a magnetic weather chart with four choices: sunny, windy, cloudy, rainy. Magnetized circles fill the cells under the possible conditions for one month. These circles stand for the weather of the day. On the first day of the month, the graph is cleared, and the data recording begins anew. Teachers make the transition from real objects to pictures and then to symbols by substituting one for another and asking the same graphing questions There is no need to rush the use of symbolic graphs such as tally marks. Most first graders can readily count by fives. At that time they can begin to use these common symbols. Other symbolic graphs for the upper grades (third–fifth grade) include line graphs and circle graphs.

Commercial material such as Unifix interlocking cubes, or Learning Links (that form a chain), lend themselves to recording data in a symbolic way. One kindergarten teacher breeds a rabbit each spring. When the one or more babies are born, a pocket chart becomes a holder for seven Unifix cubes joined together. As the pockets are filled, the class calculates the rabbits' ages in weeks and days.

Around the same time this teacher buys duck eggs from a local farmer and puts them into an egg incubator. When the baby ducks hatch, a record of their ages is made in a similar fashion. The ages of the ducks are compared to the ages of the rabbits. Unifix cubes are a practical way to create symbolic graphs.

Another way is to use Learning Links to measure everyday objects. In a science center, children measure the length of vegetables such as carrots, leeks, parsnips, and celery. The linked chains hang on pins from a bulletin board, forming an easy-to-read graph. The graphing questions include:

Which vegetable is the longest?
Which is the shortest?
How many links long is the parsnip?

Because these vegetables can be eaten raw, a taste test may be done and their preferences graphed. A lively language lesson can center on how these vegetables grow and what recipes use them. When the teacher takes the time to plan graphing activities around the birth of baby animals, or everyday foods, symbolic graphs become meaningful ways to keep track of important ideas.

Circle Graphs

Circle graphs challenge students to think in terms of 360 degrees. The center of the circle is located, and several sectors are created. These points of reference are different from the horizontal and vertical axes of bar graphs. Therefore, the study of circle graphs is appropriate for mature third graders.

Students are familiar with the 12 sectors on a clock. They may begin their exploration by dividing up how they spend 12 hours, from midnight to noon. They count the number of hours spent sleeping, eating, and studying at school. The sectors are colored and labeled. The class discusses how to handle the problem of totals that are more or less than a full hour.

Other uses of the circle graph involve putting a ring around the circumference of the circle and dividing the ring into equal parts. One graph might use "money spent from $1.00." First the outer ring is divided into 100 cents. As money is spent, the number of pennies are colored, and lines forming the sector are drawn (Figure 6–4).

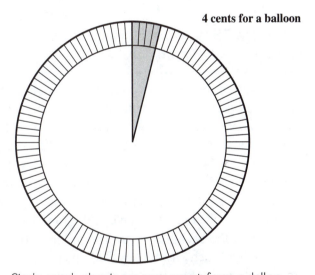

4 cents for a balloon

Figure 6–4   *Circle graph showing money spent from a dollar.*

Other circle graphs can use an outer ring with cells that can hold the students' names, each given an equal amount of space on the ring. If there are 30 children, the ring has 30 equal spots. For example, in an ice cream graph, students vote their preference for vanilla, chocolate, or strawberry by taping their curved name card on the outer ring next to other students with the same choice. Then the sector lines are drawn, and the sectors are colored. In this way, primary age students construct circle graphs from everyday experiences before they encounter more complicated ones in later years.

Line Graphs

Line graphs have numbers on both the horizontal and vertical axes. Plotting the points to create a line graph is dependent on the understanding of intersections or finding pairs of numbers on a coordinate grid. This ability involves spatial skills and geometric concepts as discussed in Chapter 4. Children need many experiences with mapping and following routes as described earlier before they grasp the meaning of a line graph. Line graphs often use data that are collected over time. Some common examples of continuous events include:

Class attendance by day/month
Temperature by hour, day/month
The height of a candle by minutes to burn down
The height of a young seedling by day/week

Construction of the graph, including measures chosen, spacing of intervals, and complete labeling, takes time and careful attention to detail. Easy-to-read graphs from everyday experiences help students analyze sophisticated commercially prepared line graphs found in the media and elementary textbooks. These kinds of line graphs challenge many adults who have not had enough positive experiences with data collection and display.

Choosing Categories That Avoid Hurt Feelings or Wanting To Be on the Winning Side

Kindergarten teachers have reported that children participating in floor mat graphing want to wait to vote their preference or change their mind after they see the popular choice. Not all classes behave in a similar way. But if the problem arises, there are some ways to counteract this problem.

In addition, some topics are sensitive issues. Most children would prefer to be tall. Graphing height might embarrass the shorter children in the group. Likewise, a teacher wouldn't create a real graph on tennis shoes versus other shoes if only the rich children could afford the popular tennis shoes. Teachers must know the backgrounds of the children. If the only children who ride the bus to school each day are disabled, then a graphing activity on "how we come to school: walk, ride, bus," might cause hurt feelings.

Most teachers feel that to grow in self-esteem means that each child's unique differences must be celebrated. This is a worthy goal for the whole curriculum. But children are eager to be "normal," and a part of the group. They do not see themselves as "ugly ducklings" waiting to turn into a swan. There are many graphing activities that can enhance everyone's chance to participate without emphasizing characteristics, possessions, or daily routines that stigmatize children.

It is natural for children to want to be on the winning side. Our society emphasizes that "more is better." And children like to vote with their friends or children who are popular. If the situation occurs, the teacher could quietly collect preferences ahead of time. For example, each child colors a picture of an ice cream cone: white, pink, brown. The teacher walks around with a paper bag and collects the creations. The whole class sorts the cones and graphs the results on the floor mat.

In another classroom, the teacher is graphing nuts in the shell: walnuts, almonds, hazelnuts. The choices are mixed together in a brown bag, and each child reaches in to pick one. This kind of "mystery bag" adds an element of chance to a choice. In addition, the "scoop and graph" activities described earlier in the chapter are free of personal preference. Teachers alternate these kinds of graphing experiences with personal preference kinds of graphings. Hopefully, children will see that they are important valuable people even if they are the only ones who "like applesauce" on the apple choice graph (see Ready-Set-Math Activities).

Probability

The NCTM Curriculum and Evaluation Standards for School Mathematics (1989) suggests that children in grades K–4 explore concepts of chance. Classroom discussions may focus on events that are certain, are likely to happen, or that are unlikely or impossible. These ideas may be contrasted with the concept of luck.

Another feature of probability is called *sample space*. Sample space refers to the total number of outcomes for a particular event. In a coin toss, there are two outcomes, heads or tails, since a coin cannot rest on a edge. In a paper cup toss, it may land on its bottom, top, or side.

Children in the early primary grades investigate these properties using simple experiments such as coin or cup tosses. They may talk about the likelihood of an event using a spinner of various colors. In an early experience, children may using a spinner of two colors, where there is a large yellow wedge and a small blue wedge. The question is, "What color is most likely?" (NCTM, 1989, p. 56).

Other activities use colored balls in paper bags, where one color predominates. For an example of a probability activity in the thematic unit, see *The Tale of Peter Rabbit* in Chapter 14.

Summary

At the start of the chapter Mrs. Romerez's class graphed peanut butter choices. The question posed was: What level of skill development in graphing was illustrated by their graph? By the conclusion of the chapter, the class had created a "symbolic graph" in which a peanut stood for a kind of peanut butter or a dislike of peanut butter. Her class is ready to go on to many wonderful experiences with other symbolic graphs such as bar graphs. Occasionally, it would be fun to create a real object graph or picture graph for variety. For a teacher with a creative mind, the possibilities are endless.

Ready-Set-Math

Ready-Set-Math

Cereal Sort

Ages: 3–4 years

Items needed: Three varieties of cereal: Flakes, Cheerios, Puffs
Three bowls per child
A small scoop
Paper plates and paper towels

The teacher mixes the three kinds of cereal together in one large bowl. The child scoops some cereal and pours it on a paper plate. The cereal is sorted into the three bowls. Then the child makes three parallel rows of cereal on the paper towels. The young child discusses, "Which row has more?" "Which row is the shortest?" "Which row is in the middle?" After the comparisons, the child may eat the results.

Ready-Set-Math

Apple Cooking

Ages: 5–6 years

Items needed: Two dozen apples
Recipe ingredients for baked apples and applesauce
Oven or microwave
Paper plates, bowls, spoons
Kitchen knife, mixing bowls
Worksheet with pictures of a baked apple, a bowl of applesauce, a wedge of apple
Kitchen timer
Graphing mat

Ahead of time, the teacher prepares the apples for the activity. One-third of the apples will be eaten raw, one-third are cored for baked apples, and the remaining eight apples are peeled and cored. They soak in water with a tablespoon of lemon juice to prevent discoloration.

Over several days or in one long session, the class prepares applesauce and baked apples. The class conducts a taste test between these choices and raw apples. The children choose their favorite and color the appropriate picture. The students place the pictures on the floor mat and answer the graphing questions.

Variation: Use a kitchen timer to watch for elapsed cooking time. While the timer goes backwards, move the hands on a teaching clock forward.

> **Ready-Set-Math**
>
> ### Favorite Toys Table Graph
>
> Ages: 6–8 years
>
> Items needed: Small collections of toys from home (15 items or less)
> Two 10-strip mats per child
> Primary story writing paper
>
> The children bring a bag of small toys from home, containing 15 or fewer items. Each child decides on two categories and sorts the bag of toys. (Have extra bags of toys ready for those children who forgot their bags or don't have toys.) The toys are placed on the 10-strip mats, and the results are discussed in a small group, or with the teacher. Each child writes a story about the experience, including a description of the two groups, and the math words: more, less, the number more than, the number less than, and the total number of toys.

Activities and Study Questions

1. Collect data from your classmates on the number of years and months they have attended college. Choose one of the following graphs to display your results: picture graph, bar graph, line graph, or circle graph. Be sure to label your graph. Bring your graph to class for further discussion.
2. Visit the library and locate a multicultural children's literature selection that could be the basis for a graphing activity. Write a paragraph or journal entry about your choice.
3. Watch a young child (3–4 year old) sort small objects using two 10-strips. Write a description of your observation. Be prepared to share your findings with the class.
4. Read the article on "Telling Tales: Creating Graphs Using Multicultural Literature" by Karp, found in the Further Reading Section. Think of other uses for a "counting rope" in a primary classroom.
5. Plan and conduct a soft drink "taste challenge." Decide on where and how to conduct the survey. Describe the limitations of the study, and how you could create a better experiment in the future. Graph your results and be prepared to explain them to a small group or the whole class.

Classroom Equipment

peanut butter	flannel board
crackers	balloons cut from flannel
peanuts in the shell	Unifix cubes
favorite foods	wooden blocks
small coins	magnetized graph or chart
M & M's	with sets of magnets
shells	learning links
large buttons	a circle graph with a
gold and silver keys	laminated ring
seeds from fruit	three kinds of cereal
a variety of leaves	bowls

Classroom Equipment (cont.)

objects that float/sink	paper plates
10-strips	apples
scoops, spoons, 1/4 cup	microwave
measuring cup	kitchen timer
floor mat	primary writing paper
a laminated picture of each child	

Further Reading

Brahier, D. J., Brahier, A., & Speer, W. (1992). Ideas: Levels K-2, Which flavor wins the taste test? Arithmetic Teacher, 40, 29–37. *Students conduct a taste test of two kinds of powdered drinks. Each drink is a different color, and the paper cups are labeled "X" and "Y." A real graph is created by stacking the preferred juice cups on top of one another, using a cardboard square as a divider. Since a tall stack might tip over, ten cups can be traded for a symbol, such as the juice container. Other graphing suggestions extend this activity or explore new areas such as the seasons or deciding on a school mascot.*

Karp, K. S. (1994). Telling tales: Creating graphs using multicultural literature. *Teaching Children Mathematics, 1*, 87–91. *Four examples of multicultural literature are given, along with the graphing activities that flow from their plots. One book,* Knots on a Counting Rope, *by Bill Martin, Jr. and John Archambault, uses a Native American custom of recording events using knots in a counting rope. A natural extension might be to have the students make a knot in an individual rope at regular intervals (10 cm) for each book read. An annotated bibliography with six other titles gives teachers additional interesting possibilities.*

Welchman-Tischler, R. (1992). Making Mathematical Connections. *Arithmetic Teacher, 39*, 12–17. *Practical ideas for graphing daily attendance, permission slips, or organizing preferences for free choice time are illustrated. Units include an excellent early introduction to circle graphs. Upper level "grouped and rounded" estimates on a variety of number lines give teachers a way to challenge capable students.*

Woodward, E., Frost, S., & Smith, A. (1991). Cemetery Mathematics, *Arithmetic Teacher, 39*, 31–36. *A unique field trip was made to a local cemetery. The article describes the data collection process. The class creates bar graphs on the age of the population at the time of their deaths. Separate graphs are constructed for men and women and month of death. The typical graphing questions are asked, along with a lively discussion of the results. The activities are suitable for mature third grade students.*

References

Baratta-Lorton, M. (1976). *Math their way*. Menlo Park, CA: Addison Wesley.

Berenstain, S., & Berenstain, J. (1983). *The Berenstain bears and the messy room*. New York, NY: Random House.

Copeland, R. (1984). *How children learn mathematics: Implication for Piaget's research (4th Ed.)*. New York: Macmillan.

Curcio, F. R., & Folkson, S. (1996). Exploring data: Kindergarten children do it their way. *Teaching Children Mathematics, 2*, 382–385.

Holabird, K. (1985). *Angelina at the fair*. New York: Clarkson N. Potter.

Leutzinger, L. (1990). Graphical representation and probability. In J. N. Payne (Ed.) *Mathematics for the young child*. Reston, VA: National Council of Teachers of Mathematics.

National Council of Teachers of Mathematics (1989). *Curriculum and evaluation standards*. Reston, VA: Author.

7 Developing Number Sense

A Cultural Perspective

Virtually every culture has a method of counting. Many Native American counting systems were based on 10s, or primary groupings of 20s, using counting words derived from fingers and toes (Closs, 1986). Closs recalled an interesting explanation of the base 20 system of the Inuits, as described by Dorothy Eber (1972). One person was worth 20 (hands and feet). Five people made 100, and 100 was called a "bundle." That was because foxes and sealskins were bundled into groups of 100.

Many North American tribes such as the Dakota, Cherokee, Ojibway, Winnebago, Wyandot, and Micmac could count into the millions. And these number systems seemed to extend indefinitely, even though it was difficult to find any utilitarian use for numbers greater than 1,000. One early source on Ojibway counting referred to 1,000,000 as the "great thousand" (Closs, 1986).

Counting is a universal skill that appears to be easily acquired at an early age. The ability to count to 100 is a generally accepted benchmark in many kindergarten curriculum assessments. However, parents, school boards, and some teachers confuse oral counting with the following more advanced ways of thinking:

- Reading numerals, for example, it's a "three"
- Writing numerals, a visual–motor task
- Matching a number to a set, or the principle of cardinality, that is, counting 5 beans and answering the question, "How many?"
- Having an intuitive feel for how big a number is, that is, "Is 15 closer to 10 or to 50?"
- Being able to make reasonable guesses using numbers, that is, the small jar could not hold more than 100 goldfish crackers
- Seeing part–whole relationships using sight or abstract thinking (without counting), that is, "I have 2 green bottle caps and 3 purple bottle caps."

Taken together, this complex set of interrelated concepts contributes to the development of "number sense." Number sense is using common sense based on the way numbers and tools of measurement work within a given culture. It involves an appreciation for the reasonableness of an answer and the level of accuracy needed to solve a particular problem. It helps students detect errors and choose the most logical way to approach a math challenge.

The NCTM Standards (1989) describe number sense and numeration and what students in the K–4 curriculum should be able to do:

- Construct number meanings through real-world experiences and the use of physical materials
- Understand our numeration system by relating counting, grouping, and place-value concepts
- Develop number sense
- Interpret the multiple uses of numbers encountered in the real world[*] (p. 38)

The development of number sense as it relates to grouping and place value concepts will be discussed in Chapter 9.

One example of lack of number sense at the upper grade level was reported by Markovits, Hershkowitz, and Bruckheima (1989). In this study, middle school students were asked to solve the following story problem:

A 10-year-old boy was 1.5 meters tall. How tall will he be when he is 20 years old?

About a third of the students chose the answer, "3 meters tall," even though from a practical standpoint a person couldn't grow over 9 feet tall. Perhaps these students did not have many concrete experiences with a meter stick or a chance to talk about and defend their ideas in the math classroom.

Developing number sense begins at a young age. Early childhood teachers make a real difference if they depart from tradition and concentrate on creating experiences based on recent research. In the past, teachers made a leap from simple counting to addition and subtraction. They skipped over essential math concepts that give meaning to number. These key ideas are explained in this chapter.

Counting: The Young Child Plays and Learns

Toddlers and preschoolers encounter numbers every day. They celebrate a birthday, "I'm three years old." Three candles light up the cake. Numbers are on appliances, the television, the mail, and the car license plate. Everyday cooking involves one cup of this, two eggs, and three cups of something else. Many things seem to come in twos: eyes, hands, feet, socks, shoes, slices of bread for a sandwich, or pieces of hamburger bun. Older brothers and sisters or cousins seem to enjoy counting how many farm animals are in a set or how many trucks fit inside the garage.

Some of the earliest language experiences come from nursery rhymes and counting books. Many songs are available as illustrated books to add pictures to the lyrics. Some of the most common rhymes include those such as *One, Two, Buckle My Shoe; Baa, Baa, Black Sheep;* and *Over In The Meadow.*

[*]Reprinted with permission from the *Curriculum and Evaluation Standards for School Mathematics* (1989) by the National Council of Teachers of Mathematics.

One, two, buckle my shoe.
Three, four, shut the door.
Five, six, pick up sticks.
Seven, eight, shut the gate.
Nine, ten, a big fat hen.

Baa, baa, black sheep.
Have you any wool?
Yes, sir, yes, sir,
Three bags full.
One for my master,
One for my dame,
And one for the little boy
Who lives in the lane.

Over in the meadow, in the sand, in the sun,
Lived an old mother frog and her little froggie one.
"Croak!" said the mother; "I croak," said the one,
So they croaked and they croaked in the sand, in the sun.

Over in the meadow, in the stream so blue,
Lived an old mother fish and her little fishies two.
"Swim!" said the mother; "We swim!" said the two,
So they swam and they swam in the stream so blue.

Over in the meadow, on a branch of the tree,
Lived an old mother bird and her little birdies three.
"Sing!" said the mother; "We sing!" said the three,
So they sang and they sang on a branch of the tree.

These songs stress rhyme and simple counting. They are available on record or cassette. (See Reference Section.)

Children's literature contains a wealth of counting books suitable for toddlers, preschoolers, and primary age children. Most computerized listings contain over one hundred titles, including picture books such as *I Can Count the Petals of a Flower* (Wahl & Wahl, 1985); African-American examples *Ten, Nine, Eight* (Bang, 1983); and *The Afro-Bets 123 Book* (Hudson, 1987). Through rhymes, books, and everyday opportunities to listen and practice, children naturally learn to count to 10.

Research and Today's Classroom

Children's cognitive math development has fascinated psychologists for many years. Some findings on number and counting are generally accepted, while many avenues of knowledge need further exploration. A reflective teacher pays attention to the implications of research in order to design the best learning environment.

Counting and number relationships develop slowly over the first seven years. Preschoolers count in a mechanical or rote fashion. This ability has three prerequisite principles or rules: the stable order rule, the one-to-one rule, and the abstraction rule (Fuson & Hall, 1983; Gelman & Gallistel, 1978; Gelman & Meck, 1986; Baroody & Ginsberg, 1986).

The *stable order rule* means that the counting words used by adults must be memorized in a certain order. Some children have one portion of the sequence stable, that is, one, two, three, four. The next part is repeated out of order on a consistent basis, that is, five, seven, six. There may be a very unstable portion of the count where they simply guess, for example, "25, 40, 12." Most children can count to 10 by the time they enter kindergarten (Baroody & Price, 1983; Fuson & Hall, 1983; Gelman & Gallistel, 1978).

The *one-to-one rule* means that children must say only one counting word for each object. By the age of four children understand that counting is a strategy to use to answer the question "How many?" (Sophian, 1987). However, most teachers notice that the accuracy of the count can be affected by inefficient methods of keeping track of counted objects, or unstable use of the counting sequence. When children master the standard sequence and can keep track of the total as the last number named, they arrive at the concept of cardinality, or matching a number to a set.

The *abstraction rule* means that children understand that they can count dissimilar objects such as a variety of farm animals (cows, ducks, chickens). The items need not be identical.

Along with the cardinality rule, children learn that they can count objects in any order: top to bottom, bottom to top, in a circle or in a line. As long as no objects were added or removed, the total remains the same. The stability of a set seems to amaze even first graders. For example, in one traditional "Pass the Bag" game, a small number of objects is placed in a brown paper bag. Music is played and the bag is passed like a "hot potato" until the music stops. The "winning child" must tell how many objects are in the bag. Naturally, since nothing happened in the few minutes of musical interlude, the number will be the same. Yet many children guess wildly, as if some magic occurred. This principle of invariance of number is also found in Piaget's Test of Conservation for number.

Three-year-olds and four-year-olds count readily when asked how many objects are in a set (Sophian, 1987). However, the evidence is less clear when preschoolers are asked to compare two sets (e.g., are these groups of animals the same?). They have trouble when asked to create a set of a particular size (e.g., make your group the same size as mine). Even when a puppet does the counting so that the procedural problems of organizing and sequencing the task is eliminated, four-year-olds cannot make good judgments about whether the puppet succeeded in comparing sets (Sophian, 1988). Kamii (1982) found that children only start to answer this question by matching up manipulatives in a one-to-one fashion at around the age of five and a half. She wrote that it took till age seven before oral counting was the preferred strategy.

Teachers in classrooms using cognitively guided instruction (Carpenter, Carey, & Kouba, 1990) describe three levels of counting to solve problems before consistently solving problems using common math facts. These strategies are direct model, counting strategies, and derived facts. In direct modeling, children physically touch and often move counters to represent the numbers in simple addition/subtraction story problems. Carpenter, Carey, and Kouba write: "By the middle of first grade, most children can solve join (change unknown) problems by direct modeling, and with experience, they can solve compare problems by matching the two sets." (1990, p. 117). The other kinds of counting strategies will be described in Chapter 8. The significance of their research for this discussion is that children readily use counting strategies to solve math problems long before they can recognize or write the symbols.

Piaget's Tests of Conservation

Piaget's tests of conservation ask children to make judgments about two sets of objects, often blocks or checkers, or two quantities of clay (mass) or liquid (capacity). In the test for conservation or invariance of number, a child observes two sets of objects (Figure 7–1):

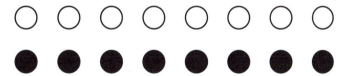

Figure 7–1

The child agrees that are the same (in number). Then, if one set is spread out, will the child still say they are the same (Figure 7–2)?

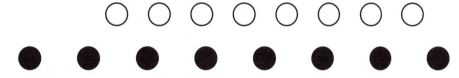

Figure 7–2

Many five- and six-year-old children say the spread out row has more because "it's longer." Therefore, if something seems to occupy more space, then there must be more items. They seem to lack the ability to abstract the concept of one-to-one correspondence once items have been shifted from a matched position. It is interesting to note that many teachers report that children try to count the objects in each row, which would indicate a more sophisticated but not complete concept of this aspect of number.

In the tests for quantity, liquid measure and clay are used. Two cups of water have identical levels of water. One cup is poured into a tall glass. Which container has more? Why? "It's taller, or it's fuller." Or two identical balls of clay are shaped. One is rolled into a snake. Which shape has more clay? Why? "The snake because it's longer." These tests rely on continuous measurement, not counting, and are even more difficult than the test for conservation of number. In all tests the key is to ask the child, "Can you tell me why you think that?"

What do these tests mean? Certainly there are limitations to a child's conception of number if the child cannot abstract comparisons among equal sets. But Piaget felt that until these kinds of concepts develop (ages 4–7), number work and counting was purely mechanical. For Piaget, classification, order, and seriation were the proper topics for the early childhood classroom. His view negated the extensive work of Montessori and her followers, who have generally found support in the academic community (Bauch & Hsu, 1988).

Piaget's findings are consistent with other researchers who have investigated children's abilities to compare sets. It would seem plausible that children view counting as a way to approach quantity serially, as if they were going up and down a mental number line. Therefore, simple tasks such as "How many?" or "How many more?" (adding), "How many fewer?" (subtracting) are reasonable challenges for young children. A compare situation or story problems such as, "There were six clowns and four balloons. How many clowns won't have a balloon if each clown gets one?" are appropriate for those children who can conserve number.

Guided Learning Activities

While conservation is a key benchmark in understanding number, classroom endeavors need not be put on hold for children who are not able to conserve. Many exciting properties of number can be explored (McClintic, 1988). These experiences include:

- counting rhymes and finger play or movement
- counting line, row, and circle games
- hide and peek games to enhance certain kinds of counting
- everyday uses of number, such as celebrating "one hundred days"
- exploration of part/whole relationships using a variety of materials
- thinking in groups
- reading and writing numerals (older children)

Examples of curricular ideas in each area may help the early childhood teacher create developmentally appropriate math adventures.

Counting rhymes rely on rhythm and enjoyment of music and movement. Rote or mechanical counting becomes rational counting when the element of one-to-one correspondence is added to the oral repetition. That is to say, children count and do something. They count and clap, or count and snap their fingers, or march to a count. Counting rhymes that go beyond the numbers 1-2-3 are helpful places to start the process. Three examples are the famous songs, "Kookaburra," "This Old Man," and "Five Little Ducks."

> *Kookaburra sits in the old gum tree-ee.*
> *Merry, merry king of the bush is hee-ee.*
> *Laugh, Kookaburra, laugh, Kookaburra,*
> *Gay your life must be.*
>
> *Kookaburra sits in the old gum tree-ee.*
> *Eating all the gumdrops he can see-ee.*
> *Stop, Kookaburra, stop, Kookaburra,*
> *Leave a few for me.*

(Note: The birds eat the berries that grow on Australian gum trees, not candy.)

The children sing the song while passing a bag containing about five or six more gumdrops than there are members of the group. Each child takes out one gumdrop, and after the song is done the class counts to see how many gumdrops the Kookaburra "left" for them.

"This Old Man" is a well known finger play and movement game that uses the counting numbers 1 to 10. Teachers often coordinate the endeavor with numeral cards to show that a sequence happens.

> *This old man, he played one,*
> *He played nick-nack on my thumb;*
> *With a nick-nack paddy whack,*
> *Give a dog a bone,*
> *This old man (point to self)*
> *Came rolling home (roll hands over each other).*
>
> *Two . . . on my shoe (tap shoe)*
> *Three . . . on my knee (tap knee)*
> *Four . . . on my door (knock forehead)*
> *Five . . . on my hive (wiggle fingers for flying bees)*
> *Six . . . on my sticks (tap index fingers)*
> *Seven . . . up in heaven (point skyward)*
> *Eight . . . on my gate (knock on imaginary gate)*
> *Nine . . . on my spine (tap backbone)*
> *Ten . . . nick-nack once again (clap hands)*

"Five Little Ducks" is one of a number of rhymes in which the audience starts with a group and loses one member during each verse. This song helps children count backwards, until all five ducks reappear at the end. A small tub of water and five plastic ducks make an enjoyable prop. Although the song does not use the concept of zero, the teacher could empty "the pond" and discuss this important number.

Five little ducks
Went out to play.
Over the hill and far away,
Mama Duck called with a
Quack-quack-quack,
Four little ducks came
Swimming back.

Four little ducks
Went out to play.
Over the hill and far away,
Mama Duck called with a
Quack-quack-quack,
Three little ducks came
Swimming back.

Three little ducks
Went out to play.
Over the hill and far away,
Mama Duck called with a
Quack-quack-quack,
Two little ducks came
Swimming back.

Two little ducks
Went out to play.
Over the hill and far away,
Mama Duck called with a
Quack-quack-quack,
One little duck came
Swimming back.

One little duck
Went out to play.
Over the hill and far away,
Papa Duck called with a
Quack-quack-quack
Five little ducks
Came swimming back!
With all their friends.

Books of songs, rhyme and fingerplays are available in most libraries. These resources make a valuable addition to any teacher's bookshelf.

Counting games include easy-to-master oral counting sequences along with music and movement. Some examples are "People Counting Games" and "The Circle Game" (1976). In one game the children form one line facing the front. They count and take one step for each number, for example, "one-two-three-fourrr," throw their hands up at 4 and turn 180 degrees. Then they mark again in the opposite direction, "one-two-three-fourrr . . ." with hands up at 4 and turn.

In row counting the teacher forms several lines, depending on the number of the count, for example, to count to four the class would make four parallel lines. Each row says its number and plops down to the ground. The children can count in unison or just say the number of their row. The count starts with the row on the children's far left. This game can also be played with ordinals. Begin by pairing the two counts: "number one—first," number two—second. . . ." Then drop the first part about number and only use the ordinal names.

In "The Circle Game," about seven to eight children form a circle. One child begins the count, with each child saying the next number until they reach the end of the sequence. For example, if the group is to count to six, the child who says "six" plops down. The count continues around the circle with the remaining children until only one child is left standing.

In another circle game children sing along to a record by Hap Palmer and join or leave the circle, depending on the lyrics. This song goes up to five. One nice feature of his work is that the pace is slow and deliberate. Too often children experience rote counting on television as a rapid-fire series of words, as if they were shot from a cannon. Because rational counting includes doing something with each number, speed is not a helpful way to develop stable counting. Any counting practice can include more than the conventional sequences 1–5, 1–10, 1–20, 1–50, 1–100. Once a particular sequence is stable, the teacher can vary the game by two different methods:

1. Count to a particular number within a sequence, e.g., "let's stop at 8," or "let's stop at 4."
2. Count on from a number, e.g., "Let's start at 6 and stop at 9."

Because oral counting is enjoyable and improves with practice, a few minutes of songs, rhymes, or games can be accomplished each day.

Counting-On Activities

A first grade teacher poses a problem—"Manuel had four trucks and two cars. How many vehicles did he have?" Many children use counters to start from the number one and model the whole problem. They put out four counters and orally say "one-two-three-four." Then they put out two more and count "one-two-three-four-five-six." While this approach is one strategy, teachers like to encourage "counting-on" from a number. In the example above, the child might start out "four," and then say "five-six."

A variety of experiences encourage counting-on from a number. These include bag games, hand games, and movement games. The activities are reversed to encourage counting back.

Bag games	The teacher and children count out a certain number of counters, e.g., five. Three are dropped into a bag. The children say "three" and count as a fourth and fifth counter is dropped in the bag. Then the teacher spills the contents of the bag, and everyone counts to affirm that there are five counters. Note: It may be helpful for each child to have a bag and counters. Variations: Use an opaque bowl and put blocks inside the bowl or under the bowl, and use a similar method.
Hand games	The children place a row of counters horizontally on the table. They count the whole row, e.g., one to five. Then they cover part of the row, e.g., "cover three" with their hand. They say "three . . . four-five."
	Variation A child divides five small counters between both hands, and closes them. One hand is opened and the audience says the count without starting from one. If the hand holds three bears, the groups says "three." Then the child opens the other hand and the group counts on, e.g., "four, five." Each child takes a turn while the rest watch and count. Suggest that the next child try a different combination.
Movement games	The children form a line in front of their chairs and count as they sit. At a certain point the teacher rings a bell, and the group must say how many are sitting at the signal, and then count on from that number until the end of the line.
	Variation: As each child in the line counts he or she turns 180 degrees. When the bell rings, the children call out the number of children who have turned around and then finish counting and turning. The child who was counted last at the bell can be the one to ring the bell on the next round.

Counting-Back Activities

Counting backwards is a skill that some children use naturally to solve subtraction problems, but many children either do not use it or use it incorrectly. Because it requires that a person reverse a well-known sequence, it is a far more difficult task. For example, on many popular IQ tests both children and adults are asked to repeat digits in the opposite order given. This task is a real challenge to a person's auditory memory.

Children often understand the process as "take away." "I have six toy cars. One less would make five." In the bag, bowl, and hand games described earlier, the total count is given and objects are removed. For example, put six counters in the bag. Take out two. Say "six, five." "How many are left in the bag?" "Four." When playing a movement game it may be best if children physically leave the line as they are counted. Example: Let's start with ten children. "Ten-nine-eight" . . . the bell rings at eight. Three children have left the circle. How many are now in line? "Seven." Children with more advanced mathematical thinking can practice counting back as an interesting challenge. They will enjoy the extra practice and will be proud to show off their abilities.

Everyday uses of number and counting are limited only by an adult's imagination. A few examples include cooking, meal preparation, toy clean-up, children's board games, and the popular tradition of celebrating the 100th day of school (K–2). These examples can help the teacher promote many more opportunities to count.

Around home children count while making meals, setting the table, and cleaning up their toys. For breakfast, juice is made with three cans of water. Two pieces of bread pop up in the toaster. For lunch, two hot dogs boil in the pan while someone prepares the two parts of each bun. When making cheese sandwiches, one piece of cheese fits nicely between two parts of a hard roll. At the table each person has a place setting of one bowl, one spoon, a napkin, and a glass of milk. It's time for the soup! Parents and caregivers can count from one to three often during the day.

Picking up toys can be a real chore, but counting makes it interesting. "How many trucks will fit in the garage?" "How many toy people came with your new play set?" Toys are counted and sorted into bins. "*All* the cars belong in the basket." "*Some* of the dolls go with your doll house, and some dolls are a part of the school house." Cleanup time can be a math experience as well as a way to put things back in their proper place.

Board games such as Candyland, Animal Crossing, or Number Guess let children use number and critical thinking to have fun. Animal Crossing and Number Guess are from a book of games called *Family Math* (Stenmack, Thompson, & Cossey, 1986). In Candyland children use one or two colored squares to make a move. In Animal Crossing the child shakes a die, labeled 1-2-3, to move around a rectangular grid.

When playing Number Guess each child covers a number from one to nine, after guessing the number by asking a clue: "Is the number greater than _____?" or "Is the number less than _____?" *Family Math* describes other games in many areas of math that are suitable for grades K through 3.

Many schools have adopted the tradition of celebrating the 100th day of school. The teacher purchases 100 straws and finds three coffee cans or three large plastic cups. Adding machine tape is used to write the numeral of each day when child actually attend class. Weekends, holidays, and snow days are not counted. Each day one straw is placed into a cup marked "1's." When 10 straws are in the cup, they are bundled and moved to the "10's" cup. This regrouping from one to tens continues until there are ten "10's" bundles (see Figure 7–3).

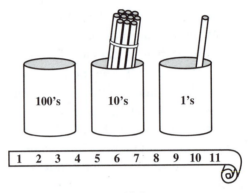

Figure 7-3 Using straws to count to 100.

On the 100th day of school, which usually falls sometime in February, the class or whole school celebrates. Each child may bring a bag from home with 100 items. The class may march 100 steps or blow out 100 candles on a cake. The teacher and children decide how to spend the day. Some teachers wear a sweatshirt with 100 buttons sewn on the front! There's no right or wrong way to celebrate, if everyone has a good time. Even though children generally experience time in the present, they enjoy anticipating a party and like to count each day as a way of marking the passage of time.

From Counting to Part-Part-Whole Activities

One of the most important recent advances in early childhood mathematics is the recognition by several researchers and writers that many teachers skip the essential building block of developing part-part-whole concepts of numbers (Resnick, 1983; Payne & Huinker, 1993; Van de Walle, 1988, 1990).

Old Schema	*New Schema*
1. Count	1. Count
2. Recognize and write numbers	2. Count on, count back
3. Attach a number to a set	3. Create and talk about "parts and wholes"
4. Learn addition and subtraction facts	4. Recognize common visual patterns
5. Solve story problems	5. Solve story problems
	6. Read, write numbers
	7. Learn the facts

Part-part-whole activities involve exploring a number as series of subsets, which when combined equal the number. For example, the number 6 can be described as: 2 + 2 + 2, 2 + 1 + 1 + 2, 3 + 2 + 1, 4 + 2, 4 + 1 + 1 and so forth. In the traditional math curriculum students often describe a number in terms of place value system, for example, 42 is 40 + 2. When asked to give another way they do not spontaneously say "39 and 3." Japanese children are encouraged to compose and decompose numbers at every grade level and for every kind of numeration system, such as fractions or decimals (Kroll & Yabe, 1987). Developing a flexible approach to numbers is one curricular goal of the kindergarten–primary curriculum. The program *Math Their Way* pioneered the careful exploration of small numbers (4–10) through the use of number stations and recording in number books (Baratta-Lorton, 1976). Since that time numerous research studies have shown the benefit of this approach. Payne and Huinker (1993) have summarized a great many research projects documenting the link of this kind of number work to problem solving. A significant amount of time in the second half of kindergarten and during the fall of first grade can be devoted to spending time on each number, using a wide variety of manipulatives. The most common materials and guidelines for each design are the following:

Toothpicks	One toothpick must touch at least one other toothpick.
Blocks	Plain one-inch cubes, or two colors.
Bathroom tiles	Plain squares, or use two colors per design.
Pattern blocks	Two shapes per design.
Jewels	These are precut in units of 1 to 5; the right number of jewels are put in a small cup (portion cup from cafeteria).
Two colored beans	Count out the number needed and put in a cup, shake and pour (use a felt square to reduce noise).
Unifix cubes	Two colors per design.
Junk or treasure boxes	Creative expression, count out the number needed per design.

Children work at tables or on the floor and fill the area with designs that each have the exact number of items for the number of the day. For example, if a child is working on the number "five" then each design contains five items (see Figure 7–4).

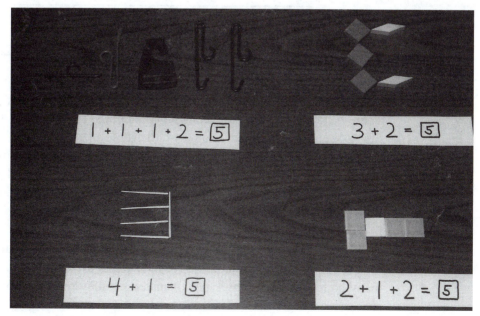

Figure 7–4   *Designs using the number five.*

Teachers may wish to have children working with a range of numbers, such as 4-5-6, 7-8-9, or 10-11-12. One day a child works with the number 6, the next day 4. In that way, children don't see the activity as a "race" to get through the numbers as fast as possible or think that higher numbers are more advanced than lower numbers.

After a child fills the table with designs the teacher asks the child to share the various subgroups for each design. A child may "see" the combinations differently from an adult. In Figure 7–5 the child may say, "it's a picture of 3 + 2 + 1."

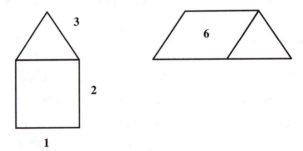

Figure 7–5   Toothpick design for the number 6.

As long as all the subparts are included to equal six, it doesn't matter how the child interprets the work.

Later children are asked to record their designs by copying them into sheets of paper, gluing down the items if they are expendable (e.g., toothpicks) or gluing down matching construction paper pieces. These designs are collected into number books such as "My Book of 5" or "My Book of 7." As children are able to recognize numerals, the teacher can label each part of the design by writing the numeral that goes with each part (see Figure 7–6).

Figure 7–6   Part–whole design using Unifix Cubes in four colors.

There is no need to write or recite an equation, such as 2 + 1 + 1 + 1 = 5 until first grade. Some teachers use part-part-whole mats (Van de Walle, 1988) in which a piece of paper has two boxes, with one picture frame around the whole thing. Children separate out a set into two subsets, such as 5 and 2 for the number 7. The disadvantages of the mat is that each number can only be decomposed into two addends, similar to the way addition facts are sometimes learned from flashcards.

When teachers take the time to explore each number over many weeks, children develop a strong foundation for later work. While the number books take many hours and use many types of materials, they represent one key to math success.

Thinking in Groups

Thinking in groups or seeing small sets and subsets without having to touch every item or count from one is strengthened by the previous counting activities, for example, counting on or back, and by part-part-whole experiences. It is also refined by practicing *instant visual recognition* of common number patterns, such as those found on dice (Figure 7–7).

Figure 7–7   *Common dot patterns and simple variations.*

Teachers begin the process by making a pattern on the overhead or on a mat in front of a small group of children. The children copy the pattern and call out the number without counting. Simple round materials such as checkers, poker chips, or small cookies facilitate instant recognition.

In another variation, teachers make "dot plates" by putting each pattern on its own luncheon-sized paper plate (Van de Walle, 1988). The collection of plates becomes a set of flashcards. The child sees a plate and says the number of dots as quickly as possible. This is one time in the mathematics program when speed becomes a motivational tool.

When using dot patterns for larger numbers, children talk about what subsets they see. For example, in a pattern of nine they might see "three groups of three." Making their own dot designs and talking about them encourages children to think about parts and wholes.

Another way to encourage recognition of number sets is to see them in relation to a "ten-frame" (Van de Walle, 1988). A ten-frame consists of two rows of five cells (Figure 7–8).

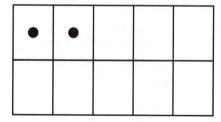   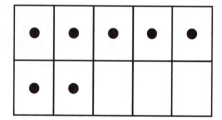

Figure 7–8   *Ten-frames for 2 and 7.*

The child places a counter in the top left cell and continues to fill each cell to make a number. In a ten-frame diagram each number relates to the number five and ten. Part-whole relationships using five and ten enhance a child's natural tendency to perform mental calculation using fives and tens to count up and back. The ten-frame patterns make interesting flashcards for first graders.

By using two ten-frames, children create the numbers from 11 to 20. For example, the number 16 is one filled ten-frame plus one ten-frame with six counters. In summary, using dot plates and ten-frames help children reach the goal of instant recognition of small sets and subsets, without resorting to counting every item. These materials strengthen a child's sense of the relations between numbers, especially the benchmark numbers of five and ten. These activities are well worth the teacher's time and effort.

Reading and Writing Numerals

Numerals are the written symbols 0, 1, 2, 3, 4, 5, 6, 7, 8, 9. In kindergarten children use numeral cards made by the teacher. They develop an awareness of the name of the symbol and its number value. As they create number books and count the pictures or parts of a design, they choose the appropriate card to glue next to the collection.

To foster number recognition many teachers play a game with a floor-size number line mat. A child says a number for each cell on the number line, from 0 to 9. Or one child picks a numeral card and reads it. The child on the mat moves to that number. The children take turns calling out the number or walking on the mat. If the teacher has more than one floor mat, more children can actively participate in the game.

Other common board games include Bingo and Concentration. In Bingo, the cards consist of cells with the dot patterns from dice, a one die to roll. A child rolls the die and covers a matching pattern. Gradually, numeral cards are substituted for the die. In Concentration the game board consists of pairs of matching numerals or dot patterns. The child attempts to make matches by remembering where the covered numerals (or dots) are.

Writing numerals is a task that first graders generally tackle. Some early childhood programs encourage the whole language approach to reading and incorporate writing stories from the first week of kindergarten. In those classrooms children attempt to write numerals along with words. But there is no rush to spend time on formal instruction. The concept of number develops slowly over many years, and tiny hands often have trouble forming the symbols correctly. When the time is right, teachers use a number of mediums to help the process. These include the following:

- Tracing a finger over sandpaper numerals
- Forming the numerals with clay
- Tracing the numerals using templates
- Forming the letters in wet sand or salt
- Forming the numerals on a chalkboard using a piece of wet sponge
- Following teacher's directions using cue words, such as "9 is a balloon and a stick."
- Tracing the numerals by connecting dots on primary writing paper

Other chalkboard exercises that benefit many children with persistent visual–motor problems can be found in Kephart's book *The Slow Learner in the Classroom* (1960).

Some children reverse the numbers, such as 6 and 9, or 5 and 2. These difficulties correct themselves as children mature, generally by the end of second grade. When reversals persist into third grade, contact a specialist in learning disabilities. This professional may wish to evaluate the child, especially if there are other academic deficiencies.

Summary

Developing number sense is an important element in a well-designed developmental math program. Many of the concepts and activities are new to teachers, even experienced teachers. Careful attention to the research on how young children think about counting and numbers results in experiences that guide development of concepts and skills in these important areas.

Ready-Set-Math

Ready-Set-Math

Toothbrush Game

Ages: 3–4 years

Items needed: Three toothbrushes
Three stuffed animals or dolls
One tall cup or glass

The teacher places the cup and the three animals on the table. The children count "one-two-three" as they put the toothbrushes in the cup. Then the teacher tells a story about how the animals wakeup in the morning and it is time to "brush their teeth." The first animal gets a toothbrush. Now there are two brushes in the cup. The story continues until there are "no brushes in the cup." The process can be done again at "bedtime."

Variation: This story can be an extension of *Goldilocks and the Three Bears* (Brett, 1987).

◆ **Ready-Set-Math**

Groups of Two and Three

Ages: 3–4 years

Items needed: Six paper plates
Twelve identical cookies in a bowl

Place the six paper plates in front of the child. Have the child sort the cookies so each plate has two cookies. Then put the cookies back in the bowl. Put out four plates. Have the child put three cookies on each plate. Watch how the child approaches the activity. Concentrate on the numbers two and three and the concept of an "empty bowl."

◆ **Ready-Set-Math**

From Tee to Green

Ages: 5 1/2–7 years

Items needed: Golf tees
Green play dough or clay
Numeral cards from 0–5
Old golf balls (optional)

Shape six rectangular tee boxes from green clay or play dough. Place a certain number of tees in the clay, e.g., the first green square gets one tee. Match the creations to the numeral cards 0–5. One tee box will have no tees (0). Note: If the dough is thick enough, the child might enjoy balancing a golf ball on each tee.

Activities and Study Questions

1. Observe a young child at home or at preschool. Listen and watch for examples where numbers are used throughout the day. Write a paragraph or journal entry about your findings.
2. Review the examples of golf tees and numeral cards in the Ready-Set-Math section. Create your own idea whereby children could match numerals to a set of everyday items. As time allows, construct your teaching aid.
3. Go to the library and read the article by Merendo on a book bag for the number 10. Find a suitable book for your own book bag creation. Write a paragraph or journal entry describing the "contents" of your bag. As time allows, construct the items you wrote about in your description.
4. Design a board game with a theme of interest to young children. Use a spinner or die with the numerals 1–2–3. Sketch out your idea. Be prepared to share your game with the class.

5. Prepare a ten-frame and collect some counters. Show a young child ($5\frac{1}{2}$–$6\frac{1}{2}$ years old) how to fill the frame. Have numeral cards ready to flash. After you show a card, have the child fill the frame. Write a paragraph or journal entry about your experience.

Classroom Equipment

nursery rhymes and counting books
records
record player
small objects
paper bag
counters
blocks
clay
two glasses of different sizes
a bell or chime
toothbrushes
three stuffed animals or dolls
floor size number line
numeral cards, 0–9
teacher-made Bingo and Concentration board games
sandpaper numerals
sand or salt boxes
small pieces of sponge
primary writing paper
six paper plates
twelve small cookies
a medium-size bowl
golf tees
old golf balls
ten-frame cards

Further Reading

Barford, J. (1994). Grade-number themes for high-profile math. *Teaching Children Mathematics, 1,* 234–241. *The author chooses a thematic approach using the number 2 for her second grade class. Stories, bulletin board displays, and trivia contests featured this theme. For example, "How old will you be on 1 January 2000?" Additional suggestions are given for grades 3, and 4, and the upper grades.*

Bohning, G. (1993). 1-2-3: Sharing and writing counting books. *Day Care and Early Education, 21,* 23–26. *The author reviews several popular counting books for preschoolers, and gives easy-to-use guidelines for selection and use of these books. A class project in which each child contributes to a page of a counting book is described. Finally, an annotated bibliography of counting books is broken down by type and suitability for preschool and primary age children.*

Merenda, R. C. (1995). A book, a bed, a bag: Interactive homework for "10"! *Teaching Children Mathematics, 1,* 262–266. *Children in her classroom take turns bringing home a book bag with a storybook (*There Were Ten in the Bed), a bed with ten tiny dolls, and a teacher-made diary notebook. Children and their parents and guardians read the story, and complete one activity about the number 10. The results are shared with the class the next morning. Examples of the materials and children's work are illustrated in the article.

Singer, R. (1988) Estimation and counting in the block corner. *Arithmetic Teacher, 35,* (6) 10–14. *The teacher organizes block cleanup around collecting and returning piles of five blocks. Sets of five are recorded using tally marks. Other ideas include predicting, counting by other groupings, and comparing totals.*

Thornton, C. A. (1989). "Look Ahead" activities spark success in addition and subtraction number-fact learning. *Arithmetic Teacher, 36,* 8–11. *Although the title of this article mentions addition*

and subtraction, the author encourages teachers to use four extensions of simple counting to improve later performance. Activities include using manipulatives to count on and count backward. Music and physical movement also help these counting skills. Finally the visual patterns of a ten-frame reinforce part-whole relationships.

Whitin, D., Milla, H., O'Keefe, T. (1994). Links to literature: Exploring subject areas with a counting book. *Teaching Children Mathematics, 1,* 170–174. *The unit begins with the book,* How Many Snails, *which lends itself to critical thinking about subgroups as well as counting. The children create their own texts and unique classification systems for animals, boats, and other modes of transportation. Children pose their own questions that require their classmates to explore the details of their drawings.*

References

Baratta-Lorton, M. (1976). *Math their way.* Menlo Park, CA: Addison-Wesley.

Baroody, A. J., & Ginsburg, H. P. (1986). The relationships between initial meaningful and mechanical knowledge of arithmetic. In J. Hiebert (Ed.), *In conceptual and procedural knowledge: The case of mathematics.* Hillsdale, NJ: Lawrence Erlbaum Associates.

Baroody, A. J., & Price, J. (1983). The development of the number word sequence in the counting of three-year-olds. *Journal for Research in Mathematics Education, 14,* 361–368.

Bauch, J. P., & Hsu, H. J. (1988). Montessori: Right or wrong about number concepts. *Arithmetic Teacher, 35,* (6), 8–11.

Carpenter, T. P., Carey, D., & Kouba, U. (1990). A problem solving approach to the operations. In J. N. Payne (Ed.) *Mathematics for the young child* (pp. 111–131). Reston, VA: National Council of Teachers of Mathematics.

Closs, M. P. (1986). *Native American mathematics.* Austin: University of Texas Press.

Eber, D. (1972). Eskimo art: Looking for the artists of Dorset. *The Canadian Form, 52,* 12–16. As cited in Closs, M. P. (1986). *Native American mathematics.* Austin: University of Texas Press.

Fuson, K. C., & Hall, J. W. (1983). The acquisition of early number word meanings: A conceptual analysis and review. In H. P. Ginsburg (Ed.), *The devel-*

opment of mathematical thinking (pp. 49–107). New York: Academic Press.

Gelman, R., & Gallistel, C. R. (1978). *The child's understanding of number.* Cambridge: Harvard University Press.

Gelman, R., & Meck, E. (1986). The notion of principle: The case of counting. In J. Hiebert (Ed.), *In conceptual and procedural knowledge: The case of mathematics.* Hillsdale, NJ: Lawrence Erlbaum Associates.

Kamii, C. (1982). *Number in preschool and kindergarten: Educational implications of Piaget's theory.* Washington, DC: National Association for the Education of Young Children.

Kephart, N. C. (1960). *The slow learner in the classroom.* Columbus, OH: Merrill.

Kroll, D. L., & Yabe, T. (1987). A Japanese educator's perspective on teaching mathematics in the elementary school. *Arithmetic Teacher, 35,* 36–43.

Markovits, Z., Hershkowitz, R., & Bruckheima, M. (1989). Research into practice: Number sense and nonsense. *Arithmetic Teacher, 36,* 53–55.

McClintic, S. V. (1988). Conservation: A meaningful gauge for assessment. *Arithmetic Teacher, 35,* (6) 12–14.

Payne, J. N., & Huinker, D. M. (1993). Early number and numeration. In R. J. Jensen (Ed.), *Research ideas for the classroom: Early childhood mathematics* (pp. 43–70). New York: Macmillan.

Resnick, L. B. (1983). A developmental theory of number understanding. In H. P. Ginsburg (Ed.), *The development of mathematical thinking* (pp. 109–151). New York: Academic Press.

Sophian, C. (1988). Limitation on preschool children's knowledge about counting using counting to compare two sets. *Developmental Psychology, 24*, 634–640.

Sophian, C. (1987). Early development in children's use of counting to solve quantitiative problems. *Cognition and Instruction, 4*, 61–90.

Stenmark, J. K., Thompson, V., & Cossey, R. (1986). *Family math.* Berkeley: University of California.

Van de Walle, J. A. (1990). Concepts of number. In J. N. Payne, *Mathematics for the young child* (pp. 62–87). Reston, VA: National Council of Teachers of Mathematics.

Van de Walle, J. A. (1988). The early development of number relations. *Arithmetic Teacher, 35*, (6) 15–21.

Related Books

Anno, M. (1977). *Anno's counting book.* New York: Crowell Junior.

Bang, M. (1983). *Ten, nine, eight.* New York: Greenwillow.

Barnes-Murphy, R. (1987). *One, two, buckle my shoe.* New York: Simon & Schuster.

Brett, J. (1987). *Goldilocks and the three bears.* Dodd Mead.

Galdone, P. (adapted). (1986). *Over in the meadow.* New York: Simon & Schuster.

Hudson, C. W. (1987). *The Afro-bets 123 book.* Orange, NJ: Just Us Books.

Jones, C. (1990). *This old man.* Boston: Houghton Mifflin.

Koontz, R. M. (1989). *This old man.* Putnam. A modern interpretation of the song. Ten little sweat-suited men are the focus of the book.

Mother Goose. (1991). *Baa, baa, black sheep.* New York: Lodestar. Exuberant art work brings new life to the traditional nursery rhyme.

Wadsworth, O. (1985). *Over in the meadow.* New York: Viking Penguin.

Wahl, J., & Wahl, S. (1985). *I can count the petals of a flower.* Reston, VA: National Council of Teachers of Mathematics.

Willebeek le Mair, H. (1989). *Our old nursery rhymes.* New York: Philomel. Thirty nursery rhymes, including "Baa, baa, black sheep," are nicely illustrated in this book that was first printed in 1913.

Related Records and Tapes

Beall, P. C., & Nipp, S. H. (1985). "Baa, baa, black sheep" from *Wee sing nursery rhymes and lullabies.* Price Stern Sloan.

Beall, P. C., & Nipp, S. H. "Over in the meadow" from *Wee sing nursery rhymes and lullabies.* Price Stern Sloan.

Beall, P. C., & Nipp, S. H. "This old man" from *Wee sing nursery rhymes and lullabies.* Price Stern Sloan.

"Baa, baa, black sheep" from *Sing-a-long.* (1987). Peter Pan.

Palmer, H. *Learning basic skills through music,* Vol. 1. Educational Activities, Inc. Freeport, New York 11520.

Scelsa, G., & Millang, S. (1979). "One, two, buckle my shoe" from *We all live together,* Vol. 3. Youngheart Records.

"This old man" from *Sing-a-long.* (1987). Peter Pan.

8 Problem Solving—Addition and Subtraction

IN MISS COOPER'S second grade classroom the children are trying to recreate the foot of the large dinosaur, a tyrannosaurus. They measure, draw, and cut out a life-size replica. They can't wait to visit the local field history museum on next week's field trip and see the dinosaur display. Miss Cooper will bring along the class's paper models for comparison to the museum's collection.

Miss Campbell's second grade class ponders a page of word problems from a well-worn textbook. The teacher urges the class to find all the answers quickly or risk having the unfinished ones assigned as homework. One problem involves comparing the height of a man in meters to the height of a camel. Some children guess wildly. "Do I add the numbers?" "Do I subtract?" No one seems interested in how much taller the camel is as compared to an adult. The children's main motivation is to finish the page.

In these two classrooms, the children are engaged in a form of math often called "problem solving", doing story problems. A visitor might think that both lessons were equally valuable. How can we judge the merits of these experiences? Teachers might ask these questions about the process:

- What is problem solving?
- How can I nurture mathematical thinking?
- How can I justify taking the time to do it right?
- Should story problems come after the children memorize the facts or before? Why?
- Aren't challenging problems only for gifted students?
- What level of students should receive challenging problems? Why?

This chapter addresses these questions as well as the operations of addition and subtraction. A thoughtful classroom environment promotes problem solving. This environment differs drastically from what many adults remember from their early school years.

Math Is Problem Solving

In one sense problem solving does not require a separate chapter. All the strands in math engage young learners in creative, persistent thinking. Matching, classifying, ordering, patterning, and thinking about numbers are a few examples of problem solving. Why probe deeper into the subject? For many years the math curriculum lost its focus on the connections between the symbols and their practical uses. Manipulation of numbers became a mechanical means to pass a course. Students did not see the relation of math to everyday life. Many teens and young adults, especially women and minorities, avoided taking more math than was required for a diploma. In short, math didn't make any sense, except to mathematicians. In the document *An Agenda for Action* (Edwards, 1980), the National Council of Teachers of Mathematics recommended that problem solving be the focus of school mathematics. Their call for reform is almost two decades old. In 1989, the Council stressed this approach when they wrote:

> In grades K–4, the study of mathematics should emphasize problem solving so that students can
>
> - Use problem-solving approaches to investigate and understand mathematical content
> - Formulate problems from everyday and mathematical situations
> - Develop and apply strategies to solve a wide variety of problems
> - Verify and interpret results with respect to the original problems
> - Acquire confidence in using mathematics meaningfully* (p. 23)

Most parents and educators agree that problem solving is a worthwhile goal of the school curriculum. All aspects of the curriculum, from science to social studies, stress logical, flexible thinking. Math is one subject in which children explore many kinds of reasoning. They see, listen and talk, touch and move to discover how math explains the real world. They write about their ideas and defend them when challenged. Math not only gives people a way to handle everyday tasks like making change, it is way of thinking.

A successful problem solving experience begins with two essential ingredients: an interesting, challenging problem and a positive atmosphere.

Choosing a Problem

Teachers study the nature of real "problems" to avoid the pitfall of using examples or exercises at the end of textbook pages as "real problems." These tasks are merely applications of a certain operation. For example, the textbook page contains computation using double-digit addition. The story problem reads:

> A boy had 76 marbles. His friend gave him 23 more marbles. How many marbles does he have?

Often students see the pattern and do not bother to read the English sentences. They pull out the numbers and add, regardless of the context.

George Polya is acknowledged as the "Father of Modern Problem Solving." In 1962 he distinguished between immediate application of known material and a real problem. He wrote:

> To have a problem means: to search consciously for some action appropriate to attain a clearly conceived, but not immediately attainable, aim. (p. 117)

---

*Reprinted with permission from the *Curriculum and Evaluation Standards for School Mathematics* (1989) by the National Council of Teachers of Mathematics.

Another author (Swenson, 1994, p. 401) refined this definition to include "finding solutions for difficulties which: (1) are seen and felt by the learner; (2) he cares about solving; and (3) seem to him to be solvable." Children need practice in solving their own problems, rather than remembering the teacher's solutions to a problem. The best problems come from children's natural interest, such as dinosaurs, or everyday living, such as buying objects at the store. Children's literature and music themes add interest to problems.

General Kinds of Problems

Word problems are classified as either closed (one solution) or open (when many solutions are possible).

For example:

Closed   Juanita receives an allowance of $2.00 each week. What are the fewest numbers of coins she could get?

Open   Juanita receives an allowance of $2.00 each week. How many different ways can she get her $2.00, using coins and dollar bills?

Closed problems lend themselves to writing one number sentence, such as $8 \times \$.25 = \$2.00$. Quarters seem the most logical answer for young children. Fifty-cent pieces are not in wide circulation. Open-ended questions lend themselves to charts, tables, and graphs in which the different solutions are displayed. Both kinds of problems present valuable learning opportunities.

Teachers search for problems where an approximate answer will suffice, as well as ones that ask for an exact answer.

Approximate answer   You and your brother are going to the movies. The ticket price is $5.00. But you might want to buy some popcorn, candy, or soda. These treats cost about $2.00 for each cup or box. Decide what you want to buy at the counter. About how much money will the trip to the movies cost?

Exact answer   Jonah fed his three cats. Then he fed his two dogs. How many animals did he feed?

Another consideration involves choosing problems that can be solved using a variety of methods: solving it in your head (mental math), paper and pencil math, or calculator math. Second grade students add five cents and ten cents in their heads. But to figure out the total grocery bill, they reach for a calculator. Overuse of paper and pencil math detracts from logical thinking about a solution, that is, "I know it! I figured it out in my head." It also limits the size of the numbers and the complexity of operations. A calculator frees the child to concentrate on the total problem rather than to just remember the facts. Modern day accountants rely on computers, calculators, and their own brains to complete an audit. If adults combine logical thinking with available electronic tools, children benefit from these same resources. (Remember: No calculator operates without brain power.)

Naturally, teachers choose interesting problems that do not promote stereotypes. Women do not do all the shopping while men buy gas and cut the grass. Sensitivity to the cultural practices of each family helps teachers make wise choices. A problem about pumpkin pie at Thanksgiving may not relate to the everyday experiences of many children who eat sweet potato pie at the holiday feast.

Problem Posing

Finally, teachers decide on how to *pose* a problem. Should the teacher read the problem aloud? Should the child read the problem? Are pictures and script helpful? How clear should the story be?

In the method suggested by proponents of Cognitively Guided Instruction (Peterson, Fennema, & Carpenter, 1989), the teacher reads aloud the problem as many times as needed. The children concentrate on listening to the problem, even though the problem may be written on a sheet in front of them. Manipulatives, such as small counters or Unifix cubes, are within reach of each child. The children solve the problem, using whatever way they wish and discuss their thinking.

Hembree (1992) reviewed a series of studies that supported the use of pictures with a full problem statement (see Figure 8–1).

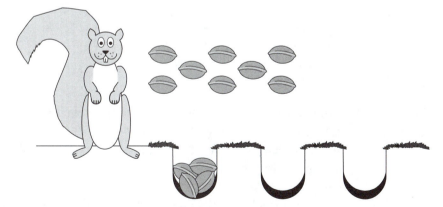

Figure 8–1   A squirrel made three holes. In each hole the squirrel buried four nuts. How many nuts did the squirrel bury?

Some authors write story problems in a clear fashion. The narrative follows the natural actions children might use as a way to solve the problem. Other problems are in mixed order. The information is out of sequence.

Clear order	Maria found six shells on the beach. She gave two shells to her brother, Peter. How many shells does Maria have left?
Mixed order	Maria gave her brother Peter two shells. If she found six shells on the beach, how many does she have left after she gave two to her brother?
Clear order	Manuel has one large box. His large box holds six cars. He has four small boxes. Each small box holds two cars. How many cars does Manuel have?
Mixed order	A large box holds six cars. A small box holds two cars. Manuel has one large box and four small boxes. How many cars does Manuel have?

Teachers choose problems that pose a challenge to young thinkers. Adding the element of a poorly constructed story, or one using mixed order, seems to be an unnecessary burden. Children want to persist, succeed, and share their solutions. Elements that create confusion detract from the enjoyment of problem solving.

A Positive Environment

A positive environment for problem solving includes many elements missing from some of today's classrooms. In an ideal environment problem solving occurs on a daily basis, not just when problems appear at the end of a chapter. The teacher allows plenty of time. Perhaps a small group solves only one problem a day, or takes many days to work towards a solution. A reflective teacher accepts unusual solutions and encourages a variety of approaches. No one "right way" takes precedence over other ways of thinking. The teacher encourages talking abut the process, not just the answer. The teacher poses many questions:

> "How did you think about it?"
> "Is her solution a good one? Why?"
> "Did anyone think about it in a different way?"
> "Let's listen to his way."

Assessment for grading includes the process as well as the product. The classroom may divide into cooperative groups so there is less risk in being wrong. But at times each person must think through the problem alone. Thinking about a problem is a very personal experience, and no one should be deprived of this valuable opportunity.

Finally, the teacher fully understands the information on the classes of problems or problem types and the mathematical operations and rules governing addition and subtraction. This valuable background knowledge gives teachers confidence that their curriculum is mathematically correct. Many modern textbooks do not contain enough background information for the teacher or interesting opportunities for children to develop into superior problem solvers. Many teachers attend classes or workshops to enhance their ability to develop curricular themes that challenge students.

General Strategies

The most common general strategy for problem solving is Polya's (1962) four-step method:

1. Understand the problem
2. Devise a plan
3. Carry out the plan
4. Look back

Instruction in a general method of problem solving appears to enhance student success, especially as children reach the upper elementary grades (Hembree, 1992). Young children naturally follow steps 1 through 3 as they investigate a problem that they think they can solve. Teachers guide children's mathematical thinking about step 4 with classroom activities that include the sharing of solution strategies and thoughtful responses to open-ended questions. The following section on how children approach story problems is organized around the four steps.

Step 1: Understand the Problem

Young children may ask to have the problem repeated in its entirety. Or they may repeat valuable parts of information aloud: "I had five cars. . . . How many did my brothers give me?" When a child has misinterpreted a piece of information, the teacher may guide the child to a better interpretation. For example, a second grade class is working on the problem:

> You have two friends visit after school. Your mom gives you five cookies. How can you share your cookies so that you and your friends have the same?

> One child draws four people at the top of a page. The teacher notices the error. She shows the child a box of small dolls. "Which doll is you? Which ones are your two friends? How many people get the cookies?" The child erases one of the people.

The teacher gives each student five paper cookies, and the class approaches the next steps in problem solving in a variety of ways.

Step 2: Devise a Plan

Children employ a number of strategies without any formal instruction. In one sense they act impulsively and do not follow "steps." These early strategies fall into three categories (Carpenter & Moser, 1984; Carpenter, Carey, & Kouba, 1990):

1. Direct model—physically moving objects or fingers for the whole problem. Counting from one.
2. Counting strategies—thinking about part of the problem as a starting place and counting on or counting back from that number.

3. Number facts—using "derived facts" or easily memorized facts to solve the problem.

Most children enter first grade with the ability to solve simple kinds of addition and subtraction story problems when counters are available. They *direct model* the following kinds of problems with no formal instruction:

1. Jayna had five crayons. Her sister gave her two more. How many crayons does Jayna have?
2. Roy had three toy cars. He gave one to Hernandez. How many toy cars does Roy have left?
3. Mrs. Peters has three yellow pencils and two white pencils. How many pencils does she have?

Modeling with counters or bars of 10 cubes, such as bars of 10 linked cubes, also helps students solve simple problems that contain double digit numbers. For example:

> Jayna had 25 crayons. Her sister gave her 12 more. How many crayons does Jayna have?

The magnitude of number size does not affect the outcome unless there is a need to change the strategy. Counters model 25 crayons as accurately as 5 crayons. However, the lack of counters for solving problems using two digit numbers appears to encourage the use of more sophisticated counting methods (Carpenter & Moser, 1984).

Counters appear to be helpful to solve the early kinds of "compare problems." For example:

> Maria had seven apples. Jose had four apples. How many more apples does Maria have? $7 - 5 = \square$ or $4 + \square = 7$

In this kind of problem, children often match the two sets to find the extra apples. Early counting skills such as counting from one and counting all the apples won't work.

In first grade, children move from direct model and counting-from-one strategies to other more sophisticated counting strategies. Some children count-on from the largest number, but many children use the first number mentioned, regardless of size. Counting-up from a given number is more popular than counting-back (Carpenter & Moser, 1984). Here is a problem solution using a counting strategy:

> Manuel had 7 trucks. Pedro gave some trucks to Manuel. Now he has 12 trucks. How many trucks did Pedro give Manuel? $7 + \square = 12$

The child says, "Let's see. Manuel had 7 trucks. Now he has 12 . . . 7 . . . 8, 9, 10, 11, 12 (holding up 5 fingers)." He beams and answers "5." In counting strategies one number is kept in the child's head as the base, and the count continues up or down.

Children gradually use number facts, including "derived facts," beginning in grade one. These derived facts are unique combinations of known facts, such as the doubles, and sums that equal ten, plus counting up or back. An answer for $12 - 7 = \square$ might be. "I know that $6 + 6 = 12$, so $12 - 6$ would be 6. But 7 is one more than 6, so the answer is 5 because I have to take one more off."

Another example might be, "What is $9 + 7$?" One child thinks, "10 is 1 more than 9, so I take off the 1 from the 7 and put it on the 9. Then I have 10 plus 6, 16." Another child thinks differently, "I know 7 and 7 are 14, and 9 take away 7 is 2. So I take the 2 off the 9 and add it to the 14, and get 16." When teachers hear these intricate calculations they think only very bright children use them. Research shows that an overwhelming majority of primary age children use them at some time in their development (Carpenter & Moser, 1984). When teachers allow children to talk about their ideas, they enjoy explaining their solutions in terms of numbers they already know. Many early childhood teachers are unaware of this critical stage. Memorization of rote facts comes more easily when these skills are integrated into the child's existing knowledge.

Direct Instruction in Diagrams.   Elementary textbooks often try to "teach" problem solving strategies such as: Draw a picture, guess and check, look for a pattern or act it out. Of all the suggestions, only one approach to problem solving appears to merit direct teaching from the early years on through college: explicit training in diagrams (Hembree & Marsh, 1993; Shigematsu & Sowder, 1994). Teachers often tell children to "draw a picture." This suggestion will not produce better results without modeling. Diagrams proceed from simple pictures with brackets, to boxes with brackets, to abstract lines. Here are some diagrams for a story problem (Figure 8–2):

Jennifer had three apples. Amy gave her some apples. Now she has seven apples. How many apples did Amy give her?

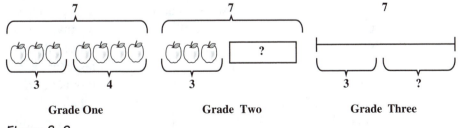

Figure 8–2

Japanese textbooks use drawings of line segments and number lines as well as conventional pictures. The diagrams are labeled with numbers, and a wide variety of problem types are represented (Shigematsu & Sowder, 1994). Because most American textbooks do not explicitly use diagrams or expose children to the whole array of problems teachers must take on this responsibility.

In summary, when carrying out step 2: Devise a Plan, most young children use informal strategies such as direct model, counting-on, or derived facts. Learning to draw simple diagrams helps them gain mathematical power. Children employ other strategies, such as guess and check, or trial and error when faced with a novel situation, just as adults do. Trial and error, or trial and success approaches, are part of any problem-solving environment. Teachers who encourage risk taking and promote a safe, supportive environment will not need to explicitly teach this method as a strategy.

Step 3: Carry Out the Plan

In step 3, children carry out the strategy or strategies they chose until the problem is solved. Many teachers ask children to write about their strategy. At times they are so busy implementing a strategy they forget where they are in the process.

Let's return to the second grade class where the pupils are dividing up five cookies among three people. Some children cut each cookie methodically into smaller but equal parts. Piles of cookie pieces sit on their desks. It seems overwhelming to give away all these slivers of cookies. The teacher guides the process so the child "gives away" the pieces to the figure on the page, deciding what to do when the count doesn't come out exactly right. The teacher says: "What can you do? You have one extra piece?" Hopefully the child will cut the remaining piece into three smaller segments, though some children may give it to "their dad," or "the dog." The original instructions were to glue down the pieces. Since the problem has so many pieces, the teacher helps the child tape down the pile as a practical alternative.

When carrying out the plan, some children get discouraged and want to quit for a time. If they have spent a reasonable amount of time on a problem, they may put it aside. Perhaps they could review the problem with others, or ask how they got started. A fresh start may bring new insight into challenging problems.

Usually a problem is stated in words, which are translated into the language of math symbols. When children write a story about how they thought about the problem, they see this task as an additional challenge. They may forget what they did first, second, or next. They may dislike invented spellings for their ideas. Many children cannot draw out their solution by using the space on a piece of paper wisely. They crowd things into one corner and cannot fit objects into the picture. For example, a first grader may wish to draw three plates of buttons. One plate holds seven red buttons. But the circle for the "plate" is so small that it cannot hold seven little circles. Teachers who think carefully about step 3, plan ahead to help children with these hurdles. They may fold the paper in threes, provide pre-drawn circles, or have children draw a circle as big as something, like a fist. Children like to be "done," or finish the problem. This step takes patience, flexibility, and creativity so all children succeed. Because some children or co-operative groups finish ahead of others, they need independent work that extends their thinking.

Step 4: Look Back

This is the stage in which good teachers take the time to let children share their results. Since children are curious and inventive, they often have solved a simple problem in many different ways. The teacher listens to each solution, and the class may need instruction in how to listen to each other. Children are often eager to share their ideas and may shout them out while others are speaking. The teacher carefully calls on girls as well as boys, early in the discussion. Also, shy children may hold back important insights because they are overwhelmed by the boisterous extroverts. These children need extra attention, as do the children who have trouble expressing themselves in English. The teacher needs to know all the different ways the class thought about the problem.

Although direct model strategies are developmentally less sophisticated than derived facts, no attempt is made to label one approach as "better" than another. When a wrong answer is given, children will change their minds when their classmates explain their answers. For example, if John gives a wrong answer, the teacher can comment: "John thought of it this way. Did anyone else get that answer? Who thought of it a different way?" Practice in talking about math, and writing about math, are essential activities in the early childhood classroom. Children may know what they want to say, but have trouble getting the words out. They need time to think aloud, or need support for their efforts, even if the results are incomprehensible to the adult. Many oral or written solutions come as a complete surprise, even to very experienced teachers. These responses are part of the delight of teaching young children.

Cognitive Background Information for Teachers: Classes of Problems

Many teachers think that there are two classes of problems. In one problem the children add the two numbers to find the sum. For example: "Dewey had six goldfish. His uncle brought him four more. How many goldfish does Dewey have?" ($6 + 4 = \square$). In the other kind of problem the children subtract. For example: Mario had seven baseball cards. He gave one to his brother. How many baseball cards does he have left? ($7 - 1 = \square$). These familiar formats fill early math textbooks. Math scholars break down the problem types in many ways. One textbook describes only one real world use for addition, which is similar to the joining of two sets in the problem about Dewey's goldfish (Kennedy & Tipps, 1994). They write that subtraction occurs in four situations. The most common is the *take-away* problem, similar to the Mario problem. Second, a *"comparison"* situation arises when children are asked to compare the sizes of two sets. For example, "Twelve people like chocolate ice cream. Nine people like vanilla ice cream. How many more people like chocolate ice cream?" Third, a *completion* problem uses subtraction to discover a missing number. For example, "Zaneta had three berets. Her sister gave her some more berets. Now she has seven berets. How many did her sister give her?" Some textbooks call this a "missing addend" problem. Fourth, a *whole-part-part* problem is used to find the size of a group within a larger group. "Aunt Edna planted twelve tulips. Five were red. The rest were yellow. How many tulips were yellow?" We know the size of the whole group (twelve tulips), and one subgroup (five red tulips). We are looking for the size of the other subgroup.

Another textbook uses a similar breakdown of problem types, but adds a fifth kind of addition and subtraction, call *incremental* problems. These problems involve measuring continuous quantities such as sand, water, or temperature. Children cannot rely on counting discrete objects (Troutman & Lichtenberg, 1991). Further discussion of these kinds of problems can be found in Chapter 10.

Another way of looking at problem types has been the basis for extensive research on how children think about addition and subtraction. Early research at the University of Wisconsin, Madison, focused on using eleven problem types, based on a different philosophy from the classification methods just described in this section (Carpenter & Moser, 1983; Carpenter & Moser, 1984; Carpenter, Carey, & Kouba, 1990; Peterson, Fennema, & Carpenter, 1989). While adults might solve many problems using subtraction, children use counting from one, or counting-on to find a solution. In effect, the children are adding. The use of the 11 problem types also encourages children to learn the standard (canonical) number sentences that mathematicians might use (Bebout, 1990). Teachers study all 11 types so they are able to approach teaching primary mathematics with confidence. Furthermore, some studies show an increase in pupils' academic achievement (Peterson, Fennema, & Carpenter, 1989).

This method uses four basic classes of problems:

Join (three types)
Separate (three types)
Part-Part-Whole (two types)
Compare (three types)

Join problems involve combining numbers, or adding, where a sequence of *actions* occur. Separate problems involve "take-away" or removing objects, where a sequence of actions occur. The difference between the three kinds of problems has to do with where the unknown number or the box symbol occurs. Watch for the parallel structure in the next two rows:

Action	*Join-Result Unknown*	*Join-Change Unknown*	*Join-Start Unknown*
An increase in the final set.	Chad had 4 blocks. Drena gave him 3 more. How many blocks does Chad have altogether. $4 + 3 = \square$	Chad had 4 blocks. Drena gave him some more blocks. Now Chad has 7 blocks. How many blocks did Drena give Chad? $4 + \square = 7$	Chad had some blocks. Drena gave him three more. Now Chad has 7 blocks. How many did he have to begin with? $\square + 3 = 7$

Action	Separate-Result Unknown	Separate-Change Unknown	Separate-Start Unknown
A decrease in the initial set.	Chad had 7 blocks. He gave 4 to Drena. How many blocks does he have left? $7 - 4 = \square$	Chad had 7 blocks. He gave some to Drena. Now he has 3. How many did he give to Drena? $7 - \square = 3$	Chad had some blocks. He gave 4 to Drena. Now he has 3 blocks. How many did he have to begin with? $\square - 4 = 3$

The order of the action in the problem determines which box is needed. This approach differs drastically from what many teachers remember from their math education. Teachers confuse the properties of numbers, such as the commutative property ($3 + 2 = 2 + 3$), with the standard way of writing a number sentence so that it matches the story problem.

In part-part-whole problems, no action occurs. The question involves the size of the final set when two subsets are known. Or the child looks for one subset, when the whole set and the other subset are known. There are only two kinds of part-part-whole problems.

Action	Part-Part-Whole Whole Unknown	Part-Part-Whole Part Unknown
None	Chad had 4 red blocks and 3 blue blocks. How many blocks did Chad have altogether? $4 + 3 = \square$	Chad had 7 blocks. Four are red. The other blocks are blue. How many blocks are blue? $4 + \square = 7$ or $7 - 4 = \square$

Two kinds of number sentences are mathematically standard ways to write part-unknown problems. Here order does not make a difference because there is no action in the story.

The final class of problems are *compare* problems. Children look at the relationships between two sets and ask the kinds of questions they ask when interpreting graphs. Which has more? Which has less? How many more? How many less? These kinds of problems lead to more sophisticated problems in which the size of one set is reconstructed, based on information about one of the sets.

If I know that I have 12 pencils, and that you have 4 more than I have . . . then I can figure out that you have *16* pencils. I know my whole set (12), and your extra pencils (4), so you must have the equivalent of my 12 pencils plus 4 more, or 16 pencils.

In another type, I know that I have 12 pencils, and I have 3 more pencils than you have . . . then you must have *9* pencils. I know my total set (12), and how many more (3), so I can construct your set.

Action	Compare Difference Unknown	Compare Quantity Unknown	Compare Referent Unknown
None	Chad has 7 blocks. Drena has 4 blocks. How many more blocks does Chad have? $7 - 4 = \square$ or $4 + \square = 7$	Chad has 4 blocks. Drena has 3 more than Chad. How many blocks does Drena have? $4 + 3 = \square$	Chad has 7 blocks. He has 3 more than Drena. How many blocks does Drena have? $7 - 3 = \square$ or $\square + 3 = 7$

Teachers learn to recognize these classes of problems and write examples of them using the themes and children's literature. Research shows that teachers who study the various types, and actively promote solving on a daily (or almost daily) basis find that their students score better on measures of both problem solving *and* computation (Carpenter, Fennema, Peterson, Chiang, & Loef, 1989). One source of story problems using multicultural children literature is *Good Books, Good Math* (Jenkins, Lehmann, Mass, Wells, & Wood, 1991). Problems written in the 11 types are available for 35 books. Gradually, elementary math textbooks will incorporate more classes of problems into their series. Until then, the resourceful teacher must write them as needed.

In another research study (Bebout, 1990), first grade children learned to write number sentences with the box in the correct place for many of the problem types. After five weeks of direct instruction, these children were successful regardless of their pretest scores on the kinds of problems and strategies they had previously mastered. Some children generalized the instruction so that they could solve the most difficult problems, where the box begins the number sentence.

Not all the problem types are equally easy to solve. Teachers who use these classes of problems easily recognize that compare problems are difficult to solve, with the problem types that have the box as the first set in the sentence being the most difficult (Join-Start Unknown, and Separate-Start Unknown).

When teachers assess children's abilities they chart the kinds of problems they can solve *and* the method used to solve it. The best way to find out about the strategy is to have the child tell you *how* they thought about the problem. Did the child use a direct model, counting, or derived fact approach? Looking at both the problem types and the level of sophistication in strategy gives primary teachers a powerful assessment guide for future planning.

Rules of Operation

In addition to classes of problems, teachers need information on the mathematical properties of addition and subtraction. These rules of operation govern what is mathematically possible using the addition and subtraction symbols. Addition is a *binary operation*. Two ("bi") numbers combine to make one and only one number. The properties of addition are the commutative property, the associative property, the transitivity of equality, and the identity element. Young children use these properties informally. Students in upper elementary school learn to explain them and demonstrate them with manipulatives and number sentences. Many adults have heard of these operations, but cannot remember what they mean.

Math property	*The Identity Element* Zero is the identity element for addition. a + 0 = 0; 0 + a = 0
Children's use of the identity element	"If I have a million caps and add zero, I still have a million caps."
Math property	*The Commutative Property* When I have two addends, I can write them in any order. The sum is the same. For whole numbers a and b, a + b = b + a.
Children's use of the commutative property	"If I know 8 + 5 = 13, then I know the commutative property 5 + 8 = 13, because they are both the same." This helps me learn my facts.
Math property	*The Associative Property* When I have *three* or more addends, I can put any two whole numbers together, and then add that number to the third number. For whole numbers a, b, c, (a + b) + c = a + (b + c).
Children's use of the associative property	"What is 6 + 8?" "I know. I know the associative property that 6 + 6 is 12, and 6 + 2 is 8. So I take the 2 off the 8, and add it to the 12. The answer is 14." Children use the associative property when constructing knowledge using derived facts. 6 + 8 = 6 + 6 + 2 = 14. They know they can start anywhere and add 2 numbers, and put on a third number to get the sum.
Math property	*Transitivity of Equality* Any two addends that have the same sum are equal to each other. For whole numbers a, b, c, d, e, f, if a + b = c and d + e = f, then c = f, if c and f are the same whole number. 5 + 2 = 4 + 3.
Children's use of transitivity	"There are many ways to make the number 6." When I made my block designs I found: 4 + 2, 5 + 1, 6 + 0, 3 + 3. I put these designs into my *Book of 6*."

The *identity element* for subtraction is zero. There are two ways to show the role that zero plays in a number sentence using subtraction: 7 – 0 = 7 and 7 – 7 = 0. Children need experiences with both kinds of problems. If I have 7 pieces of candy and I eat 0 pieces, I still have 7 pieces left. If I have 7 pieces and I eat all 7 of them, I have 0 pieces left. Zero plays a dual role in subtraction number sentences.

Helping Children Write Their Own Problems

Children enjoy writing and sharing their own stories. Generally they write problems they can solve. One child may write about spending 10 cents and 15 cents on two toys. How much did she spend altogether? Another child in the same class might write about having enough pennies (37 cents) to buy a certain toy that was originally 60 cents, because it was on sale at $1/2$ off. Occasionally a problem loses its focus when children try to include very large numbers or create a complicated plot. The teacher guides the child to see what parts of the problem are confusing or missing. If other children try to solve a poorly written problem, they may act as editors and help straighten out the puzzle.

To begin, children often need a model of a problem, and a way of recording their findings. The following are some examples of ideas for children's problems:

Kindergarten	The children have finished weighing various pieces of fruit (apples, bananas, oranges, grapes, and grapefruit) in a pan balance scale. Each piece weighs "so many" dinosaur counters.
	Now the children think of things to weigh, and vary the counters, e.g., pears and teddy bear counters, a staple and wooden cubes. They write a problem, draw a picture, and solve it.
First grade	In Piggy Bank Math, the teacher puts one penny in a clear "piggy bank" jar for each day of the year. The teacher models story problems such as, "When I went to the store. . . ." or "When I went to the fair. . . ."
	The children use the money count of the day in a story problem of their own.
Second grade	The teacher reads the story *Ten Black Dots* (Crews, 1986). On each page one more dot makes a new picture.
	Members of the class pick a particular page and change the theme. They write stories about "what if each person in the class made a picture with three dots?" How many dots does the teacher need to buy for the whole class?
Third grade	The teacher reads the story of *The Nice Mice* (Irons, 1995). Mother mouse has 3 children, who must share many things. On one page the mice must share 9 tiny shirts; on another, 12 cakes. The children invent their own problems, where there are fewer people than treats, or fewer animals than food or nests.

Children appreciate having a recording sheet (or math journal entry form) that has lined space to write the story, open space to draw and figure out the solution with symbols, and another section to explain the approach. On the back of the paper might be a section called "More Ideas." After hearing how other children solved the problem, they may wish to expand on their own thoughts.

Very young children may need help spelling some essential vocabulary. Word cards overcome some children's natural reluctance to use invented spelling for every word.

Occasionally children tire of journal writing, about their own stories, or other's problems. They expend so much energy on the problem, and during the classroom discussion, that they feel they are done with the problem. However, writing about math is one way to reflect on the process and to explain and defend ideas. Children may write more thorough explanations if they are encouraged to complete this task *before* sharing with the group. Also, not every problem needs to be recorded. Variety increases motivation and attention to detail. Models of excellent work can be shared with an authority figure, such as the principal, or parent, or displayed in the classroom or hallway. Public recognition and encouragement help stimulate reluctant writers to new levels of enthusiasm.

Summary

At times, teachers feel torn between developing a problem solving curriculum and using a textbook approach based on writing numerals and teaching standard algorithms. However, these skills come naturally as children explore mathematical ideas. Children are capable of solving many complex problems using a variety of strategies. They enjoy solving challenging problems. They share their solutions with enthusiasm, often inventing ways of thinking that the teacher has never heard before. A problem-solving curriculum moves beyond merely using manipulatives to demonstrate and entertain the class. It promotes critical thinking and the discovery of the power of math.

Ready-Set-Math

Ready-Set-Math

Drops on a Lid

Ages 3–4 years

Items Needed: Eye dropper
Small lids from ketchup, salad dressing bottles
Paper towels
Colored water
Newspaper

Each child has a dropper and a few small lids. The teacher spreads old newspapers and paper towels on a table and gives the child a small container of colored water. The teacher explains that the goal is to fill each lid with colored water without going over the top. The child devises a plan and explains how the problem might be solved. Which lid will be the first? How will you know when to stop? If the child's lid overflows, new toweling is provided.

Variation: For older children, the teacher gives each child a penny. The child thinks of a way to count the number of drops on the coin.

Ready-Set-Math

Our Book of Favorite Foods

Ages 5–6 years

Items Needed: 100+ recording sheets for drawings and stories about favorite foods
Crayons, markers, pencils

The class decides to make a big book after reading *The Wolf's Chicken Stew* (Kasza, 1987). The wolf likes the number 100, so the book will have 100 pages. The class must decide how many pages each person will need to write in order to reach the goal. Younger children draw pages with pictures and text about their favorite foods. Older children put 100 items on their pages. For further ideas and explanation see "Scrumptious Activities in the Stew" (Schneider, 1995).

◆ **Ready-Set-Math**

Dots on the Dice

Ages: 5–6 years

Items Needed: Pairs of dice
                     Recording paper

The teacher poses the question, "How many dots are on a pair of dice." The class discusses the vocabulary concept of "a pair." Each child works on the problem alone, then shares the solution with a small group or the whole class. The students are encouraged to draw and show their work as well as write a narrative about the strategy.

◆ **Ready-Set-Math**

Time to Compare: When Were You Born?

Ages: 7–9 years

Each member of the class brings information on the date and hour of birth. Children who cannot find out about this data may choose their own information (generally the time of day). The class decides how to organize themselves in order to portray this data. The children display the data in a table or graph, and draw conclusions about their findings. Some teachers have found two children who were in the same hospital on the same day or within one day of each other.

Activities and Study Questions

1. Create a calendar of activities for a week or a month, similar to the ones described in the article by Saarimaki (1994). Use local events and landmarks to promote problem solving as a family.
2. Review the 11 problem types as described in this chapter. Chose a favorite book for children and write an example of each type using the book's characters and plot.
3. Create your own glyphs for an elementary social studies unit, using the example in the article by Harbaugh (1995). Try out your glyphs on another member of your class.
4. Visit your local library and locate its collection of primary math textbooks (college libraries with teacher certification programs collect instructional media). Make a chart of the problem types found in grades 1 through 3. Which problem types are missing? Evaluate the series for its overall ability to promote problem solving. Explain the criteria you chose for your analysis.
5. Select a favorite children's book and create a problem-solving activity to accompany the text. Write a paragraph or journal entry about your ideas.

Classroom Equipment

large sheets of newsprint
markers
calculators
pieces of fruit
a pan balance scale
toy counters
real or play money
stick-on dots from an office supply company
journal or recording paper
children's literature

Further Reading

Fairbairn, D. M. (1993). Creating story problems. *Arithmetic Teacher, 41,* 140–142. *The author gives examples of ways to update old problems by giving them a new context. Old problems can be appealing when the names, places, and the context are changed. For example, a hotel setting with three adults is transformed into a ski trip for middle schools students. Many good problems survive decade after decade with just a cosmetic facelift.*

Harbaugh, K. N. (1995). Glyphs? Don't let them scare you! *Teaching Children Mathematics, 1,* 506–511.

A glyph is a picture symbol that represents certain information. One drawing, such as a person, may be covered with symbols telling about age, eye color, pets, and siblings. For example, a certain number of strands of hair indicates age in years. Jewelry worn around the neck may have a symbol for a pet dog. Learning about symbols, drawing and interpreting them, and creating new symbols, help children think about how to display data. Several good examples with full-page illustrations are given for a second grade unit. This kind of problem solving helps children with good visual–spatial skills use their talents to succeed in math.

Saarimaki, P. (1994). Calendar mathematics. *Arithmetic Teacher, 41,* 528–532. *The Toronto Public Schools published a monthly "math" calendar for the 1993–94 school year. Each day list-ed an open-ended problem that parents and children could investigate together. Problem difficulty ranged from preschool through upper elementary school. References to local landmarks and holidays, children's books, and nature walks added interest to the activities. Parents were encouraged to try the ones that appealed to their family members and not to worry about doing everything.*

Swenson, E. J. (1994). How much real problem solving? *Arithmetic Teacher, 41,* 400–403. *The author discusses ways to relate problem solving to children's everyday experiences. She distinguishes between real problems and exercises by giving examples that teachers understand. Aspects of problem solving include selecting data and deciding when a solution is acceptable. Guidelines for improving classroom climates are given.*

Wesson, J. B., & Lawhorn, C. (1992). Standards in the methods class: An example. *Arithmetic Teacher, 40,* 38–39. *College methods classes use base-ten block manipulatives to discover the principles of rounding decimals in various bases. The general rounding rule was extended into two places to the right of the decimal point for odd numbered bases. These exceptions were found after experimenting with the blocks and the usual rule. Classroom discussion, experimentation, and pattern development helped the class achieve a positive math climate.*

References

Bebout, H. C. (1990). Children's symbolic representation of addition and subtraction word problems. *Journal for Research in Mathematics Education, 21*, 123–131.

Carpenter, T. P. & Moser, J. M. (1983). The acquisition of addition and subtraction concepts. In R. Lesh & M. Landau (Eds.) *The acquisition of mathematical concepts and processes* (pp. 7–44). New York: Academic Press.

Carpenter, T. P., & Moser, J. M. (1984). The acquisition of addition and subtraction concepts in grades one through three. *Journal for Research in Mathematics Education*, 15, 179–202.

Carpenter, T. P., Carey, D., & Kouba, U. (1990). A problem solving approach to the operations. In J. N. Payne, (ed.), *Mathematics for the young child.* (pp. 111–131). Reston, VA: National Council of Teachers of Mathematics.

Carpenter, T. P., Fennema, E., Peterson, P. L., Chiang, C. P., & Loef, M. (1989). Using knowledge of children's mathematics thinking in classroom teaching: An experimental study. *America Educational Research Journal, 26*, 499–532.

Edwards, E. (Ed.). (1980). *The agenda for action.* Reston, VA: National Council of Teachers of Mathematics.

Hembree, R. (1992). Experiments and relational studies in problem solving: A meta-analysis. *Journal for Research in Mathematics Education, 23*, 242–273.

Hembree, R., & Marsh, H. (1993). Problem solving in early childhood: Building foundations. In R. J. Jensen (Ed.) *Research ideas for the classroom: Early childhood mathematics* (pp. 151–170). New York: Macmillan.

Jenkins, M., Lehmann, L., Maas, J., Wells, K., & Wood, P. (1991). *Good books good math.* Madison, WI: Madison Metropolitan School District.

Kennedy, L. M., & Tipps, S. (1994). *Guiding children's learning of mathematics 7th Ed.* Belmont, CA: Wadsworth.

Peterson, P., Fennema, E., & Carpenter, T. (1989). Using knowledge of how students think about mathematics. *Educational Leadership, 46*, (4) 42–46.

Polya, G. (1962). *Mathematical discovery.* Volume 1. New York: Wiley.

Schneider, S. (1995). Scrumptious activities in the "stew." *Teaching Children Mathematics, 1*, 548–552.

Shigematsu, K., & Sowder, L. (1994). Drawings for story problems: Practices in Japan and the United States. *Arithmetic Teacher, 41*, 544–547.

Swenson, E. J. (1994). How much real problem solving? *Arithmetic Teacher, 41*, 400–403.

Troutman, A., & Lichtenberg, B. K. (1991). *Mathematics a good beginning: Strategies for teaching children.* Pacific Grove, CA: Brooks/Cole.

Related Books

Crews, D. (1986). *Ten black dots.* New York: Greenwillow Books.

Irons, C. (1990). *The pirate's gold.* Crystal Lake, IL: Mimosa.

Irons, R. (1955). *The nice mice.* Crystal Lake, IL: Rigby.

Kasza, K. (1987). *The wolf's chicken stew.* New York: Putnam.

9 Understanding Our Place Value System

THE CHILDREN IN MISS JOHNSON'S class are investigating numbers by using beansticks to symbolize a certain value. One child volunteers the number "83," and the second graders readily put out eight sticks and three loose beans. (A beanstick is a Popsicle stick with ten small beans glued on it.) Another child asks the class to make "47." Again, the class has no problem arranging four sticks and seven beans. A third child suggests the number "11." Because the class is just beginning to develop an understanding of base-ten numeration, many children struggle with the problem. The other numbers, 83 and 47, contain the pattern within the English name, that is, 80 plus 3. But the word eleven doesn't give a clue. It's not "ten-one." The numbers 11 to 19 pose a special challenge. It will take many years to develop an understanding of the relationships in our numeration system, including decimals. But the journey is essential to grasping the power of mathematics as a universal language of commerce and science.

A Brief History of Base-Ten

Very early cultures appear to have used pebbles, tally systems, sticks, notches on a stick, scratches on a stone, or marks on pottery. When commerce and the need for taxes developed, civilization made marks up to 10, with a special symbol for 10. For example, the Egyptians wrote numbers from right to left, using these hieroglyphs (Figure 9–1):

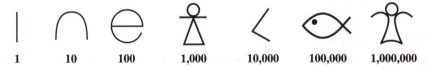

| 1 | 10 | 100 | 1,000 | 10,000 | 100,000 | 1,000,000 |

Figure 9–1

The Egyptian system was based on powers of 10, but had no zero. It was not a true positional system. If the number was 352, the symbol was written (Figure 9–2):

Figure 9–2

The Egyptians used numbers into the millions when managing large estates or building pyramids.

Our present system is described as a Hindu–Arabic numeration system. The Hindus developed it and the Arabs spread it throughout Europe. For a short time it coexisted with a system of Roman numerals, but replaced that system by the sixteenth century. The system included the symbol for zero, although the exact origins of zero are a subject of controversy. One author believed that zero did not appear until the ninth century in India (Smith, 1953). A base-ten system was by no means the only method of grouping. For in-depth description of various systems used by Native Americans see *Native American Mathematics* (Closs, 1986).

Our culture uses base-twelve in measurement of length (inches), quantity (a dozen), and time (twice 12 hours in the day). We use base-twelve to run the modern computer. The machine distinguishes between two possibilities, 0 and 1. Although written numbers may become very long, the simple "on-off" method is easier than finding a way to encode the 10 possibilities of the numerals 0 to 9.

The Unique Features of the Base-Ten System

There are four unique features of the base-ten system:

1. The system uses the numerals 1, 2, 3, 4, 5, 6, 7, 8, 9, and 0. Zero is a place holder; for example, 405 indicates that there are no tens. It also represents a quantity or an empty set. There are "zero elephants" in the room.
2. Base-ten is a positional system. The one's place is on the right. The next position is the base, then the base times the base, and so on (b = 10).

$$b^4 + b^3 + b^2 + b + 1s$$

3. The value of the whole number is the sum of its parts or the value assigned to each digit.
4. People use the system to perform all the basic calculations, using procedures called *algorithms*. These paper and pencil tasks include addition, subtraction, multiplication, and division. The base-ten system extends to decimals and is used in the metric system of measurement. Calculators and computers also accomplish this task, using their own system. Children still need to master common procedures to see how the base works. In addition, there are times when it is not efficient or practical to locate a device. A calculator cannot solve a problem using large numbers or decimals without the help of a person who has acquired number sense about the base-ten system.

Teachers use the base-ten numeration system on a daily basis, without thinking about the way it is constructed. Many instructors in math methods classes use activities around other bases to show the versatility of our system.

Readiness for Place Value

Children enjoy oral counting by ones. In kindergarten they learn to recognize and write the numerals 0 to 9. They also explore part-whole relationships, decomposing numbers into a variety of arrangements. For example, the number 6 might be 5 + 1, 4 + 2, 3 + 3, 6 + 0. In base-ten, children will discover the properties of units of tens and ones (23 is two ten's and three one's). Gradually children connect knowledge of the English word, the written symbol and positional units. The child thinks, "I can say thirty-five, and write 35 and add 35 to another number such as 24 by thinking of 3 ten's and 5 one's added to 2 ten's and 4 one's." As soon as physical quantities become bigger then single digit numbers, it becomes more efficient to break them apart by units of ten. Consider the story problem: "Belita had 17 pieces of candy. Andrew gave her 20 more pieces of candy. How many did Belita have altogether?"

One child solves the problem by directly modeling the quantities or counting out the candy one piece at a time. Another child models the problem by taking units of Unifix cubes already made into tens. This child takes one ten and seven loose cubes, and two tens. Then the child counts, "ten, twenty, thirty, thirty-one, thirty-two . . ." and so on. A third child solves the problem in her head, "I put the 10 from the 17 together with the 20 and got 30. Then I added on the 7 to the 30 and got 37." The transition from counting by one's to counting by units of ten occurs over the course of many years. Eventually, children see that units of ten can be grouped or ungrouped. For example, the number 36 has many names:

> 36 = 1 ten and _____ ones
>
> 2 tens and _____ ones
>
> 3 tens and _____ ones

These properties of the system deserve an extended period of instruction and discourse. How does a teacher guide learning in our place value system? Recent research about children's natural preference and the conventional use of many forms of visual imagery help the process.

Children's Natural Preferences

Many children face the challenge of adding or subtracting multi-digit numbers sometime during second grade. The traditional method emphasizes learning to line up digits and computing from right to left often using boxes as a visual aid. Practice consists of doing 30 problems a day, in class or as homework.

The method is not the way children think about solving multi-digit computations. When allowed to approach the process on their own, children universally begin on the left, and regroup back and forth until they arrive at an answer (Madell, 1985; Kamii & Joseph, 1988; Kamii, Lewis, & Livingston, 1993; and Wearne & Hiebert, 1994).

Here is an example:

The traditional approach: 673

+<u>241</u>

"I added the 3 and the 1 and got 4, so I put down the 4. Then I added 7 and 4 and got 11, so I put down the 1 and carried the 1. Six plus 2 is 8 and 1 more makes 9, so I put down the 9."

Children's invented approach: 673

+<u>241</u>

"I added 600 and 200 and got 800. Then I added 70 and 40 and got 110. I put the 800 and the 110 together, and I got 910. Then I added 3 + 1 and got 4. So the answer is 914. I put down the 914."

Children who use their own abilities to solve these kinds of problems show good number sense about place value. If they make errors, the wrong answers are small computing errors. In contrast, in one study of second through fourth graders, fourth graders who were taught the traditional method "did considerably worse than the second graders who did their own thinking" (Kamii, Lewis, & Livingston, 1993, p. 202). Fourth graders' errors were also of a large magnitude, showing that they did not use number sense to see that they were way off the mark. Adults understand place value and can use the conventional algorithm with confidence. Children will see the logic to the traditional method and see it as "another way" to compute when they eventually change over to it. The standard method becomes more efficient with very large numbers where there are multiple opportunities to regroup, for example, 1,658,249 + 3,480,167. (Of course, this kind of calculation may be more suited to a calculator.) When adding 87,001 + 40,010, going from left to right makes good sense.

Classroom Learning with Manipulatives

Young children like to touch and move objects. Kamii and her associates prefer to present a problem on the board and listen to the classroom conversation without the use of any learning aids. They feel that materials might interfere with the development of a mental representation of a unit of ten (Kamii, Lewis, & Livingston, 1993). However, most educators feel that these objects represent numbers in ways that are more helpful to children than just talking and listening.

Adults also appreciate their versatility. In a case study of elementary teachers attending a math institute, the participants reported that base-ten blocks really helped them perform the algorithms in a new base, "X mania" (Schifter & Fosnot, 1993).

The key is whether the child understands the process, rather than simply moving cubes and rods around on a mat. There are probably as many wrong ways to teach with manipulatives as there are to teach without them.

General Kinds of Manipulatives

There are three general kinds of materials used to help children appreciate the concept of place value. These ways can be classified as follows:

1. Proportional (nonlinked)
   a. drinking straws/rubber bands
   b. sticks, or coffee stirrers/rubber bands
   c. Unifix cubes
   d. beans/cups or plates or counters
2. Proportional (linked)
   a. beansticks
   b. base-ten blocks
3. Nonproportional
   a. money (pennies, dimes, dollars)
   b. abacus

Proportional materials show relationships by size. The beanstick has ten beans glued on a stick. It is ten times bigger than one bean. In the base-ten materials, a flat of 100 is the size of 100 loose unit cubes. Linked materials come preformed and cannot be taken apart to form loose units. Nonlinked materials either stick together (Unifix cubes) or a person bundles them using rubber bands or containers.

Nonproportional materials use units of a certain value for exchange, for example, money. A dime isn't ten times the size of a penny. An abacus uses beads or plastic chips that derive their symbolic value by location on the row.

Activities can be organized around these three kinds of manipulatives:

1. Count and group—nonlinked proportional
2. Using beansticks/base-ten blocks with mats and blackboards—linked proportional
3. Creating numbers and exchanging values—nonproportional

Some of the earliest place value activities involve count and group. The teacher decides on a group of a certain quantity and uses that quantity to solve a problem. In one article on estimating and the block corner, the author has the children put blocks away in groups of five. When almost all the blocks are shelved she asks, "Do we have another group of five left?" The children estimate by looking at the remaining pile. Are there more than five? The children decide when there are too few blocks to make a group (Singer, 1988). Many classrooms celebrate the "100th day of school." For everyday of school they add one straw to a cup and bundle groups of 10. They have a big part on the 100th day, usually sometime in February. Everyday counting activities go smoothly when groups of 10 help organize the chore. For example, the estimating jar holds a mystery number of cotton balls. The children take turns guessing and recording their guesses on the classroom number line. Then one child counts out a group of 10 and squeezes them into a ball. The class counts first by tens and then by ones.

With nonlinked proportional materials such as Unifix cubes, children may practice creating units in several bases (Baratta-Lorton, 1976). In the "Zurkle game," base-four uses four linked cubes and loose cubes. Units and loose cubes are placed on a two-color mat (Figure 9–3):

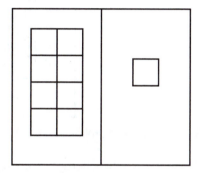

Figure 9–3   "2 Zurkles and 1."

Silly names are created for each unit, until the children reach units of 10. There is no need to attach conventional numerals to the bases.

Teachers use preformed or linked proportional materials such as beansticks and base-ten blocks in conjunction with place value mats to add, add and regroup, subtract, subtract and regroup, and multiply (one-digit by two-digit numbers). It is complicated, but possible, to demonstrate simple division using these materials, especially the base-ten blocks, which represent numbers up to 9,999.

Children begin by creating numbers using units of ten and ones. The beansticks are helpful because they are inexpensive to make, and model numbers 1 to 99 very well. Teachers pay careful attention to the numbers 11 to 19, since these numbers do not readily decompose into tens and ones using the English word as a cue. Also, they sound very much like other numbers, such as, fifteen . . . fifty.

Teaching with Beansticks or Base-Ten Blocks

The teacher gives each child a place value mat, a set of sticks, and a cup of loose beans. To subtract, the students also need an envelope with two sets of numeral cards, 0 to 9.

To add:	The teacher or a student writes a problem on the board. The children create each number by representing the tens with sticks and the ones with loose beans. The teacher has the children "join" or "put together" the sets and count by tens and ones to find the total. Note: Children may prefer to add the tens first, and then the ones.
To subtract:	The children make the top number with sticks and beans. The bottom number is made by using two numeral cards (Figure 9–4).

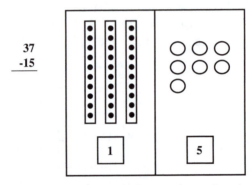

37
-15

Figure 9–4   Subtraction using beansticks, cards, and a place value mat.

The teacher gives a story problem using action. For example, "There were 37 pieces of candy in the box. My friends and I ate 15. How many pieces of candy are left in the box?

The teacher stresses that the class knows "the whole," or 37, and "one part," or 15. They are looking for the other part.

The children place 1 stick and 5 beans on the numeral cards and remove them from the mat. The answer is the remaining stick/bean number.

To add with regrouping:	After combining the sticks and beans the children see that are 10 or more loose beans. They trade 10 beans for 1 stick.
To subtract with regrouping:	When the children try to remove the ones, they see that they do not have enough. They trade 1 stick for 10 loose beans.
To multiply:	Early multiplication is similar to repeated addition. For example, teacher writes on the board: *3 groups of 12.*
	The children put out 3 sets of sticks and beans and join them. They trade loose beans for sticks as needed.
To connect the materials to paper and pencil computation:	The teacher puts the children in groups of two. One partner has a small chalkboard, while the other partner uses the beansticks After a few problems they exchange materials. In Figure 9–5, one child solves the problem, 26 + 46, using the board, while one solves the same problem using the sticks.

Figure 9–5   *Second-grade students using beansticks and the chalkboard.*

Children use base-ten blocks in a similar fashion, with a mat that has three sections: hundreds, tens, ones. These mats generally come with the materials. Some teachers use the vocabulary "flats for the hundred square, rods for the ten piece, and cubes or units for the ones." This circumvents the problem of using number words twice to describe a particular position, for example, the number 87 could be 8 ten's and 7 one's, or 8 rods and 7 units. For some children, hearing a stream of number words is confusing. They may think, "Did the teacher say, 1 ten or 10 ones?"

Some teachers use base-ten blocks from the beginning of study, skipping beansticks. This practice makes sense when a school can afford the expense of a classroom set at each grade level. However, beansticks are inexpensive. Children can make them themselves, repair them, and large lima beans are easy to grasp. Both materials have a place in the curriculum.

Teaching with the Abacus and Money

Both the abacus and money are nonproportional systems. The abacus shows numbers into the billions. It is also helpful to demonstrate zero and its value as a place holder. For example, in Figure 9-6 the number 7,600,502 illustrates no ten thousands, thousands, or tens.

Figure 9–6   A third-grade student using an abacus.

As children encounter large numbers in science and social studies, they can recreate them on the abacus. For example, when a third grade class studies mountain ranges in the Northwest, they find that Mt. McKinley, located in south central Alaska, is 20,320 feet high. Mt. Rainier, a famous peak in the state of Washington, is 14,410 feet high. The students may wish to illustrate the difference in their notebooks by drawing two abacuses with the corresponding number of counters for each mountain's height.

Play money helps students see relationships based on value. Games such as Dollar Digit from *Family Math* (Stenmark, Thompson, & Cossey, 1986) use pennies, dimes, and dollars. Some children understand money well because it is a part of their everyday lives. Money may be especially helpful to explain decimals.

In another money activity, the teacher assigns a value to each day of the month. For example, the date is equal to $100 times the number. January 1st equals $100, January 2nd equals $200, and the 3rd is worth $300. By the third day of a new year, the students have $600. On February 1st, the system begins anew; February 1st equals $100. Students trade hundreds for thousands and so on through the year. They may wish to set a goal of a certain amount and change the value of each day to meet their goal. Using a base of $100 means that the class will soon work with larger numbers. This activity may be done once or twice a week, as an excellent "sponge" activity for unexpected free time.

Estimating and Rounding Larger Numbers

As children work with larger numbers they need experiences that give them a sense of how big something is. One famous book, *How Much Is a Million?* (Schwartz, 1985), helps children relate to large numbers. Some teachers attempt to collect a million metal pull tabs from soda cans, stringing them across the classroom.

Another number activity involves having students participate in teams of four pupils. The teacher prepares a deck of cards by removing the face cards and tens. Each card is worth its face value, with an ace equal to one. Each member of the team picks a card and the group forms a four digit number, making the largest number they can. The members position themselves and display the number to the class. The class reads the number and the highest number wins. The students write a story about something that could have happened with the winning number. The plot should be realistic. For example, the student probably did not eat thousands of cookies, but could have purchased a used car priced in the thousands.

Often children are asked to round numbers based on place value. This concept needs careful attention. Students need to see:

1. Rounding is relation to position, that is, the tens will be rounded up or back from 10 to 100. The hundreds will be rounded from 100 to 1,000, to the closest 100, and so on.
2. When a number is halfway or more than halfway we round up.

   Examples:

1–10	5 and up
10–100	The number between the tens, that is, 15, 25, 35, etc.
100–1,000	The number between the hundreds, for example, 150, 250, 350, etc.

One helpful way to illustrate rounding is by the use of separate number lines. Students practice choosing a "home base" for a pet (animal counter) by using a number line from 0 to 10. They cover the 5 with a clear plastic chip (Figure 9-7). The teacher calls out a number. The student places the counter on the number and moves the animal to the closest house, 0 or 10.

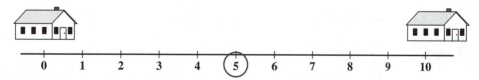

Figure 9–7   Rounding board 0–10.

They graduate to number lines from 10 to 100 (Figure 9–8).

Once they have the concept, students practice with numbers in the hundreds and thousands. They fill in the base numbers on a blank number line, cover the middle, and make a decision (Figure 9–8).

0	1	2	3	4	5	6	7	8	9	10
10	11	12	13	14	15	16	17	18	19	20
20	21	22	23	24	25	26	27	28	29	30
30	31	32	33	34	35	36	37	38	39	40
40	41	42	43	44	45	46	47	48	49	50
50	51	52	53	54	55	56	57	58	59	60
60	61	62	63	64	65	66	67	68	69	70
70	71	72	73	74	75	76	77	78	79	80
80	81	82	83	84	85	86	87	88	89	90
90	91	92	93	94	95	96	97	98	99	100

Figure 9–8   Rounding board 0–100.

Rounding numbers occurs in everyday life with sales tax and tips. It will also be helpful later in division and decimals.

Assessing Children's Understanding of Place Value

One common method of assessing a child's understanding of place value is to ask the child to perform the following task (Ross, 1989):

1. "Count out 25 sticks from a bag of sticks."
2. Tell me, "How many are there?"
3. "Write down the number."
4. Then the teacher circles the 5 and asks, "Does this part of the 25 have anything to do with how many sticks you have?" The teacher circles the 2 and asks the same question.

Based on her own research, and the research of many authors, Ross (1989) described a five-stage model of interpretation.

Stage 1, whole numeral. The child sees a two-digit number as one whole amount. For example, 47 means 47 objects.

Stage 2, positional property. The child recognizes that there is a "ones place" and a "tens place," but does not connect this knowledge to numbers.

Stage 3, face value. The child can identify which number is in the ones place, and which number is in the tens place. But the child does not see that 3 tens is 30.

Stage 4, construction zone. At times the child calculates the tens and ones correctly, but this knowledge is unreliable.

Stage 5, understanding. The child sees the parts correctly and can describe the whole number in terms of tens and ones. The child can take a nonstandard partition, that is, 2 tens and 18 ones, and create a standard partition (p. 49).

Ross found that many students succeed at stage 3 when they match materials to the spoken word, such as 27 would be two of the rods and seven of the cubes. They can succeed in a wide variety of manipulatives without being able to explain place value with understanding. Manipulatives may or may not interfere with a child's thinking about a base.

Summary

Children in first and second grade naturally combine or subtract multi-digit numbers using a variety of strategies (Kamii & Joseph, 1988). Children graduate from counting by ones to counting by units, such as tens and ones. Instructional planning for the use of place value materials needs to carefully integrate the children's current thinking with the visual aids. The classroom climate must challenge the child to think. Careful assessment, using what the teacher already knows about how children think about place value, will help the teacher decide on the next level. Children develop an understanding of place value over many years, with much exposure to everyday situations using larger numbers. It does not happen after a brief unit "covering the material" at a certain grade level. The reflective teacher takes the time to guide learning in this important topic using many opportunities for high-interest mathematical problem solving.

Ready-Set-Math

Ready-Set-Math

More Than Five

Ages 3–4 years

Items needed: A variety of small counters, or food such as cereal, a bowl, a more/less chart

The teacher puts a group of objects in a bowl. The amount is either more than 5 or less than 5. The teacher asks, "Are there more than 5 pieces or less than 5 pieces? When the child guesses the correct answer, a star is put in the appropriate column on the chart.

Ready-Set-Math

Race to 100

Ages 6–7 years

Items needed: Beansticks
Loose beans
Two dice
A tens/ones recording
Sheet and pencil
A calculator

Two to four players take turns rolling the dice. They take the sum in tens and ones. They trade 10 loose beans for 1 stick as needed. They write each move on a recording sheet. The winner is the first person to reach 100. To check the result, they add up their throws with a calculator.

Variation: Begin with 100 (10 sticks) and subtract each throw of the dice until a winner reaches zero.

Ready-Set-Math

The Newspaper Ad Game

Ages 7–9 years

Items needed: Newspaper ads for inexpensive items
                         A shopping list recording sheet and pencil

The teacher decides on the amount to be spent: $1.00, $5.00, or $10.00. Students work in teams to find items to purchase. They must spend as close as the whole amount as possible, buying a minimum of three items. They write the name of the store, the item, and the amount on their "shopping list."

Ready-Set-Math

Create a Board Game

Ages 7–9 years

Items needed: Spinners or dice
                         Cardboard
                         Markers/crayons
                         Play money (pennies and dimes)

Teams of students decide on a theme and make up their own game. Players advance with pennies and dimes. The game may include an adventure with a beginning and an end. Players may collect pennies and trade them for dimes along the way. However, the students have the final say on how the rules work. Other classmates try the game to see if it works.

Note: This activity may take an extensive amount of time.

Activities and Study Questions

1. Visit the library and locate information on another culture's numeration system. Prepare a chart illustrating the method and be ready to describe how it was used in everyday life.
2. Prepare a sample lesson showing the use of one kind of material that is commonly associated with place value: using building sticks or straws, using beansticks or base-ten blocks, using Unifix cubes, or using the abacus. Be prepared to share your ideas with the class.
3. Prepare a deck of cards by removing all face cards and tens. Draw four cards at random and create a four-digit number (ace = 1). Write a paragraph or journal entry using your number in a story. The story does not need to be a word problem, but the number should be used in a realistic way.

4. Administer the informal assessment for understanding of place value to a child. Decide which of the five levels described in this chapter best describes the child's comprehension. Write a paragraph or journal entry about your experiences.

5. Using a theme from children's literature, think of a word problem where children would put items into bags or boxes by tens and ones. Be prepared to share your problem with a partner or a group of your classmates.

Classroom Equipment

coffee sticks	numeral cards/envelopes
straws	deck of cards
rubber bands	dice
tall cups	spinners
Unifix cubes	rounding boards
large lima beans	small clear plastic counters
beansticks	small counters, such as
cafeteria portion cups	teddy bears
base-ten blocks	a bowl
play money	newspaper ads
an abacus	markers
building blocks	crayons
cotton balls	bags, small
an estimating jar	boxes
place-value mats	

Further Reading

Bove, S. P. (1995). Place value: A vertical perspective. *Teaching Children Mathematics, 1, 542–546. The author suggests using a strip of adding machine paper, where zero is at the bottom, and the numbers are written vertically up the paper in one column. Two-digit numbers will show how a new position, left of the ones place, occurs. The number line is coordinated with the place value mat. The teacher facilitates a classroom discussion of the relationship of the written symbol to the cubes on the mat to promote a better understanding of the concept.*

Gluck, D. (1991). Helping students understand place value. *Arithmetic Teacher, 38, 10–13. The author demonstrates a variety of ways to link concrete experiences with manipulatives to the abstract or the paper and pencil algorithm. She gives ideas for games and extension of the basic concepts.*

Ross, S. H. (1989). Parts, wholes, and place value: A developmental view. *Arithmetic Teacher, 36,* 47–51. *The author conducted an extensive study on the acquisition of place value concepts in students in grades 2 to 5. Five stages of development were used to show understanding. Approximately half of the fifth graders could not demonstrate real understanding. Many younger children seem to know more than they do. Teachers need to take more time to explore numeration. The role of manipulatives is clouded by uncertainty as to whether they help or impede successful learning.*

Schifter, D., & Fosnot, C. T. (1993). *Reconstructing mathematics education: Stories of teachers meeting the challenge of reform.* New York: Teachers College Press. *The authors follow a group of teachers and record their thoughts as they struggle with the challenge of creating a new base called "X mania." Their thinking is described, along with illustrations on how the various systems worked. This activity involved base-five, so the teachers had to discover the properties of a base, just as primary children do, including making many of the initial errors that children make. The teachers' comments show as much "perspiration as inspiration," making the challenge of math learning real.*

Wearne, D., & Hiebert, J. (1994). Research into practice: Place value and addition and subtraction. *Arithmetic Teacher, 41,* 272–274. *Second-grade children were interviewed as they solved place value computations. The authors illustrate the importance of listening for understanding, not just the right answer. Implications for teaching and learning emphasize the latest research on acquisition of this knowledge.*

References

Baratta-Lorton, M. (1976). *Math their way.* Menlo Park, CA: Addison-Wesley.

Closs, M. P. (1986). *Native American mathematics.* Austin: University of Texas Press.

Kamii, C., & Joseph, L. (1988). Teaching place value and double-column addition. *Arithmetic Teacher, 35,* 48–52.

Kamii, C., Lewis, B. A., & Livingston, S. J. (1993). Primary arithmetic: Children inventing their own procedures. *Arithmetic Teacher, 40,* 200–203.

Madell, R. (1985). Children's natural processes. *Arithmetic Teacher, 32,* 20–22.

Ross, S. H. (1989) Parts, wholes, and place value: A development view. *Arithmetic teacher, 36,* 47–51.

Singer, R. (1988). Estimation and counting in the block corner. *Arithmetic Teacher, 36,* 10–14.

Smith, D. E. (1953). *History of mathematics.* Boston: Ginn.

Stenmark, J. K., Thompson, V., & Cossey, R. (1986). *Family Math.* Berkeley: University of California Press.

Wearne, D., & Hiebert, J. (1994). Research into practice: Place value and addition and subtraction. *Arithmetic Teacher, 41,* 272–274.

Related Books

Anno, M., & Anno, M. (1983). *Anno's mysterious multiplying jar.* New York: Philomel Books.

Schwartz, D. (1985). *How much is a million?* New York: Scholastic.

10 Measurement

IN THE KINDERGARTEN CLASS at Martin Luther King Elementary School the teacher greets each pupil, "Good morning, Charles." "Good morning, Rhea." She continues, "Tomorrow is Lian's birthday and we are going to have a party. We've waited a long time to have a birthday!" The teacher models the measure of time by carefully talking about sequence and duration.

Down the hall in first grade two children tackle the problem of "how tall the amaryllis is." The carefully staked flower sits on a low table. One child guesses, "I think it's 8 inches, no 9 inches." The other child says, "I think it's 12 inches." First they put a ruler in the dirt. "It's more than 12." They reach for the yardstick. "It's over 30. It's more than 30 inches."

It's late spring and the second grade class is growing pea plants. Now it is time to measure and chart their growth. Each week the students record their results in inches on a graph. The plants in the sunny window are making good progress. The ones in the dark corner are turning yellow and seem stunted. In science class the children learn that plants need many things to flourish. Some of these experiments are headed for the compost pile.

In each classroom children work with the concept of measurement by talking, using the tools of measurement, guessing, and recording the results. Are these children engaged in learning activities that are appropriate to their developmental level? How does the teacher guide measurement experiences, and assess their usefulness? Both new and experienced teachers benefit from studying *the process*, as well as the common textbook approaches to the subject. Most professionals feel confident that this is one area they have mastered. Yet children score poorly on national tests such as the National Assessment of Educational Progress, illustrating the simplest elements of measurement (Kouba, Brown, Carpenter, et al., 1988). This chapter describes the concept of measurement, the general foundations of the process, the methods, and some cautions about the way we assess readiness. Teachers benefit from a deeper understanding of how the procedures of measuring interact with the basic concepts.

Definition

Measurement involves assigning numbers of units to physical quantities (such as length, height, weight, volume) or to nonphysical quantities (such as time, temperature, or money). Physical quantities such as the length of table may be measured by repeated application of the unit *directly* on the object. This process is called *iteration*.

Nonphysical quantities such as time use an *indirect* method. Clocks and calendars are two instruments used to measure time. Temperature measures use a thermometer. Money measures worth or value, and coins and bills are used.

Young children discover the properties of formal measuring systems by using informal or arbitrary units. These units may be body units: thumbprints, hands, feet, or the length of their arms. Or they may measure in paper clips, blocks, Unifix cubes, beans, or paw prints of common animals. Older children begin to use customary (English) units or the metric system. With either system the method is the same. However, it takes many years before a secure foundation, or a way of thinking, regarding measurement, is in place.

Principles of Measurement

1. A number line is paired with units of measure. Each unit is the same, and by repeated measure a total or final count is made.
2. A measure usually starts at the endpoint (0) and continues until the end of the quantity. If a person measures somewhere in the middle of the series, subtraction of unused numbers helps find the correct response (see Figure 10-1).

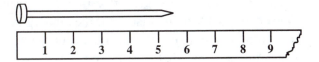

Figure 10–1

3. Formal measurement uses a variety of units, including two units with the same name (ounce for capacity, ounce for weight). The unit must match the quantity. For example, area needs a two-dimensional unit, such as the square yard.
4. Most measures are additive, such as the length of two pieces of rope. Some are not, such as the example of volume: 1 cup of sugar and 2 cups of water. This mixture is not 3 cups.
5. Measurement is approximate. There is usually a finer gradation of measure that is more accurate. For example, on a sports watch, time is reported in minutes, seconds, and hundredths of seconds.
6. Measurement is transitive. If the length of my paper (A •———• B) is 11 inches on the ruler (C •———• D), and the length of my book (E •———• F) is also eleven inches, then my book and my paper have the same length. That is, if AB = CD, and EF = CD, then AB = EF. Using a measuring tool, such as a ruler, we can compare objects without having to line them up next to one another. The height of a window frame can be compared to the length of the floor.

Children acquire knowledge and application of these foundational principles over many years in the Pre K–8 curriculum.

The General Method

Most professionals agree that the method for measuring for physical quantities is the following:

1. Choose the appropriate unit.
2. Use the unit to cover the object with no spaces or gaps.
3. Count the units.
4. Decide on what to do with leftover parts (round-up or back, ignore, use a different unit).

Before and after the process of measuring children guess and/or estimate the results. Guessing occurs when the child pulls an answer out of nowhere—a wild stab at the result with no forethought. Hopefully, the guess will demonstrate number sense. For example, a large mayonnaise jar cannot hold "a million cookies."

An *estimate* takes more logical thinking. Perhaps the task is broken down into reasonable subparts, and a method is applied. For example, a child estimates the number marbles in a jar by counting the marbles on the bottom layer, and counting the number of layers. Or children rely on past experiences. For example, a class of first graders estimates the number of seeds in a pumpkin. One child volunteers that last year the kindergarten class found over 100 seeds in their pumpkin. In estimating area, children may choose to pace off the room using "giant steps" that approximate one yard per step. To estimate seconds, children learn to count "one thousand and one, one thousand two. . . ." Children use benchmarks to guide their estimates, just as adults often use them. For example, adults may use miles-per-gallon to estimate how far to drive before looking for a gas station to refill the tank.

Estimating occurs after a measure when children see that a whole unit isn't used. The table is "almost 14 inches" long. Is the table closer to 13 inches? A decision needs to be made. Parts and wholes play a role in most measurement activities. In the early childhood curriculum measurement is not meant to be as exact or sophisticated as in high school vocational classes. For example, when covering a picture of a mitten the student uses whole tiles, and some parts of tiles. The total area might be 10 whole tiles and 18 parts of tiles. A good estimate might be 19 tiles.

The Young Child Plays and Learns

Children enjoy playing with sand in the sandbox and at the beach. They fill containers, dump them, mold mountains and houses. They pour water into "lakes" and into coffee cups for a tea party. Play helps children discover when the water is too cold to swim in, or what amount of wet sand is too heavy too carry.

Creative play includes pretending to be a doctor who takes the sick child's temperature and says: "You are too hot. You're sick. I'll give you medicine." Or children visit the grocery store in their imagination, "I want two pounds of hamburger." Over time children learn whether they like hot chocolate or cold milk, how much cereal they want in a bowl, how tall they are, and the length (size) of their feet. Many informal learning experiences occur using the comparing words "more-less-the same." Cooking activities blend formal units such as cups and teaspoons with informal units like "a pinch of salt." Measurement is a way to answer questions like, "Is it too warm outside for our jackets?" Or it offers a way to put together the right amount of ingredients. "If we put too much milk in our play dough, we can't make biscuits. It's too gooey to stick together." Children who attend day care centers for much of their early years benefit from these kinds of sand, water, and cooking experiences as well as dress-up and pretend opportunities. Puzzles, coloring, and cut and paste worksheets offer few measurement episodes.

Gradually preschoolers graduate to arbitrary units such as measuring by hands, feet, containers, scoops or the weight of bags of rice (generally in kindergarten and early first grade). The American curriculum seems to stress formal units beginning in first grade and rushes through too many concepts in second and third grade. Some school districts may demand proficiency in the following topics:

Grade 1   Inches, pounds, temperature, cups, pints, quarts, centimeters, kilograms, liters, pennies, nickels, quarters

Grade 2   All of the above plus dollars, perimeter, area, feet, yards, gallons, meters, kilograms

Grade 3   All of the above plus AM and PM, elapsed time, the calendar, ounces, ½ inches, the mile, measuring angles

These units are developed in one chapter of the math textbook at each grade level. The sheer number and diversity of quantities and systems confuse many students. The reflective teacher realizes that such a mix of topics detracts from the essential task of learning how to measure.

Two Measurement Systems

Children generally encounter the English system of units. These units arose over many centuries in Europe and were derived from natural measures. An inch was three barley corns, a foot was the length of a human foot, a yard was the distance from the tip of the nose to the end of an outstretched arm (Figure 10–2). Yards were handy for measuring cloth.

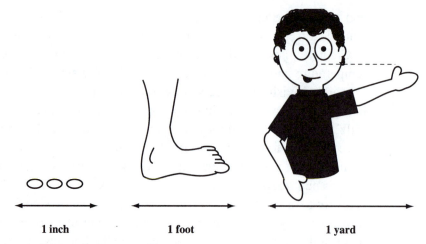

Figure 10–2 Early measurement.

An acre was the amount of land a horse could plow in one day. The system was standardized when the foot was defined by a metal bar of a certain size. This fundamental unit became the basis for all other measurements of length, area, and volume.

We measure temperature in degrees Fahrenheit, using the freezing point of water (32°F) and the boiling point of water (212°F) as points of reference. Ounces, pounds, and tons are common measures of weight in the English system.

One unit of measure within any English system does not easily convert into the next unit. Therefore, children face the task of memorizing a great many relationships. For example, there are 12 inches in 1 foot, 3 feet in 1 yard (or 36 inches) and 5,280 feet in 1 mile (or 1,760 yards). In contrast, the metric system uses units that are based on multiplication or division by 10.

The metric system uses the meter as the standard unit. This system was developed in Europe over a relatively short period of time in the late eighteenth century. All measures of capacity, mass (weight), and area can relate to the meter. The entire world, except for the United States, uses the metric system. In our country scientists rely on metrics. In everyday life some units such as grams and liters are fairly common. In the future, children will live in an all-metric world. Until that time, they must study both systems.

Children do not need to convert measures of one system into another. Instead, benchmarks that link the two systems help children see relationships. Some examples are:

$2\frac{1}{2}$ cm   = about one inch

a meter   = a little longer than a yard

a kilogram = slightly more than 2 pounds

a liter   = a little more than a quart

a kilometer = a little more than $\frac{1}{2}$ a mile

These concepts help children estimate in one system by using what they know about the other system.

Difficulties in the Measurement Process

Children like to count to solve problems, but counting involves *discrete* objects, like finding out how many pieces of candy are in the bag. Measurement is a *continuous* process. To find the weight of a piece of fudge, the child needs to read the number of units from a scale. *One* piece of fudge weighs many units, such as three ounces. In pouring water, so many cups fill the jug. To find out how tall a child is, an adult might use a yardstick and put a line on the kitchen wall. Children must make the transition from counting separate units to using units that vary by quantity.

In addition, Piaget demonstrated that children are easily fooled by appearances. Something must weight more if it's bigger in size. So, to a child, a *larger* ping-pong ball is heavier than a *small* rubber ball. Two balls of clay start out as equal in size. One ball is transformed into a snake. The child might say that the snake has "more clay because it's longer." Complete conservation of length and area may not occur until the child is 8 to $8\frac{1}{2}$ years old, while measurement of volume occurs in stages from around 7 to 11 years of age (Copeland, 1984). At around 8 years old children recognize that a ball of clay changed into a snake has the same amount of clay, but still feel that the snake would displace more water than the ball when put in a bowl of water. The latter concept is attained around the age of 11 years (Piaget, Inhelder, & Szeminka, 1960). Measurement relies on the concept that the object maintains the same volume or weight if it is moved or divided into parts.

Because children vary widely in their abilities to conserve length, area, and volume, a reflective teacher guides learning activities that seem developmentally appropriate. Once the concept of a unit and the process of measuring are mastered in one system, curious young minds easily transfer these relationships from one system of units to another. There is no need to rush learning beyond the child's capabilities.

Other difficulties occur around the concept of a unit, the relationship of unit size to the number of units needed, and how to apply the units. For example, very young children will think that a strip covered with "more" smaller units is longer than an identical strip covered with larger units (Carpenter & Lewis, 1976). The National Assessment of Educational Progress reported several common misconceptions about reading units. If an object was not placed at zero on the rule, most third graders and half of the seventh graders read the number at the end of the line, instead of counting units (Figure 10–3). The study also found that most third graders confuse area with perimeter (Kouba, Brown, Carpenter, et al., 1988).

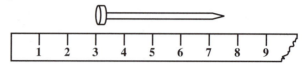

Figure 10–3   Measurement when an object is not placed at zero.

Another difficulty arises because although measurement is a widely used application of math, young children do not naturally use measurement tools in everyday life. They think in comparisons "I'm taller than you are." "You got a bigger piece of cake." "It's too cold to go outside to play." They do not pick up a ruler to measure their desks or weigh fruit on a pan balance scale at the market. Measurement activities must involve ideas children can enjoy and that have significance for their lives. For example, second graders might investigate these problems: "How heavy is my book bag when I put in all my books?" "What if I remove my science book?" "Now how much will my book bag weigh?" "What weight is too heavy to tote?"

One final measuring difficulty appears in elementary textbook illustrations. These drawings are a poor substitute for hands-on experiences. Publishers portray the inch and centimeter in scale, but must use parts of rulers. Other measures are left to the imagination of the readers. In addition, pages are crowded with examples and text. Often, more than one unit appears on the same page. Teachers must use these teaching aids with caution.

Guided Learning—Physical Quantities

Length and Height

The study of length typically begins by using informal units such as thumbs, paper clips, or a piece of chalk. Children measure everyday objects such as books, boxes, and pencils with these nonstandard units. They may draw and write stories about their findings (Whitin & Gary, 1994). They tackle larger objects such as a desk. An investigation ensues. Perhaps it would be better to measure the desk using hand prints. One aspect of the process becomes clear. Different-size units help speed up the activity.

The teacher shows the group a ruler. A lively discussion centers on questions such as: "What is a ruler?" "Do you have one at home?" "Who uses a ruler?" "What are the marks for?" "What are the numbers for?" Talking about the tools of measurement sets the foundation for making rulers.

In the English system, children study inches, feet, and yards early in their schooling. Projects include rulers made of ink print thumbprints or paper clips glued to a strip of heavy cardboard. Children make "tape measures" from heavy two-inch ribbon, marking the distance between hand prints. Ribbons provide an interesting way to cover larger distances. Eventually children progress from informal units to standard units such as the inch and the foot.

In metrics the primary grade curriculum emphases the centimeter and the meter. Centimeter cubes facilitate the drawing of a meter stick. Centimeter graph paper (Stenmark, Thompson, & Cossey, 1986) provides an easy way to color and count these small units. In general, millimeters are too small a unit to be of importance to young children. Likewise, the kilometer, a very large unit, may be associated with driving or walking fairly long distances (about .6 mile).

Many teachers conduct indoor or outdoor scavenger hunts for objects of a certain length (Souchik & Meconi, 1994). Having a variety of items such as bread boards, jewelry boxes, and children's books in many sizes makes the hunt an interesting challenge!

Area

The measuring process for area uses the two-dimensional unit square, rather than the one-dimensional line segment unit of length. Experiences begin by covering a surface, such as an outline of a mitten, with small beans or counters. Other seasonal shapes include a shamrock, a kite, or a beach ball. Handprints or footprints cover the area of a floor rug. Children estimate how many informal units they need. The teacher asks: "Will there be any spaces uncovered?" "How can we count these parts?" After covering the objects, the children count the units and compare their results to the estimates. They decide on how many whole units solve the problem and how many parts of wholes complete the coverage.

Children advance by using one-square-inch pieces of paper. They cover an object such as a book, paying careful attention to avoid overlap or gaps. Square centimeters are so small that teachers often have the child trace around the object on centimeter grid paper. Children lightly color the units and count them.

Different shapes may have the same area. Bathroom tiles provide an excellent opportunity to build designs using the same number of tiles. The teacher explains, "Each design has eight tiles. The rule is that the tiles must touch each other on one whole side." Children record the designs on one-inch graph paper, color them lightly, and count the units. The children outline the perimeter in another color or marker. This line defines the boundary between what is inside (the area) and the rest of the space.

The concepts of area and perimeter pose a challenge to many second graders. One helpful tool is the geoboard. Children create boundaries with rubber bands. Felt or paper squares cover the area of the design. The boundary may be described as a "fence for a cow." One unit of fence is from post to post (nail to nail). The teacher creates the challenge, "Make a pasture for your cow with twelve units of fence." Children record their designs on geoboard dot paper (see Figure 10–4). They color and count the area in square units. Then they compare their results with other children's pictures.

Figure 10–4   A third grader using a geoboard to find area and perimeter.

Even older children enjoy using the familiar tune, "Old MacDonald Had A Farm" as a springboard for building enough pens and pastures for the farmer's large number of animals (cows, pigs, ducks, horses, donkeys, and chickens). One question might be, "How much room does each kind of animal need?" These answers may be in meters and kilometers. Third graders may be able to translate these needs into a simple scale, that is, one square centimeter = one square meter.

If there is a construction project going on at school, the students can observe the measuring and ordering of flooring such as carpet and linoleum. Perhaps a field trip to a local floor center or a guest speaker could show how adults make basic decisions about something as important as a floor. Finally, newspaper ads for carpet cleaning stress the size of the rooms covered under the sale price. The teacher might pose the question, "If our classroom floor needed to be cleaned, how much would it cost?" Inventive teachers look for ways the concept of area relates to students' everyday lives.

Volume and Capacity

The fundamental unit of volume is the cubic inch or the cubic centimeter. Cubic inches are combined to make cubic feet and cubic yards. Cubic centimeters build into the liter (1,000 cm^3). In addition, one cubic centimeter is one milliliter. A wooden block makes a good arbitrary unit of volume. First, children estimate how many blocks they need to fill a box. Then, they fill boxes with one-inch cubes or 1-centimeter cubes, count them, and record the results.

The same volume can take many shapes. Children build designs with a certain number of blocks, such as 12 blocks. The rule is that each block must touch another block on one side. A flexible teacher may wish to use sugar cubes. Children glue their block designs together and display their creativity. Because blocks come in standard sizes (1 inch and 1 centimeter) as well as non-standard sizes (2 centimeters), standard unit blocks are important tools to solving early problems in volume.

Many people use the term *capacity* for liquid volume. They remark, "My car's gas tank has a 14 gallon capacity." Informal or nonstandard units of capacity include using a baby food jar to fill various containers (Liedtke, 1993). Colored water gives children a picture of how full the jar is in a clear view. Standard customary units of capacity include cups, pints, and quarts. One experiment involves taking unopened containers that claim to hold a quart (e.g., of milk) and pouring them into standard measuring pitchers. The teacher posses the question: "Did the product really contain the amount that label said it did? Why or why not?"

Metric units of capacity emphasize the liter, which is the familiar size of some soda bottles (1 or 2 liters). Eventually older children study milliliters, which are like large drops of water. About five milliliters will fill one teaspoon. Milliliters are often used in medicine.

Weight and Mass

Technically, weight is the term used in the English system of measure. It refers to mass plus the effects of gravity. A person weighs less on the moon because the force of gravity on the moon is about one sixth of what it is on earth. In the metric system, *mass* is the term used for the amount of material in an object.

Young children use the term weight because they hear it often in everyday life. The doctor weighs the baby at each visit. The clerk at the checkout counter weighs the fruit to find out what to charge. Some things feel heavier than others just by holding them or lifting them. The teacher asks one child, "Which box of cereal seems heavier?" (One box is full, the other is almost empty.) But sometimes the physical sensation is too vague. Children need pan balances and spring balances to test their predictions. Teachers purchase pan balances or make them from simple materials, such as a coat hanger, string, and two Styrofoam soup bowls (see Figure 10–5).

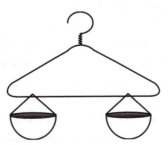

Figure 10–5   A simple balance scale.

Parents, friends, or relatives may have a simple spring balance used for weighing foods up to one pound. Houseware departments and diet centers sell many of these small scales to people who are trying to control the portion size of foods. Some authors suggest filling film containers with different materials, such as sand, salt, small stones, paper clips, and buttons (Porter, 1995; Liedtke, 1993). Because these black cases are of equal size, children must weigh the materials using a pan balance to determine the order of their weight. Children weigh each container on a spring balance to find the weight in ounces.

A bathroom scale is a handy tool for weighing pounds or kilograms. Watermelons, pumpkins, buckets of water, and book bags make interesting objects of investigation. Unfortunately, our society is very weight conscious, and some young children fear ridicule if they seem to weigh more than others. A teacher may wish to proceed with caution, depending on the makeup of the group.

Guided Learning—Nonphysical Quantities

Time

Time involves duration, or how long something takes (elapsed time), and sequence. One sequence is the concept of age. According to Piaget, a five-year-old may believe he is older than his younger brother because he is "bigger." But mother and grandmother are the same age. They are "both old." Grandmother isn't older than mother because aging stops when you grow up. Physical size is confused with time. Piaget felt that children understood both *succession* of events (people being born in different years or order in time) and *duration* (If I'm three years older than my brother, I will always be three years older.) around the age of eight (Copeland, 1984).

Researchers have found some aspects of measuring time that are accomplished in the primary years. Friedman and Laycock (1989) found that first graders can order common activities of the day, such as "having breakfast, arriving at school, eating lunch, and coming home from school." Second and third graders learn to order hours and relate clock time to everyday activities, such as knowing breakfast is at 7:00 AM and understand AM/PM.

First graders tell time accurately to the hour, both digitally and by using an analog clock. Second through fifth graders tell time to the five-minute interval, and the one-minute interval more accurately on an analog (customary) clock. They count by fives and then ones. Ten-year-olds to adolescents have the ability to represent week and month order (Friedman, 1986). The research of Piaget and more recent investigations suggest that reflective teachers realize that children's understanding of time takes many years to develop.

One goal of the preschool/kindergarten curriculum is to help children sequence events in the daily program. A picture chart of "Our Daily Schedule" focuses on ordering common reoccurring activities such as story time or out-door time (Schwartz, 1994). Some events such swimming or gym occur once or twice a week. A weekly schedule helps children anticipate tomorrow and the next day. From weekly calendars emphasizing key activities the teacher may wish to make a transition to the traditional calendar. Here special events such as birthdays and holidays create interest in numerals and months. Preschool and early kindergarten children need calendar experiences that fit their unique per-spective on time. These methods of recording sequence enable the teacher to plan child-centered time activities.

Most curriculums prescribe that children learn "to tell time" in first grade. One method that builds on children's natural ability to count by fives is the "Whole Clock Method" of telling time (Lipstreu & Johnson, 1988). First, chil-dren master the hours in the traditional fashion. Then, instead of studying the half-hours, the method relies on the natural movement of the hands "clockwise around the circle." The children learn to read the minute hand by fives with the help of a minute circle (Figure 10–6).

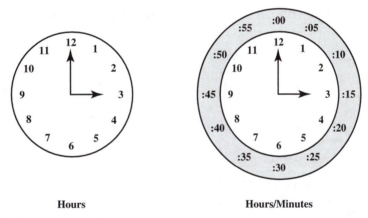

Hours   **Hours/Minutes**

Figure 10–6   A clock with a minute circle.

The minute hand is large enough to cover the hour and point at the five-minute interval. First graders learn to read the clock digitally by fives, for example, 9:55. They often see the marks between the numbers and spontaneously begin to count by fives and ones, for example, 7:34. The language concepts such as "half-past, quarter to, or counting back from an hour, such as 10 minutes to 3:00" are appropriate objectives after the essential task of reading the clock face has been mastered.

Likewise, adults know that the hour hand "creeps" as time progresses. In the beginning children read hours and minutes in a straight forward fashion. When this skill seems secure, the teacher introduces a new difficulty into the process. A clock face situation shows an hour hand between two numbers. Some teach-ers use the phrase "it doesn't count until it gets there," to help with the decision.

Because children read digital clocks easily, they may transfer their analog clock reading into the digital form throughout the unit. One advantage of learning to read an analog clock is that elapsed time (+30 minutes, +50 minutes, +43 minutes) appears to be more easily calculated using the round face of an analog clock (Friedman & Laycock, 1989).

The concept of duration, or how long something takes, occupies an important place in the time curriculum. Sand timers and kitchen timers record duration and give a sense of time intervals. For example, children close their eyes and open them when they think a minute has elapsed. Many good minute curricular ideas are found in *Family Math* (Stenmark, Thompson, & Cossey, 1986).

Everyday classroom activities provide opportunities to estimate time. For example, children guess how long it will take to recopy a story, or color a picture, or put up a bulletin board. Field trips provide opportunities to estimate time. How long does it take for all of us to board the bus? How long is the drive to the zoo? How long is the train ride around the zoo? What time do we need to reboard in order to return to school at 3:00 p.m.?

Second through third graders may plan their homework using a checklist and estimates of time. They see how close they came to judging their ability to finish certain tasks (without rushing or skipping parts of the assignments). Being on time and paying attention to time are integral parts of our society. While other cultures may have a different view of time, eventually children must adapt to the highly scheduled world of adult business and cultural life. Time to do nothing and the ability to ignore time and live by the movement of the sun, moon, and the seasons seems a real luxury in this harried world.

Temperature

Children experience temperature as the seasons change. Clothing needs may range from a T-shirt and shorts to a parka, depending on the local climate. Activities often relate to the seasons, from sledding to swimming. In some parts of the country a person can be on a beach one day and in the upper elevations of a mountain range the next. Many teachers chart the weather (sunny, cloudy, windy, rain, snow) along with the daily calendar activities. Second and third graders keep daily temperature logs, which are easily turned into graphs.

The primary curriculum focuses on reading a thermometer in the standard units of Fahrenheit or Celsius degrees. The units in F are calibrated so that the freezing point of water is 32 degrees, and the boiling point of water is 212 degrees. Conventional ovens use Fahrenheit degrees. Large demonstration thermometers make reading the units easier. Celsius units are developed around 0 degrees as the freezing point of water, with 100 degrees as the boiling of water. These units appear in science lessons, but are not as apparent in everyday life.

Teachers purchase thermometers with a movable red band or make one with ribbon. The band shows the "alcohol" going up and down. Experimenting with hot water and ice cube water will illustrate the dramatic effect of temperature on the instrument. Children need benchmark temperatures for hot, freezing, beach and sweater, or lakeside weather. This is especially true for Celsius temperatures. A cool day may be 15 degrees, while a hot day may be 35 degrees.

Each day weather data appears on television, in newspapers, and on telephone hot lines and computer networks. Temperature plays a key role in agriculture. The relation of climate to culture as found in social studies units, current events, literature, migration patterns, and numerous other subjects brings temperature into our everyday lives.

Money

Money plays a recurring role in everyone's life. Children receive allowances and buy things. By kindergarten and first grade students learn to name the coins and give their value in cents. They enjoy matching real coins to pictures. Teachers use real money or plastic coins. When possible, real money provides a better hands-on experience. One school received a "loan" of 50 dollars in coins from the parent's organization. A class "checked the money out of the bank" (the school safe), counted it, and used it for unit activities. At the end of each day the money was returned to the safe.

In a simple version of "The Store," the teacher prices small items in amounts of pennies. The children take turns spending 10 pennies. They play with their purchase a certain amount of time and return it at the end of the day.

In a more complicated version the students form teams of four participants. The teacher locates small toys from items left behind by previous classes or perhaps purchases them at a resale shop. Two members of the student team are "buyers." They decide on which five items their shop will sell. The two sellers price the objects and take care of business transactions. Each team has a certain amount to spend, for example, 10 dollars. The two buyers roam the various shops looking for items that will add up to the amount they have to spend. One goal might be to spend as much of the 10 dollars as possible. If the sellers price the items in odd amounts, for example, $1.43, the buyers' job becomes a real challenge. The sellers use a money box to make change. At the conclusion, the team plays with the toys for a certain amount of time and returns them at the end of the day.

One song that lends itself to simple buying of objects is "Hush, Little Baby."

> *Hush, little baby, don't say a word,*
> *Papa's going to buy you a mockingbird.*
>
> *If that mockingbird won't sing,*
> *Papa's going to buy you a diamond ring.*
>
> *If that diamond ring turns brass,*
> *Papa's going to buy you a looking glass.*

> *If that looking glass gets broke,*
> *Papa's going to buy you a billy goat.*
>
> *If that billy goat won't pull,*
> *Papa's going to buy you a cart and bull.*
>
> *If that cart and bull turn over,*
> *Papa's going to buy you a dog named Rover.*
>
> *If that dog named Rover won't bark,*
> *Papa's going to buy you a horse and cart.*
>
> *If that horse and cart fall down,*
> *You'll still be the sweetest little baby in town.*

Pictures of the items from the song such as a ring, or a looking glass, are sequenced and purchased with money. Third-grade children might investigate how much each item would cost in today's market and find Papa's total bill.

Money is a nonproportional system. A dime is not 10 times the size of a penny. Therefore, children must memorize the values of coins. One teaching aid to help children count money and make change is a money mat (Stevenson, 1990). The mat uses a 20×5 chart to replace the usual hundreds chart (Figure 10–7). Rectangular coin pieces have a grid side and a coin side (Figures 10–8 and 10–9). The Stevenson approach seems to be the best system as far as combining the elements of counting by fives and seeing spatial relationships of the value of coins in relation to 100 cents. Her task analysis for adding coins includes the following:

1. Covering the mat with the rectangular pieces with the grid side up staring at the top
2. Using the grid side to make a certain amount without the mat
3. Repeating the procedures with the coin side up
4. Putting real money on the areas of the mat, for example, a quarter on 25, a dime on 35, three pennies on 36, 37, and 38
5. Using only real money to make an amount

When making changes she suggests:

1. Putting a counter on the amount spent
2. Covering the rest of the grid with the rectangular pieces, using the smallest pieces first
3. Counting the pieces *up to a dollar*
4. Removing the mat and practicing with coin pieces and then real coins.

1	2	3	4	5
6	7	8	9	10
11	12	13	14	15
16	17	18	19	20
21	22	23	24	25
26	27	28	29	30
31	32	33	34	35
36	37	38	39	40
41	42	43	44	45
46	47	48	49	50
51	52	53	54	55
56	57	58	59	60
61	62	63	64	65
66	67	68	69	70
71	72	73	74	75
76	77	78	79	80
81	82	83	84	85
86	87	88	89	90
91	92	93	94	95
96	97	98	99	100

Figure 10–7   A 20 × 5 grid to replace the usual hundreds chart. From *Teaching Money with Grids.* by Cathy L. Stevenson. Reprinted with permission from the Arithmetic Teacher, copyright April 1990 by the National Council of Teachers of Mathematics. All rights reserved.

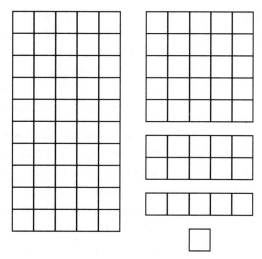

Figure 10–8   Grid side of the rectangular coin pieces.

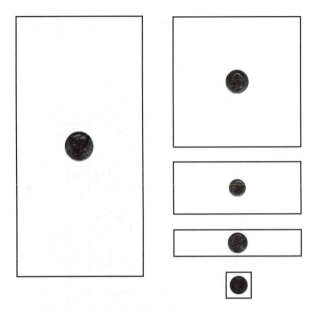

Figure 10–9   Coin side of the rectangular pieces.

In second and third grade, children also enjoy "ordering" from their favorite fast food or local restaurants. The teacher collects menus or creates simulated ones. The children write out their order and add up the bill. Grocery ads and toy catalogs provide opportunities to plan menus or get ready for a birthday or holiday. It is easy to spend amounts up to 100 dollars.

Finally, the units of pennies, dimes, and dollars may be a practical way to reinforce the concept of place value system. In the game "Dollar Digit" (Stenmark, Thompson, & Cossey, 1986), the player uses a two column mat (dimes and pennies) and rolls a die. The player takes *either* dimes or pennies and puts them in the appropriate column. Pennies are traded for dimes as needed. Each play has seven turns. The goal is to come as close to one dollar without going over. One variation might be to extend the playing board to include dollars. The play continues until one person reaches five dollars. While learning the name and value of coins is relatively easy, counting coins and making change takes many years of practice. A game format encourages active learning in an enjoyable environment.

Summary

Measurement includes many attributes, such as the number and units, the appropriate unit, and the exact or approximate answer. The tools of measurement include a variety of rulers, containers, scales, and thermometers. Children's levels of understanding of measuring concepts develop over many years, and vary widely from child to child. All of these complex factors make the teaching/learning process quite complicated. Time spent mastering one system of units in a thorough fashion will reap benefits in later study of other units. Patience, listening to children's explanations of the process, and lots of practice fosters success.

Ready-Set-Math

Ready-Set-Math

Make a Mountain

Ages 3–4 years

Items needed: Moist sand, or a large quantity of clay/play dough
String or heavy yarn

The material is divided into two piles. The child uses one pile to make as high a mountain as possible. The challenge is to create another mountain of equal height. The child measures one mountain with a piece of yarn. Then the yarn is cut and used to measure the second mountain until they are "both the same."

Variation: Play the record and sing the song, "She'll Be Comin' Round the Mountain." Talk about how people travel around mountains. How is this different from a flat road?

Ready-Set-Math

Measure My Jump

Ages 4–5 years

Items needed: long rectangular building blocks or cardboard
kindergarten blocks or a piece of smooth wood (no splinters)
Optional: Plastic whiffle balls used by golfers, wads of newspaper
yardsticks

Children work in pairs. One child takes a "giant step" and the other child places blocks end to end to measure the distance. The children reverse roles and try it again. They may experiment to see if they can take a longer step. This activity works well on a sunny day, using a grassy area (to avoid injury if someone tries too hard and falls). They report their findings to the group.

Variation: One child throws a whiffle ball and stands by it, as the other child (or team) measures the distance in yardsticks. The teacher may want to color code the white balls with a marker, so the teams can find their own on the field. The class makes a graph of the results.

Ready-Set-Math

Beat the Clock

Ages 6–8 years

Items needed: Bowls of small objects such as cereal, nuts/bolts, macaroni, buttons
Plastic spoons
Paper plates or trays
A kitchen timer

The teacher gives each child a bowl of small objects, a spoon, and a plate. The goal is to scoop as many objects onto the plate within one minute. The rules include no fingers—only use the spoon. Any dropped items that don't make it to the plate will be subtracted from the total on the plate. (Children competing against one another should have similar items, for example, everyone has cereal.) The action stops when the bell goes off. Each child counts the total on the plate, subtracts the dropped ones, and submits a score. The highest number wins the game.

Ready-Set-Math

Animal Puppet Patterns

Ages 7–9 years

Items needed: The storybook and song for "There Was An Old Lady (who swallowed a fly . . .)"
Tongue depressors
Glue
Heavy construction paper

Children draw the animals swallowed by the lady (fly, spider, bird, cat, dog, cow, horse), color, and cut them out. The creation is traced and measured in inches or centimeters, depending on the unit of study. These puppet patterns are exchanged with other classmates, who try to use the pattern to make one animal of their own. The animals are glued on or stapled on tongue depressors, and the class acts out the story while singing along to the record. The class may wish to order the sizes of each animal, from smallest to largest.

> ### Ready-Set-Math
>
> #### Food Labels and the Way We Eat
>
> Ages 8–9 years
>
> | | |
> |---|---|
> | Items needed: | A variety of products such as bottles of ketchup, BBQ sauce, salsa, salad dressing; jars of peanut butter, mayonnaise, mustard; a container of sour cream |
> | | Soup spoons |
> | | A tablespoon for measuring |
> | | Styrofoam paper plates |
>
> Many nutritional food labels use 2 tablespoons as the recommended serving. Students measure out various ingredients in two ways. On one plate they put the amount of the product they think they usually eat as a serving. On another plate they carefully measure out 1 or 2 tablespoons of the ingredient. The class discusses whether the standard serving size is appropriate (i.e., "Are 2 tablespoons of peanut butter enough for your average sandwich?") Students write up their results in a summary paper or as a journal entry.

Activities and Study Questions

1. Choose either the English (customary) or metric system and research its historical development. Write a paragraph or journal entry about your choice.
2. Invent a coin identification game using a familiar format, such as Bingo or Concentration. If possible, create the materials and try it out on a first grade student.
3. Visit the library and locate a children's picture book on time. Critique the book on how it sequences activities or how it shows duration of time. For what age group does this book appear to be best suited? Describe your findings in a paragraph or journal entry.
4. Read Souchik and Meconi's article on "Ideas: Classroom Activities in Measurement" and create an indoor or outdoor measurement hunt. Decide on the unit (centimeter, meter, foot, etc.) and write out your ideas. Be prepared to share them with the class.
5. Watch a kindergarten or first grade child measure an object using arbitrary units. Listen to the child explain how he or she approached the process. How did the child talk about getting close, but not needing a whole unit? Write a description of your observation. Be prepared to share your findings with the class.

Classroom Equipment

tall plants	moist sand
clocks (digital/analog)	yarn
real or play money	record player
large paper clips	classroom blocks
measuring cups/spoons	plastic whiffle balls
rulers (inches, yards)	bowls

Classroom Equipment (cont.)

meter sticks
kitchen timers
sand time, stopwatch
estimating jar
bathroom tiles
playdough/clay
indoor/outdoor thermometer
body temperature thermometer
ink pads
crayons/markers
wide ribbon
one-inch graph paper
centimeter graph paper
geoboards/bands
geoboard recording paper

plastic spoons
paper plates
tongue depressors
glue
heavy construction paper
grocery items with serving
    sizes of 1–2 ounces
balance scale
spring scale
film canisters
one liter bottle
baby food jars
two color lima beans

Further Reading

Andrade, G. S. (1992). Teaching students to tell time. *Arithmetic Teacher, 40,* 37–41. *Children use two colored beans to create desk-size or floor-size clocks. Each minute is represented by a bean. For example, four red beans are for the first four minutes. The fifth minute is a white bean. Students cut out hands and numeral cards and place them on the clock. This activity involves the geometry of making a round circle, and shows the minutes quite clearly. Students walk around the floor-size version as "the caller" gives a comment to make a certain clock time..*

Cook, M. (1989). Ideas: Figuring weight and temperature problems. *Arithmetic Teacher, 36,* p. 27. *First or second graders develop a chart on baby's weight. They follow the guideline that a baby doubles its weight by six months. A vertical bar chart illustrates the baby's weight, while a horizontal chart shows another infant. Children discuss the results. They may wish to collect statistics on themselves and chart the results.*

Markle, S. (1986). Hands on science: Keeping warm. *Instructor, 96,* 123–125. *The author gives the history of musk oxen and the current efforts to raise them for wool. Temperature experiments include finding out how a mitten pot holder and a regular mitten trap air. Children practice reading thermometers to conduct these experiments.*

Ramondetta, J. (1994). The hot cup caper: Probing for scientific knowledge. *Learning, 22,* 65. *Many computer software programs in science include temperature probes. The students test a variety of cups (ceramic, plastic, metal, glass) to see which cup will keep hot chocolate warm the longest. Temperatures are plotted at intervals up to 20 minutes. Students discuss and compare the data. They defend their answer on the best material suited for this use.*

Souchik, R., & Meconi, L. J. (1994). Ideas: Classroom activities for measurement. *Arithmetic Teacher, 41,* 253. *Children conduct an outdoor hunt for a twig, a leaf, a blade of grass, or something else that is about the size of a hand, finger, or thumb. They measure using centimeters as well as informal units. One suggestion has the students weigh a bag of leaves on a seesaw, along with a student whose weight is known. These activities add variety to primary units on length and weight.*

Whitin, D. J., & Gary, C. C. (1994). Promoting mathematical explorations through children's literature. *Arithmetic Teacher, 41,* 394–399. *The authors use* The Line-Up Book *(Russo, 1986) to tell the story of Sam. Sam measures the distance from his bedroom to the kitchen with wooden blocks, books, and bath toys. He doesn't have enough of any one item. A classroom discussion revolves around what else Sam could use. Then the children choose their own units, such as hands, pencils, and erasers, to measure their desks. They draw and write about their findings. Most students used several units in one measure, such as "12 hands and a sticker."*

References

Carpenter, T., & Lewis, R. (1976). The development of the concept of a standard unit of measure in young children. *Journal for Research in Mathematics Education, 7*, 53–58.

Copeland, R. W. (1984). *How children learn mathematics*, 4th ed. New York: Macmillan.

Friedman, W. J., & Laycock, F. (1989). Children's analog and digital clock knowledge. *Child Development, 60*, 357–371.

Friedman, W. J. (1986). The development of children's knowledge of temporal structure. *Child Development, 57*, 1386–1400.

Kouba, V., Brown, C., Carpenter, T., Lindquist, M., Silver, E. A., & Swafford, J. O. (1988). Results of the fourth NAEP assessment of mathematics: Measurement, geometry, data interpretation, attitudes, and other topics. *Arithmetic Teacher, 35*, 10–16.

Liedtke, W. W. (1993). Measurement. In J. W. Payne (Ed.), *Mathematics for the Young Child*. (pp. 229–250). Reston, VA: National Council of Teachers of Mathematics.

Lipstreu, B. L., & Johnson, M. K. (1988). Teaching time using the whole clock method. *Teaching Exceptional Children, 20*, 10–12.

Piaget, J., Inhelder, B., & Szeminka, A. (1960). *The Child's Conception of Geometry* (E. A. Lurnzer, Trans.). New York: Basic Books.

Porter, J. (1995). Balancing acts. *Teaching Children Mathematics, 1*, 430–431.

Schwartz, S. L. (1994). Calendar reading: A tradition that begs remodeling. *Teaching Children Mathematics, 1*, 104–109.

Souchik, R., & Meconi, L. J. (1994). Ideas: Measurement scavenger hunt. *Arithmetic Teacher, 41*, 253.

Stenmark, J. K., Thompson, V., & Cossey, R. (1986). *Family math*. Berkeley: University of California.

Stevenson, C. L. (1990). Teaching money with grids. *Arithmetic Teacher, 37*, 47–49.

Whitin, D. J., & Gary, C. C. (1994). Promoting mathematical explorations through children's literature. *Arithmetic Teacher, 41*, 394–399.

Related Records and Tapes

Beall, P. C., & Hagen, S. (1990). "She'll Be Comin' Around the Mountain," from *Wee sing sing-along*. Price Stern Sloan.

Beall, P. C., & Wipp, S. H. (1979). "Hush Little Baby" from *Wee sing children's songs and fingerplays*. Price Stern Sloan.

Beall, P. C., & Wipp, S. H. (1979). "Old MacDonald Had a Farm" from *Wee sing children's songs and fingerplays*. Price Stern Sloan.

"Hush Little Baby" from *Sing-a-long*, Peter Pan.

"She'll Be Comin' Round the Mountain" from *Bert & Ernie sing-a-long*, Sesame Street, 1975.

"There Was An Old Lady" from *Sing-a-long*, Peter Pan, 1987.

11 Problem Solving— Multiplication and Division

MR. GERSTER GIVES his second grade class the following problem:

> You invite two friends over to play after school. There are five graham crackers left in the box. Show me how to divide up the crackers so each of the three people gets the same.

The children work with paper crackers and a blank piece of paper. First they solve the problem, and then they will write a story about their solution. The teacher holds up three small dolls to illustrate the concept of three people. Most children draw three people at the top of their page. One child asks if they may use scissors. The teacher's permission to use scissors evokes a flurry of activity. All the children cut the crackers in some way. In this session no one gives away three crackers and works on the remaining crackers. One child methodically cuts each cracker into small equal strips. He isn't satisfied with his drawing of the people and crumples the sheet. Now he is left with the pile of strips. While other students are gluing down their solutions and moving on to writing a story, the teacher approaches this boy. The teacher gives him a fresh sheet of paper, holds up the three dolls, and repeats the problem. The boy puts the dolls on the sheet and proceeds to distribute "graham cracker" pieces one by one to the dolls. He is left with two long strips. The teacher asks, "How can you give these away so everyone gets the same?" He cuts one strip into three pieces and gives them away. Then he does the same with the last strip. He succeeds in thinking through the problem (Figure 11–1).

Children have many experiences in everyday life that involve sharing or grouping. The coach makes equal teams of players. After the game everyone goes out for pizza. The teacher collects a fee per child for a field trip. The class calculates the total amount, if everyone contributes to the event. In social studies, the textbook presents data about population and leading crops in terms of pictures. One picture of a person stands for a certain number of people. From kindergarten on, many children solve multiplication or division problems when allowed to use their own natural ways. Typically, formal use of the symbolic language of multiplication begins at the end of second or the beginning of third grade. The division algorithm is taught later and often presents a challenge to upper grade students. This phenomenon may be the result of inadequate preparation in the early years.

Figure 11-1   *One child's solution for the graham cracker problem.*

Definition

Multiplication is the operation used to find a product when two factors are known, that is, factor × factor = product. Division is used when a person knows the product (the whole) and one factor, that is, dividend ÷ divisor = quotient + remainder. In addition and subtraction problem solving we are working with situations involving one-to-one correspondence. In multiplication and division the relationship changes to a *one-to-many* correspondence.

Readiness for Multiplication and Division

One of the earliest challenges for very young children is the concept of a set or a group. In mathematical terms, 3 + 2 is the joining of three objects and two objects. In one kind of grouping problem, 3 × 2 means that a correspondence of 1 : 2 has been decided. For example, one box has 2 cookies. There are 3 boxes or 3 groups of 2.

Children benefit from many experiences in classifying objects, such as buttons or shells. They are able to talk about a group and assign a number to it. They say, "I have one group for red buttons, and it has 6 buttons." To further expand the idea, children collect pictures of objects that have multiple identical parts. For example, a child glues down three pictures of cars cut from magazines. Each car has 4 tires, and 3 cars have 12 wheels. Or there are 8 crayons in a small box, or 8 per box. The child tapes down 2 containers. The 2 boxes hold 16 crayons in all.

Another activity that builds on children's enthusiasm for counting is skip counting. Many kindergarten classes count by 10s as well as 1s. First graders enjoy counting by 2s and 5s. The 5s are useful when telling time, as well as for multiplication or division. Some children double the 2s to count by 4s. (Kouba & Franklin, 1993)

Readiness for multiplication problem solving is enhanced by differentiating rectangles from non-rectangles. Bathroom tiles make excellent manipulatives. Every rectangle has only four corners. Here are some examples:

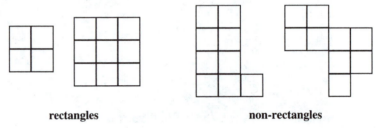

rectangles   **non-rectangles**

Figure 11–2

Children create as many rectangles as they can and record them on one-inch graph paper. Practice with rectangles lays the foundation for later work with arrays, rows and columns, or similar charts.

Children's Natural Strategies

Children appear to go through the same developmental sequence of strategies for problem solving in multiplication and division as they do in addition and subtraction.

1. **Direct model**—Children use counters to represent the problem. They count the objects to arrive at an answer.
2. **Counting strategies**—Children use skip counting, or skip counting in combination with counting by ones, to find a solution.
3. **Derived facts**—Children use the multiplication facts they already know as a starting point to find a fact they don't know.
4. **Standard math facts**—Children use the facts efficiently, but can also explain how the story problems might be interpretations of a given fact (Anghileri, 1989; Carpenter, Ansell, Franke, Fennema, & Weisbeck, 1993; Kouba, 1989).

Here is an example of children's thinking in each of these stages. The story problem is:

There are seven apples in each bag. How many apples are there in six bags?

1. Direct model—The child counts out 7 counters, then another set of 7 counters until all 6 sets are made. Then the child counts the total set "42 apples."
2. Counting strategies—The child thinks 7, 14, 21, 28, then counts out by ones using fingers to keep track of groups of seven . . . 29, 30, 31, 32, 33, 34, 35 . . . until the child reaches 42.
3. Derived facts—The child says, "I knew that 7×5 was 35, and I needed 7 more. So I put 7 on the 35 and got 42."
4. Standard math facts—"I knew that 7×6 was 42, so if there are 7 in a bag, and there are 6 bags, then the answer is 42."

There are slight variations in how children directly model the easiest kinds of problems. These differences will be explained in the next section. Carpenter and colleagues (1993) found that with only a few exceptions, kindergartners in their study successfully solved many kinds of multiplication and division story problems using the direct model strategy.

In a study of 90 children (ages 8–0 to 11–10) Anghileri (1989, p. 380) found that "multiplication facts were used infrequently, even among the older children who continue to use number patterns when the application of a single known fact would present a more economical solution." The story problems in the study involved products of whole numbers no greater than 5×4. Yet the vast majority of the students preferred modeling, counting, or other calculations (derived facts). Only 6 of the 90 children used multiplication facts to solve all 6 tasks. The children who attempted to use number facts were classified by their teachers as "above average." The researcher also found that:

> Calculation or modeling with materials was used by the "average" children on 79% of all items. Upon consideration of the "below average" children, direct modeling was most popular being used [by] 44% of all successfully completed tasks. (p. 383).

Only seven children used the same strategy to solve all the problems. Children use a variety of approaches, depending on how they view the problem. More examples of how children think about the various types of multiplication and division follow in the next section.

Cognitive Background for Teachers: Classes of Problems

Teachers benefit from studying the wide range of problem types that use the operations of multiplication or division. Most researchers divide these situations into two general categories (Kouba & Franklin, 1993). These categories are:

1. Asymmetrical—problems in which the numbers are *not* interchangeable. Each element of the story problem plays its own role and can be modeled very clearly by children.

a. Grouping situations—two boxes of six cans, *not* six boxes of two cans.

b. Rate situations—five pencils at three cents, *not* three pencils at five cents.

c. Comparison situations—mother rabbit (four lbs.)—weighs three times as much as the baby, not the baby rabbit weighs three times as much as the mother.

2. Symmetrical problems in which the numbers *are* interchangeable. For practical purposes, it doesn't matter which number is the multiplier. These problems often use charts, arrays, and area models as illustrations.

a. Area—while we frequently say that length is the longer side, and width the shorter side, the sides play similar roles. $l \times w = w \times l$.

b. Selection (also called combination or Cartesian product problems)—when calculating sandwich combinations: three kinds of bread (white, wheat, rye) and four fillings (cheese, peanut butter, bologna, tuna fish). We can match each kind of bread to 4 fillings or each kind of filling to 3 kinds of bread.

Another way to classify problem types is by what happens in the problem and the strategies children use to solve them. This analysis is an extension of the work on addition and subtraction described in Chapter 8. Hendrickson (1986) described four general categories:

1. Change problems
2. Comparison problems
3. Rate problems
4. Selection problems

In each general category specific subtypes are given, depending on which variable is unknown. Teachers of young children need to familiarize themselves with the various types, the level of difficulty of each type, and how children attempt to solve them. Some problems are clearly easier than others. Teachers assess the kinds of problems their children can solve and the sophistication of their solution strategies. These categories have slightly different names, depending on the researcher. Similar names appear in the text, after the most common name for a category.

Change Problems

Here is a story: Brendan has 4 boxes of cans. He has 6 cans in each box. Altogether he has 24 cans.

We can make three kinds of change story problems from this information.

1. Repeated addition—Brendan has 4 boxes of cans. He has 6 cans in each box. How many cans does Brendan have?

Children generally model the kind of problem by counting out 6 boxes of cans, one group at a time. Then they count all the objects, $6 + 6 + 6 + 6 = 24$.

Children who use counting strategies skip count by 6s, using their fingers, tally marks, or head nods to keep track of the number of boxes, 6 – 12 – 18 – 24.

2. Repeated subtraction—Brendan has 24 cans. He puts 6 cans in each box. How many boxes does he fill?

Children generally count out 24 cans and then count out groups of 6. If boxes or plates are available, they may put the objects in the boxes or on the plates. Then they count the number of boxes.

3. Partitive division—Brendan has 24 cans. He puts them into 4 boxes, with the same number in each box. How many cans are in each box?

In this kind of problem children can count the total number of cans. But then they cannot form groups by counting. Two methods have been described by researchers (Kouba & Franklin, 1993). In one method children count out 24 cans. They make a guess about the answer. They think, "Maybe there are 5 cans in a box." They put 5 cans in each group, but there are more cans left over. So they put an extra can in each group. Since all the cans are gone, the answer must be 6 cans in each box. The approach is called "systematic trial and error."

Another solution strategy involves "dealing-out" the 24 cans one-by-one into 4 groups. Boxes or plates help some children keep the groups separated. The child distributes all the cans and then counts the number in a box.

Some children, who use skip counting, say the numbers 6 – 12 – 18 – 24, and stop when they reach the total. They may also use a "derived fact" strategy by thinking, "I know 6 + 6 = 12, and 12 + 12 = 24, so the solution would be 4 groups of 6."

The three *change* problems present a challenge to primary age children, but are considered within their grasp. They enjoy trying to solve them using their own ways of thinking. However, the next three categories of multiplication and division problem solving pose more difficult situations. Except for rate problems using money, these problems need careful introduction to both the English language meaning of the problem and ways to conceptualize the information.

Comparison Problems

In addition and subtraction story problems, "compare problems" use words like "how many more than . . . or less than . . ." In multiplication and division the problems change to "how many times more than or how many times as many." For example:

Addition/subtraction compare problem	Cecil has 12 pencils. Mary has 3 pencils. How many more pencils does Cecil have than Mary?
Multiplication/division compare problem	Cecil has 4 times as many pencils than Mary. Mary has 3 pencils. How many pencils does Cecil have?

The vocabulary of "times as many" prevents many primary age children from modeling the problem.

Another difficulty arises when children sort out the information. Here is an example of a problem.

> There were 3 times as many boys as girls at the dance. If there were 12 boys at the dance, how many girls came to the dance?

Occasionally young students model this situation by drawing 12 boys and a picture of 1 girl. They have difficulty going beyond this way of interpreting the problem, and therefore cannot solve it. Hendrickson (1986) lists 8 different compare subtypes, depending on the relationships between the sets and the kind of questions asked. These problems seem better suited to the upper grades.

Rate Problems

Rate problems use ratios or two variables in relation to one another. Easy to understand rates include money (a piece of gum costs 5 cents per stick) and everyday happenings, such as a cat who eats 2 cups of cat food per day. Many rate problems can be modeled by using counters or skip counting. Ratios of miles/hours, feet per second, cents per kilowatt hour, or dollars per pound pose new challenges if the child doesn't understand how the two variables are related. Adults use predetermined rates everyday, such as pay per hour. Children may not conceptualize exactly what is occurring in the story. It would be especially difficult for primary age children to be given the figures and be asked to calculate the rate. For example, Helen bought 8.5 lbs. of chicken for $12.95. How much did she pay per pound? Children who are unable to think about rates and ratios often revert to substituting numbers into memorized formulas. Practice weighing food, such as chicken, including weighing one pound of chicken, helps children see that a *whole* chicken is made up of many pounds. The chicken's price depends on multiplying the number of pounds by a fixed ratio. The process can be reversed when a person knows the total weight and the total amount.

Selection Problems

Selection problems are also called combination problems or Cartesian product problems. In these situations objects are matched to find all the possible ways they may be grouped. For example: "I have four blouses and three pairs of pants. How many different outfits can I make?" Choosing from combinations occurs often in everyday life, such as ordering a sub sandwich or a pizza.

Since ordered pairs of data require some way of checking, matrices or factor trees provide useful visual diagrams. Selection problems are generally considered too difficult for very young children.

Children must recognize that a blue blouse with a yellow shirt is a different combination from a yellow blouse and a blue skirt. In addition, young children experience difficulty in keeping track of their outfits. They may make only a few choices and decide that they have made enough.

English (1992) found that four-and five-year olds could not distinguish between the blue blouse and yellow skirt pattern when it was reversed. In her study, children ages 4 to 12 years dressed plywood bears with self-adhesive tops and pants. Some four-year-olds used pants only, explaining that it was a hot day. Children aged seven years and over began to invent ways of keeping track of the combinations. Effective monitoring of their strategies contributed to successful problem solving. Teachers may wish to try the bear problems with primary age children who are ready for a challenge.

Remainders

Problem types such as repeated subtraction or partitive division lend themselves to a discussion of remainders. In some story problems remainders do not make sense. Here is a problem:

> The soccer team has 26 players. The coach recruited some drivers of minivans to transport the team to the next game. Six people can ride in each van. How many drivers are needed?

The answer must be five drivers, since two children are not going to ride in one third of a van.

At times a fractional part makes sense. In the introductory classroom scene of this chapter, it was perfectly logical for children to split the whole graham crackers into pieces in order to give 5 crackers away to 3 people.

In more complicated story problems, the remainder is the answer to the problem:

> The coach has 8 soccer balls. There are 26 children on the team. The coach gives each group of 3 players a ball for the first drill. How many children will not be able to practice this drill?

Of course, many times young children ignore the remainder. In the graham cracker problem, some children give the extra crackers to "dad or the dog."

Illustrations

Children often draw pictures showing groupings as needed in a problem. If the problem is about goldfish in fish bowls, they produce bowls and fish. Representations for multiplication and division include number lines, arrays, charts, pairings, matrices, and tree diagrams (Figures 11–3, 11–4, 11–5, and 11–6). These illustrations occur spontaneously in the work of some children.

Other children need a chance to experience how these pictorial representations may help them organize their thinking.

The kangaroo made four hops of two meters each. How far did it hop?

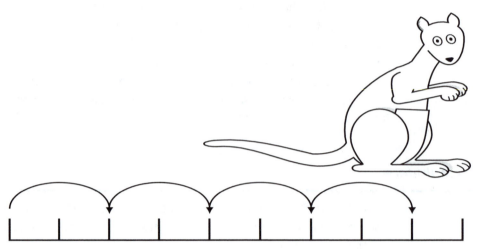

Figure 11–3   Number line.

The classroom has five rows of six desks. How many desks does the room have?

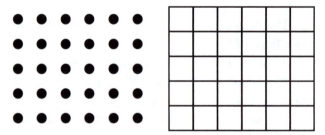

Figure 11–4   Classroom desks in arrays.

Here is another problem:

John has a yellow T-shirt and a red T-shirt. He also has blue pants, black pants, and gray pants. How many different outfits can he make?

Shirts	*Pants*
yellow T-shirt	blue pants
yellow T-shirt	black pants
yellow T-shirt	gray pants
red T-shirt	blue pants
red T-shirt	black pants
red T-shirt	gray pant

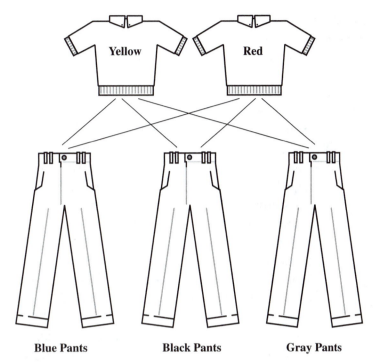

Figure 11–5   Pairings.

	1. Yellow Shirt	**2. Red Shirt**
A. Blue Pants	A, 1	A, 2
B. Black Pants	B, 1	B, 2
C. Gray Pants	C, 1	C, 2

Figure 11–6   Matrix.

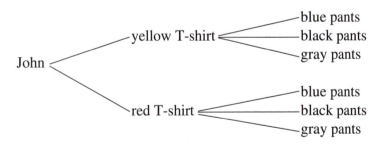

Tree Diagrams

All of these visual diagrams give children ways to think about multiplication and division.

Linking Problem Solving to Symbolic Representation

Children can solve many kinds of problems before they are ready to write abstract number sentences. Gradually children learn to link pictorial representations to the number sentence.

Marilyn Burns (1991) suggests a game called "Circle and Stars" as a way to make the connection. Each child plays with a booklet of seven blank pages. When it is the child's turn, he shakes the die once. The number on the die means draw that many circles (4 = 4 circles). Then he shakes again. The number equals the number of stars to draw in each circle (3 = 3 stars). The student writes *4* groups of *3*, $4 \times 3 = 12$. Students see the operation of commutativity when the picture of 3×4 differs from the one for 4×3 but the number of stars is the same.

The author also has the class fill boxes of candy, write stories about their findings, and explore patterns of multiples on the 0 to 99 chart. In these ways, children have many opportunities to successfully represent multiplication and division.

Early work in double-digit multiplication can be modeled using base-ten blocks and mats. The process is similar to repeated addition, using larger numbers. The method works well for one digit by two digit numbers, as described in Chapter 9.

Rules of Operation

In addition to classes of problems, teachers need information on the properties of multiplication and division. The properties of multiplication are the commutative property, the associative property, the distributive property, and the identity element. Zero has a special role in multiplication and division.

Math property	Identity Element—One is the identity element for multiplication and division $1 \times a = a$; $a \times 1 = a$; $a \div 1 = a$
Children's use of the identity element	"If I multiple or divide by 1, I still have the same number. $6 \times 1 = 6$, or $6 \div 1 = 6$."
Math property	The Commutative Property—When I have two factors, it doesn't matter which way they are arranged. The product remains the same. $4 \times 8 = 32$; $8 \times 4 = 32$.
Children's use of the commutative property	"If I know $8 \times 5 = 40$, then I know $5 \times 8 = 40$. This helps me learn my facts. I can prove they are the same by drawing an array."
Math property	The Associative Property—In multiplication of three or more factors, I can work with pairs of factors in any order. For all whole numbers a, b, and c: $a \times (b \times c) = (a \times b) \times c$.

Children's use of the associative property	"If the volume of a box is 2 cm. × 4 cm. × 10 cm., I can multiply 2 cm. × 4 cm. = 8 sq. cm. and then multiply 8 sq. cm. × 10 cm. = 80 cm. Or I can multiply 4 cm. × 10 cm. = 40 sq. cm. Then multiply 40 sq. cm. × 2 cm. = 80 cm."
Math property	The Distributive Property—In multiplication or division, I can think of one factor as composed of two addends. I can multiply the other factor by these numbers. For all whole numbers a, b, and c: $a \times (b + c) = (a \times b) + (a \times c)$.
Children's use of the distributive property	"If I am multiplying 6×43, I can think of it as $6 \times 40 = 240$, and $6 \times 3 = 18$. I can add the 18 onto the 240 and get 258."

The Role of Zero

Zero plays a unique role in multiplication and division; $a \times 0 = 0$ and $0 \times a = 0$ for all whole numbers. In multiplication you might have a problem, "There are 3 plates of 0 beans. How many beans in all?" The number sentence is "$3 \times 0 = 0$." There are no beans.

Here is another problem using zero:

Children who visit Dr. Jones, the dentist, receive 2 toys each after a check-up. On Monday, 4 children went to the dentist. How many toys did Dr. Jones give away? The number sentence is $4 \times 2 = 8$. Eight toys were given away.

On Tuesday no children visited the dentist. How many toys were given away? The number sentence is $0 \times 2 = 0$. No toys were given away.

Zero plays a different role in division. It is impossible to divide by 0; $0 \div a = 0$ where $a = 0$. Any number could be a, so there is more than one possible replacement for a. This violates the rules of operation where the result must be one and only one number.

Helping Children Write Their Own Problems

When children are ready to write their own story problems, there are several common themes that teachers often integrate into lessons.

Grouping Situations	
wheels/bikes	eggs/baskets or nests
cars/vans	snacks/children
silverware sets/people	fish/bowls
flowers/vases	crayons/boxes
beans/cups	pencils/pencil cases
balloons/clowns	buses/children

Grid Situations	
sheet cake/people windows/panes	bathroom floor/area

Selection Situations	
ice cream/cones frostings/cake tops/pants/skirts	toppings/pizza fillings/sandwich breads

Children may wish to directly model a problem with physical materials or draw a picture or chart before writing the problem. Sharing a problem with a partner, a group, or the whole class extends a child's ability to explain and defend a solution. The whole process takes time, but everyone reaps the rewards of critical thinking.

Summary

Multiplication and division are operations that provide interest and challenge from kindergarten through the upper grades. A reflective teacher recognizes the kinds of problems available and how children typically approach their solutions. Real world applications with these situations abound. These opportunities provide options for creative challenge and extend children's thinking. Not all classes of problems are suitable for young children, but many situations are accessible and enjoyable. Knowledge of multiplication and division gives the teacher an extensive collection of novel ways to encourage problem solving.

Ready-Set-Math

Ready-Set-Math

Bunches of Grapes

Ages 3–4 years

Items Needed: Large bunches of grapes
Scissors
Small paper plates
Paper towels

For snack time, a few children are assigned the job of preparing the grapes. After washing and drying the food, a child cuts off a small bunch of 4 or 5 grapes and puts it on the plate. If there are enough grapes after filling all the plates one time, a second bunch may be added to each serving.

Ready-Set-Math

My Book of Many

Ages 5–7 years

Items Needed: A book with blank pages for each child
Magazines/garden catalogs
Scissors
Glue
Markers or crayons

Children create a page illustrating groups of each number. For example, on the 2's page, children cut out faces that show two eyes. Other pages might be 3's—bundles of three flowers each; fours—car wheels, fives—gloves, sixes—soda packs and so on. Items for some pages may take time to find. Children glue their pictures on a page and label it by number, e.g. "Things that come in 2's."

Note: The book, *How Many How Many How Many* (Walton, 1993) gives children examples of things that come in sets of various numbers (see Related Books).

Ready-Set-Math

Beach Scene

Ages 7–9 years

Items Needed: Large blank sheet of drawing paper per child
Pencils
Crayons or markers

Children plan a picture that includes sets of people doing a variety of outdoor activities. The class may wish to brainstorm ideas: six people at each picnic table; two people per beach blanket; four people per row boat; three people per tent; or clotheslines with wet bathing suits. Each child draws, colors, and writes a story about the scene.

◆ **Ready-Set-Math**

The Multiplication Game

Ages 7–9 years

Items needed: Construction paper
                    Cardboard for game board
                    Two dice per team
                    Scissors
                    Glue
                    Crayons or markers

Teams of two to four students design a game using multiplication to move from start to finish. They chose a theme, obstacles to success, and chances to double or triple their moves. They share their game with other members of the class. Other teams evaluate the clarity of the rules, the theme, and the overall design.

Activities and Study Questions

1. Choose a theme from children's literature and write examples of each kind of problem type. Write three kinds of change problems, as well as a compare, rate, and a selection problem. Be prepared to share your examples with the class.

2. Use a set of multiplication and division story problems to assess an older child's ability. Record the kinds of problem types solved and which of the four strategies the child used. Write a short description of your findings.

3. Read the article by Englert and Sinicrope (1994) listed in Further Reading, and create an illustration of two-digit multiplication using square-centimeter grid paper. Write a description of the method you used to solve a problem.

4. Practice problem solving using "lattice multiplication" as described in Further Reading (May, 1994). Be prepared to demonstrate the method to a partner or a small group.

5. Reproduce the game board, "Froggy Frolic," found in Further Reading (Whitman, 1992), and practice playing the game with another person. Write a paragraph or journal entry to explain how the game teaches multiplication of positive and negative numbers.

Classroom Equipment

base-ten blocks/mats
square-centimeter grid paper
black paper for drawing
paper graham crackers
scissors
glue
plates
boxes
counters
stapler
dice
markers
crayons
grapes
paper towels
magazines
newspapers
seed/garden catalogs
cardboard

Further Reading

Englert, G. K., & Sinicrope, R. (1994). Making connections with two-digit multiplication. *Arithmetic Teacher, 41,* 446–448. *The author uses base–ten blocks and square-centimeter graph paper to help students conceptualize multi-digit multiplication. Partial products are color-coded and labeled. Students who understand the algorithm need less time for review and reteaching.*

English, L. (1992). Problem solving with combinations. *Arithmetic Teacher, 39,* 72–77. *The author uses wooden bears and self-adhesive clothing to explore selection problems with 4- to 12-year-olds. Children at each developmental level chose to approach the problem in a variety of ways. Everyone, even 12-year-old students, enjoys the activity. Patterns for the bears and outfits are provided.*

Hopkins, M. H. (1992). Ideas: Computational court: You be the judge. *Arithmetic Teacher, 39,* 27–33. *Students solve real-world cases involving all the operations and determine correct from incorrect solutions. They discuss their findings and defend their answers. This novel format may be a springboard for children's own problems.*

May, L. (1994). Teaching math: Extending the meaning of multiplication and division. *Teaching Pre K–8, 25,* 14–15. *The author discusses calculator applications and lattice multiplication as a way of extending knowledge about the process. Writing assignments encourage students to explain their thinking.*

Quintero, A. H. (1986). Children's conceptual understanding of situations involving multiplication. *Arithmetic Teacher, 33,* 34–37. *The author describes a variety of pictorial representations and games to help children relate a problem situation to the proper math process. The domino game helps children distinguish between addition and multiplication. Her ideas have many practical applications for the classroom.*

Whitman, N. C. (1992). Multiplying integers. *The Mathematics Teacher, 85,* 34–38, 47–51. *The author describes a game, "Froggy Frolic," which is designed to help students look for patterns and to discover how to multiply positive and negative numbers. The game improves students' confidence and motivation to study math. The game board and pieces are reproducible.*

References

Anghileri, J. (1989). An investigation of young children's understanding of multiplication. *Educational Studies in Mathematics, 20*, 367–385.

Burns, M. (1991). *Math by all means: Grade 3*. New Rochelle, New York: Cuisenaire Co..

Carpenter, T. P., Ansell, E., Franke, M. C., Fennema, E., & Weisbeck, L. (1993). Models of problem solving: A study of kindergarten children's problem-solving processes. *Journal for Research in Mathematics Education, 24*, 5, 427–440.

English, L. (1992). Problem solving with combinations. *Arithmetic Teacher, 39*, 72–77.

Hendrickson, A. D. (1986). Verbal multiplication and division problems: Some difficulties and some solutions. *Arithmetic Teacher, 34*, 26–33.

Kouba, V. L. (1989). Children's solution strategies for equivalent set multiplication and division word problems. *Journal for Research in Mathematics Education, 20*, 2, 147–158.

Kouba, V. L., & Franklin, K. (1993). Multiplication and division: Sense making and meaning. In R. J. Jensen (ed.), *Research Ideas for the Classroom: Early Childhood Mathematics* (pp. 103–126). New York: Macmillan.

Related Books

Anno, M., & Anno, M. (1983). *Anno's mysterious multiplying jar*. New York: Philomel Books.

Barry, D. (1994). *The rajah's rice: A mathematical folktale from India*. New York: W. H. Freeman.

Walton, R. (1993). *How many how many how many*. Cambridge: Candlewick.

12 Assessment

Most second grade teachers want to find out whether their pupils can tell time to the hour and the minute. In the past, the students may have taken a written multiple choice exam. For example (Figure 12–1):

Directions: Circle the answer that matches the time.

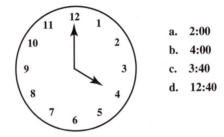

a. 2:00

b. 4:00

c. 3:40

d. 12:40

Figure 12–1   *An example of a multiple choice exam.*

The test repeats the same procedure for time to the minute, such as identifying 6:40.

Today, a teacher may conduct a formal or informal interview. In a *formal interview* each child spends time alone with the teacher. The teacher uses a clock model and asks the child, "Show me 4:00. Show me 6:40." On an assessment form, the teacher records the child's actions. Then the teacher asks, "How did you figure it out?" The child verbalizes a strategy. The teacher rates the total response in three categories: not understanding; developing understanding; and understanding/applying (adapted from Ann Arbor Public Schools, 1993). The child's progress is viewed as a continuum from no knowledge . . . to some idea of how clocks work, but with errors . . . to accurate answers with a reasonable explanation of the process.

If the teacher wants to conduct an *informal interview*, the teacher might pose many of the same questions during a small group lesson on the clock. The teacher jots down information on many students on cards or in a notebook.

Which method takes more time? Naturally a formal interview is time consuming. What has the teacher learned? Why is the movement to more authentic assessment an important part of today's reform efforts?

As school districts move from using one means of evaluation—paper and pencil tests, to multiple ways to collect valuable information, many important issues surface. Professionals assess what they value. The public, including school boards and parents, want results. The National Curriculum and Evaluation Standards for School Mathematics (1989) set guidelines for the kind of mathematics curriculum everyone should experience. Math educators have faced the challenge of convincing the general public that implementing the goals of the standards means a better mathematics curriculum. In many parts of the country this battle has been won.

However, progress in aligning testing, grading, and program evaluation has not kept pace with curricular changes. Traditional standardized tests often do not match the curriculum. While it is easy to determine mastery of facts and common computation, important concepts such as mastery of problem solving or the development of mathematical power are too complex for a typical multiple choice exam (NCTM, 1995, pp. 2–3).

> In NCTM's Standards documents (1989), the phrase *mathematical power* has been used to capture the shift in expectations for all students. The shift is toward understanding concepts and skills; drawing on mathematical concepts and skills when confronted with both routine and non-routine problems; communicating effectively about the strategies, reasoning, and results of mathematical investigation; and becoming confident in using mathematics to make sense of real-life situations.

It is hardly possible to capture this powerful sense of mathematics on one or two exams.

Furthermore, traditional assessment methods have acted as screening devices to keep people out of higher math. The future of our world depends on reaching all students, while setting high standards that students are expected to reach. In 1995, the National Council of Teachers of Mathematics published the Assessment Standards. These standards built upon the foundation of the original work, *Curriculum and Evaluation Standards for School Mathematics*, published in 1989. This new guide clarifies the direction of mathematics assessment in the years to come.

Assessment and Evaluation Defined

The NCTM Assessment Standards (1995) define assessment and evaluation:

> In this document, assessment is defined as the process of gathering evidence about a student's knowledge of, ability to use, and disposition toward, mathematics and of making inferences from that evidence for a variety of purposes . . . Furthermore, by evaluation we mean the process of determining the worth, or assigning a value to, something on the basis of careful examination and judgment. The term evaluation as used in this document refers to one use of assessment information. The focus on gathering evidence and making inferences emphasizes that assessment is a process of describing what mathematics students know and can do. (p. 3)

The Assessment Standards (1995) describe the purposes of assessment in four broad categories:

1. monitoring student progress—to promote growth;
2. making instructional decisions—to improve instruction;
3. evaluating students' achievement—to recognize accomplishment;
4. evaluating programs—to modify the program[*] (p. 25)

Let's say that a school district wishes to assess the learning outcome, "to measure linear distance in centimeters and inches." Here are some examples that illustrate the four purposes.

Monitoring student progress—The teacher observes that Chad uses the side of the ruler that measures with inches, when the problem calls for centimeters. Chad needs help in choosing the right unit. The teacher gives Chad some centimeter cubes and some one-inch bathroom tiles. Chad makes a design with each set and records the results. He orally describes the different units to his teacher.

Making instructional decisions—The teacher notices that many children in the class do not begin measuring with the end of the ruler. The class needs more experience with lining up units and counting them. Perhaps pairs of students should create a ruler using arbitrary units of their own choosing. The partners will explain to the whole class how their creation works.

Evaluating students' achievement—At the end of the instructional unit, the teacher asks each student to measure three objects (the length of a chalk eraser, the width of a book, the height of a chair) in inches and centimeters. First, the student estimates the outcome, then measures each item and records the results. The teacher observes how each pupil performs this task.

Evaluating programs—District personnel review the state competency exam results that are given to all third graders. They find that a significant percentage of their pupils did not score well on linear measurement. Now the math committee must collect information on why this occurred. Was the test item ambiguous? Did the students receive sufficient instruction? What changes, if any, need to be made in the primary curriculum? Some kinds of assessment provide feedback about pupil progress as a group. Professionals must make informed decisions about their results.

To promote the best assessment practices, the NCTM standards (1995) include six benchmarks of excellence. Briefly, they are the following:

1. The mathematics standard—assessment should reflect the mathematics that all students need to know and be able to do.
2. The learning standard—assessment should enhance mathematics learning.
3. The equity standard—assessment should promote equity.
4. The openness standard—assessment should be an open process.
5. The inferences standard—assessment should promote valid inferences about mathematics learning.
6. The coherence standard—assessment should be a coherent process. (pp. 11–22)

[*]Reprinted with permission from the *Assessment Standards for School Mathematics* (1995) by the National Council of Teachers of Mathematics.

A teacher might think of the standards in terms of these questions (NCTM, 1995):

- How does the mathematics of the lesson fit within a framework of overall goals for learning important mathematics?
- How do these activities contribute to students' learning of mathematics and my understanding of what they are learning?
- What opportunity does each student have to engage in these activities and demonstrate what he or she knows and can do?
- How are students familiarized with the purposes and goals of the activities, the criteria for determining quality in the achievement of those goals, and the consequences of their performances?
- How are multiple sources of evidence used for making valid inferences that lead to helpful decisions?
- How do the assessment and instructional content and process match broader curricular and educational goals?* (p. 46)

Within a comprehensive system of assessment students learn to assess their own progress and to set goals. They receive feedback that is timely, encouraging, and specifically relevant to their own insights and errors. Both oral and written feedback can enhance learning, if it is readily usable by the student. Ongoing assessment answers the question, "How am I doing?" This information is especially important for students who do not seem to be able to sustain attention, follow directions, or succeed in arriving at a satisfactory solution.

The *Assessment Standards for School Mathematics* (1995) assume that the curriculum is organized around important mathematical ideas that match the developmental levels of the class. They assume that students will be able to demonstrate their knowledge in multiple ways, that do not discriminate or penalize a person who has apparent disadvantages, such as a child who does not speak English as a first language, or a child who has a disability. They assume that the results of assessment will be used in open and valid ways to make reasonable decisions for pupils, for improvement of instruction, and for formulation of future district, state, and national policy.

What are the various means of collecting data? How can they be made equitable for all students? These questions are addressed in the following sections.

Curriculum Reform and Alignment

In the movement to make schools more accountable to the general public, several states and local school districts have adopted ambitious K–12 math outcomes. Key outcomes are identified by grade level, with the expectation that teachers will ensure student achievement over many topics. These lists of com-

---

*Reprinted with permission from the *Assessment Standards for School Mathematics* (1995) by the National Council of Teachers of Mathematics.

petencies may become extremely lengthy, with as many as 30 or more outcomes to be assessed at each grade. For example, a second grade teacher who has 30 students may be asked to rate these students on 30 tasks. This teacher must keep track of 900 outcomes. If a reasonable system of record keeping and appropriate assessment processes are not available, the teacher may resort to checking off lists without valid data.

Beginning users of alternative assessment need to focus on a limited number of behaviors or students to be observed. It may be more valuable to choose one key outcome and list it at the top of a notebook page. In addition, the page would hold a list of the students' names. The teacher keeps the notebook handy and comments on examples of the outcome that occur throughout the day. Alternative assessment methods will only become commonplace if they meet the needs of busy teachers.

Besides knowing the content and methods for a particular grade, teachers must know the common errors children make on key math concepts. Experienced teachers often discover these misconceptions by observing children perform year after year. These valuable data need to be shared, so teachers can make valid inferences. Generally, if children make errors, it is because they are thinking, curious beings. There is a reason why they approach a problem a certain way. Children who have a chance to hear other children's thinking, or see other work samples, will change their minds when the evidence convinces them that they have made a mistake. Errors are a valuable source of information for all teachers.

Assessment Strategies

Five common assessment strategies are:

1. Observation
2. Interview
3. Performance tasks
4. Student writing, including self-assessment
5. Portfolio

Each method has unique advantages, and some methods incorporate more than one kind of assessment. Some strategies are more appropriate for very young children because they are not capable of writing, or sophisticated selection and reflection about their work.

Very Young Children *(ages 3–5 years)*	*Older Children* *(Ages 6–9 years)*
Observation/listening	Observation/listening
Interview	Interview
Performance tasks	Performance tasks
Simplified self-assessment	Journal writing
	Sophisticated self and group assessment
	Portfolio

Generally, very young children should not be asked to write unless fine motor assessment requires it, such as writing your name, drawing a person, or copying shapes.

Observation

Observation is a natural part of the teaching/learning process. The teacher is alert to when children display signs of catching-on or discovering a solution, or a behavior that signals that the class seems confused. The teacher may have to change the lesson midstream or redirect the focus of the activity. Success varies from group to group and from year to year. Kindergarten teachers are very familiar with an activity, like a counting game, that works well with the morning class, but baffles the afternoon group. Observation is familiar to parents and teachers.

A parent notices many things at home:

- When the adult puts a toy in front of a six-month-old, the child grabs it. It's normal for the child to explore the toy by using the eyes, hands, and mouth.
- When the child is two, she may count with the adult while making juice, "One, two, three."
- The three-year-old child enjoys hearing the same story over and over and can repeat and anticipate what's happening next.

A teacher notices many things at school:

- Three-year-old Jesse stacks the blocks to make the highest tower possible.
- Four-year-old LaQuiesha carefully sets the table for snack time, remembering every item and location.
- Five-year-olds, Angelica and Tia, arrange peanuts carefully around the perimeter of the table. They work cooperatively, while other partners argue about where to keep the bowl of peanuts and who should cover a particular side.

Because so many things happen in a day, the teacher must devise a workable way to keep notes. Later, these observations are summarized into a more formal report. When a child seems to struggle with what appears to be a simple activity, such as sorting everyday objects, it is even more important to investigate what the child can do. All children have strengths as well as weaknesses. We need to build on these strengths so school is a positive experience.

Kamii (1990) encourages teachers to play card games with children and to observe their numerical reasoning. In the game "War," children turn up cards and the person with the highest number gets the pile. In "Double War," each child turns up two cards and adds them. The child with the highest total keeps all four cards. In the game of "Ten," the teacher creates a deck using the playing cards 1 though 9. A 3 + 3 matrix of cards is dealt. The person takes all the combinations that make 10. New cards replace the ones removed. A teacher can tell which children recognize the pairs instantly, and which children use a counting method. Stenmark and colleagues' book, *Family Math* (1986), contains other challenging games for young children.

Interview

Observation involves watching and listening. Interview involves asking good questions to assess whether the child really understands the concept. A performance task combines an interview technique with a script, materials, and a quiet setting to more formally assess a child's thinking. Good teachers use informal interviews as a part of the daily class routine.

Not all children respond well to a typical interview situation. Very young children construct meaning through play, and their ability to express themselves often lags behind their thinking. In a similar way, children whose first language is not English, and children with disabilities in speaking and listening, may just stare blankly when confronted by a teacher's question. How does a teacher guide learning when complex mathematical ideas escape expression?

Schwartz and Brown (1995) suggest three teaching strategies that foster communication without overwhelming a child. These strategies are validating, reviewing, and challenge.

The validating strategy involves catching the child in a moment of insight and agreeing with the child. A teacher might possibly give a reason for supporting the child's thinking. This reason helps the child organize his thoughts using language.

The reviewing strategy involves discussing what happened and repeating the event. It gives the child another change to experience insight and practice what has been learned. Children enjoy repetition, and rehearsing ideas builds a sense of confidence.

The challenge strategy involves extending children's thinking by adding a new element to the activity. The teacher scaffolds on what has been learned with a "what if" situation. Perhaps the mathematical relationship is extended to new materials, new locations, or other mathematical topics.

Here is a preschool example. The classroom teacher has been preparing the snack table when she is briefly interrupted by a visitor. At the point of departure, several of the plates have three crackers, while some have only two crackers. Max reaches the table early and declares, "These plates have more."

The teacher hears the conversation, and wants to use the opportunity to talk about the language words: more, less, one more. She *validates* Max's observation; "Yes, Max, you're right. Some plates have more. I can see that too." She may *review* the situation: "Does anybody else's plate have more? How many more?" She may extend or *challenge* their thinking by pouring juice into two cups, "Which cup has more? How do we know? How can I make them the same?" As time allows, the children practice pouring until the cups are the same.

The use of these three strategies involves waiting and watching, rather than lecturing. Communication about mathematical ideas evolves naturally from the everyday life of the classroom.

These methods will work well with older children who are learning English or with children with disabilities. The key is to take the time to listen to the students. Students who have difficulty communicating may sit quietly day after day. Their needs can be easily overlooked by a busy teacher.

Good questioning techniques are especially key in the planning or "getting started" phase of an activity and at the conclusion. While some questions may elicit information during the child's work (or the group's work), it is important to listen and let children try to struggle with a problem. Too much prompting, overcorrecting, coaching or actually doing the children's work, should be avoided. It only convinces children that if they wait long enough, an oversolicitious adult will do it for them.

In the planning or "getting started" stage, a teacher might ask:

What do we need to get started?
How do you want to try this?
How long do you think it will take?
What do you want to do first? Next?

For children who seem confused:

Do you want me to repeat the problem?
Do you need to hear it again?
Tell me what you think you are supposed to do?

Impulsive and disorganized children need help with making a good beginning. They may benefit from temporarily working with a child who can explain the directions or repeat the problem. At times, they need to hear it again. Or they need to verbalize their first steps (think aloud).

After the children have finished their work, the teacher might ask:

How did you figure it out?
Can you tell us how you did it?
Why did you think about it that way?
Did anybody think of a different way?
Is there another way to do it?

These kinds of questions assess a child's understanding, not just a right or wrong answer. Interviewing techniques are key to the success of many problem-solving curriculums.

The first-grade child in Figure 12–2 has just finished writing a story and number sentence about three groupings of buttons. Each child received a bag of buttons and three plates.

After sorting the buttons, the teacher interviewed each child. "What groups do you have? Why did you choose these groups? Is there another way?" The buttons are put back in one pile, and the child tries again. Eventually the child

Figure 12–2   Story writing about groups of buttons.

settles on one way and writes a story. Children share their choices with the class, so other children can see the variety of options possible. The teacher asks, "How may different ways did we sort our buttons?" The teacher records the answers on the board. "How many different number sentences did we have?" The class responses are listed. "If we tried these tomorrow, do you think we could find more ways?"

Class discussions elicit the idea that there are probably many ways to classify buttons. One child suggests that the class keep a running list on the bulletin board. Students can work on adding to the list during free time.

Performance Tasks

Students are asked to do many things during or after math class. Performance tasks include assignments, homework, quizzes, exams, class presentations, and creating products. Good performance tasks help teachers assess progress on attainment of key outcomes. Student achievement is judged by awarding points based on a scoring system that establishes the criteria for success. Points are often awarded in three areas: general understanding; the use of an appropriate strategy, including computation if needed; and a correct solution. Many newer performance tasks stress open-ended problems, encourage group work, and offer more than one way to display results.

Some performance indicators assess progress by grade level and content area. One book of performance activities, *Alternative Assessment: Evaluating Student Performance in Elementary Mathematics*, complete with scripts and scoring systems, has been published by the Ann Arbor Public Schools (1993). These classroom tested measures are easy to administer, align themselves well with most math curriculums, and cover a broad range of topics. One interesting set of activities for kindergarten include the following content areas:

1. One-to-one correspondence
2. Conservation of number (6) objects
3. Number to 5 (part-part-whole)
4. Instant number recognition (2–5)
5. Identifying shapes (circle, triangle, rectangle, square)
6. Number order cards (0–10) (put numeral cards in sequence)
7. Sort and classify (four categories for crayons are given by the teacher)
8. Numeral recognition (1–20)
9. Graphing—making a Unifix cube color graph with four colors, and interpreting the results (pp. 15–18)

Activities for grades 1 to 3 include virtually all the strands of the primary math curriculum, including mathematical thinking, geometry and spatial sense, measurement, estimation and mental math, and statistics and probability.

The Ann Arbor Public Schools (1993) devised a scoring system using a "target approach." These professionals realized that teachers felt comfortable thinking about student progress in three stages:

1. Consistently hits the mark—understands the outcome
2. Starting to catch-on but doesn't seem to have a complete grasp of the outcome
3. Misses the target completely—has no idea about the outcome (p. 3)

These three categories translate into *Not Understanding*, *Developing*, and *Understanding/Applying*.

Beginning teachers and professionals interested in authentic assessment may use both this excellent resource and materials developed by other groups working in many school districts and states. Another worthwhile resource is the material, including scoring system, developed for the Minneapolis/St. Paul Public School System by Equals Minnesota Working Group on Assessment (1995). Much work in assessment has been accomplished in the past decade. There is no need to start from scratch when devising an appropriate assessment and evaluation system.

Student Writing, Including Self-Assessment

In today's math class, primary age students write about math in a variety of ways. They may, for example:

- Keep a math journal
- Write an investigative report

- Write math problems
- Solve problems and explain their solutions
- Examine their own feelings
- Write a self-assessment.

Student writing includes pictures, diagrams, and charts. It provides a way to record student thinking and assess attainment of a concept. It demonstrates clarity of written communication in a subject area. Students may share their writing with others, which expands the repertoire of ideas among the group. Writing samples are easily saved and may become a part of a larger assessment, a portfolio.

In the story below (Figure 12–3), a third-grade student has composed an early multiplication story about groups of fish in a number of oceans. She has lived in the United States for less than two years. How would you score her work? What comments would you write back? Writing to students shows you think that writing is an important means of communication.

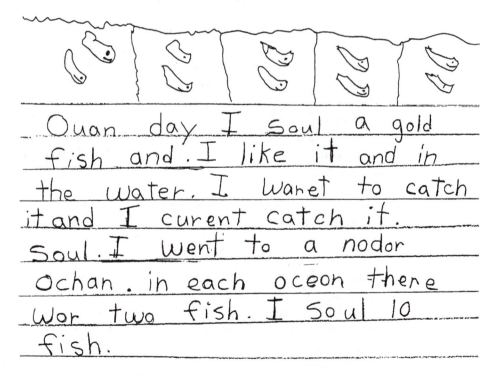

Figure 12–3 Story writing about groups of fish.

One day I saw a goldfish and I like it and in the water. I went to catch it and I couldn't catch it. So I went to another ocean. In each ocean there were two fish. I saw 10 fish.

Students often write journal entries in which they solve a problem and explain their solution. Or they might respond to these kinds of self-assessment questions:

1. How did you feel about today's problem?
2. Do you feel that you were able to figure out a way to start today's problem?
3. What do you like best and least about math class?
4. What did you learn this week that you didn't know before?
5. Explain to a friend what _____ (current class topic) means.
6. How well did you and your group (partner) work today? What went well? Is there anything about your group you want to improve?

Realistic self-assessment shows an ability to see one's own strengths and weaknesses. It may result in increased self-confidence, including the ability to ask for help when it is really needed.

Portfolio

A portfolio is a collection of a student's work along with the student's self-reflection on the process of math. A portfolio encourages students and teachers to take a comprehensive view of assessment. This strategy has several unique advantages:

- It shows student progress over time, usually a semester or a year.
- It contains a wide variety of work samples and performance indicators.
- It focuses on the student's strengths and accomplishments.
- It helps students take ownership over their own learning.
- It gives teachers a vehicle to communicate more effectively to parents about a student's progress.
- In some school districts, it may be a means to evaluate instructional programs.
- Its organization and presentation fosters critical thinking and other higher level mental processes.

These skills improve with practice across curricular areas and with practice at each grade level.

A portfolio is more than a folder of papers. It may contain:

- Individual or group work samples
- Audiotapes or videotapes
- A math autobiography
- Entries from a math journal
- Charts, photos
- Dictated reports
- Student self-assessments
- Peer reviews
- Computer printouts
- Report card information checklists
- Standardized test information
- Pre and post quizzes
- Their best tests
- Their worst tests

Most teachers develop a workable format that includes a cover, a table of contents, a small number of items (perhaps five or six), and a written narrative on why each piece was selected. The self-evaluations and reflective statements are a key component of a good portfolio. Students take an active role in *collecting*, *selecting*, and *reflecting*.

A beginning teacher needs to preview many portfolios before it is possible to compare samples and to get ideas for grading. Over time, certain patterns will emerge that set the criteria for excellence. Portfolios must reflect progress on major math outcomes. Some kinds of student work may best exemplify change over time. Experience with portfolios will give teachers important information to aid in evaluating them (Knight, 1992).

Scoring Methods

Observation, interview, performance tasks, and portfolios cannot be scored like standardized tests. Human judgment is involved and can be subject to bias. To be fair to the student, the criteria for success need to be shared both with them and with family members. An established set of criteria is called a *rubric* (Hart, 1994). Points are awarded for certain levels of performance. In holistic scoring, points are awarded for the whole product, based on a scale from 0 to 3 or perhaps 0 to 5. The criteria might range from no response, to a partial response with a strategy, to a complete response with a clear explanation. In analytic scoring, points are awarded for various traits or dimensions. For example, points might be given for overall organization, neatness, grammar, strategy solution, and self-assessment. Analytic scoring lends itself to providing descriptive feedback on complex assignments. Greater weight may be given to higher priority dimensions, depending on the abilities of the students and the time of year.

Scoring the new assessment types often takes longer than scoring traditional quizzes and tests. If the tasks are well-designed, they become learning opportunities as well as evaluations. Summaries of different kinds of rubrics can contribute to a teacher's decision on an overall grade. However, the major purpose of scoring systems is to provide valid and reliable measures of student progress.

Alternatives for Students with Special Needs

In some school districts, children come to school speaking 40 or more different languages. In all schools, some children have been diagnosed as having significant learning disabilities or having an Attention Deficit Disorder. The Equity Standard of the NCTM Assessment Standards (1995) stresses that teachers should use practices that promote fairness. This standard means that it is not possible to treat all children the same. Teachers must use multiple sources of information to tap into the unique ways that students may demonstrate their understanding.

Non-native speakers of English may wish to respond in their native language, while learning English. The Standards stress:

Equity can be addressed by English-enhancing preparatory activities such as:

- Using pictorial and manipulative materials
- Distinguishing between the language used in daily communication and the language of mathematics
- Controlling the range of vocabulary and the use of idiomatic expressions. (p. 52)

Special attention to the language of math means encouraging the use of the wide variety of math vocabulary found in Chapter 2. Young children need opportunities to experience and use these words in dramatic play, song, story, and physical activities. Many of the suggestions that are commonly written into the education plans for children with disabilities (the IEP) are helpful for non-native speakers of English too.

Children with disabilities have the legal right to alternative instruction and assessment under the Federal laws, IDEA and Section 504. Besides the legal mandate, teachers of young children want to do their best to reach these children. It's important to realize that language difficulties are often at the heart of a learning disability. Many of these children receive speech therapy, beginning at the age of three. It makes sense that listening and speaking problems interfere with classroom success. School professionals often remark, "Some of your best math students may be your LD kids." That is because having a disability in reading, writing or oral expression often is not accompanied by a disability in math. Most students with learning disabilities do not have a math disability (Bender, 1995).

But the trend toward explaining math in words or in writing puts a number of children in serious jeopardy. Some options that are commonly written into a child's Individual Education Plan (IEP) include:

Time

1. Give additional time.
2. Give shorter assignments.
3. Give breaks in routines and vary an activity often.
4. Omit copying from an activity.
5. Avoid timed tasks as a measure of proficiency.

Presentation of Oral Material

1. Get the child's attention first.
2. Break down directions into smaller steps.
3. Speak clearly and a bit more slowly.
4. Use visual aids such as picture or three-dimensional models along with words.
5. Use a tape recorder to replay the material for older primary children.
6. Have patience while the child gets started.

Alternatives to Writing

1. Listen and write down a child's response.
2. Have the child dictate an answer or explanation into a tape recorder.
3. Have the child draw out an explanation or make a three-dimensional model.
4. Have the child demonstrate knowledge by using manipulatives.
5. Use appropriately lined paper, with enough spacing.
6. Have extra paper and pencils available.
7. Do not penalize poor spelling or the use of a mix of cursive and manuscript letters.
8. Allow older primary children to use a computerized spelling aid.

Agitation Under Pressure

1. Remain calm. Divert the young child's attention to something enjoyable or a project where success is possible.
2. Take a break. Try again later.
3. Stress effort and persistence over accomplishment. Have the child repeat affirming phrases, such as, "I can do this if I try." Or, "I can slow down and figure it out."
4. Try a game format and see if it has a calming affect.

Each child has a unique way of interacting with the world. At times parents and special education professionals have insight that provides valuable information for the classroom teacher. Asking for ideas from these important resources is a good way to expand one's options.

Record Keeping

Teachers of young children constantly watch, listen, question, and challenge their students' thinking. Much valuable information will be lost unless the teacher organizes and uses some form of record keeping. An assessment management system is a high priority for beginning teachers. Several common approaches include:

- Notecards with each child's name
- A three-ring binder with tabs that hold each child's name
- A calendar system to ensure that everyone will have an opportunity for a more personalized assessment
- Checklists with student names in one column, and outcomes across the top

The notecard and binder systems rely on a teacher's ability to record anecdotal evidence as it unfolds. The essential math ideas are well-known to the teacher, who watches for evidence pertinent to assessment of the child's progress.

In the calendar system each child is assigned to one day per month. On that day the child receives special one-on-one time with the teacher. The teacher may use any of the methods described earlier to assess progress on an individual basis. This approach assures that a more in-depth interview on a performance task can be given throughout the school year, not just before report card time.

A checklist system might list key outcomes across the top, with the children's names down the side. For example, the matrix might include the following student performance or attitudes toward math: rote counting; one-to-one correspondence; pattern recognition and extension; and part-part-whole understanding with the number five. Any combination of notes and scoring may be used. Teachers often record success with +, –, or perhaps a "P" for progress in understanding. Ample room for comments, and room for dates, makes the system more valuable.

Some school districts provide a system of observation forms, checklists, and calendars. It is up to the teacher to make record keeping a manageable part of classroom life. Without good organization skills, teaching becomes an overwhelming profession. For an in-depth look at recording forms and methods, see the models developed by the Ann Arbor Public Schools (1995).

Summary

The National Council of Teachers of Mathematics (NCTM) has set an ambitious agenda to reform the teaching and learning of school mathematics. One key component is the Assessment Standards for School Mathematics (1995). The document ensures that all aspects of the school program, including individual and program evaluation, are conducted in an authentic, fair, and open way. One major shift is towards multiple sources of evidence and methods that mirror real-life understanding of concepts and skills. As with any reform movement, changes take time and run the risk of being derailed before they have a chance to prove themselves. Teachers of young children have always relied on many of the methods currently espoused by professionals. The newer methods, such as performance tasks, problem-solving interviews, and portfolios, add to the repertoire of assessment tools used by experienced teachers with young children. They help teachers make better decisions about teaching and learning.

Activities and Study Questions

1. Choose a concept or process, and think of one interview question that might help you assess student progress. Try out your question on two or three students. Be prepared to share your findings with the class.
2. Decide whether you prefer a particular record-keeping method, such as notecard, binder, calendar or checklist. Write a paragraph or journal entry about your decision.
3. Choose one of the six assessment standards and describe its intent and impact on the early childhood classroom. Prepare a five-minute presentation and be ready to share your ideas with the class.

4. Choose one important math outcome for your children and write a scoring rubric for its assessment. Decide on whether you will use holistic or analytic scoring. If possible, try both methods and be prepared to discuss the advantages and disadvantages of each approach.

5. Interview three or more parents and find out what assessment methods are currently being used in their children's classrooms. Ask about their opinion on the use of typical grades (A-B-C) in the primary classroom. Summarize your findings in a one- to two-page paper.

Further Reading

Greenwood, J. J. (1993). On the nature of teaching and assessing "mathematical power" and "mathematical thinking." *Arithmetic Teacher, 41,* 144–152. *The author describes the concept of "mathematical power" and explains a variety of ways to establish learning criteria to assess this key math idea. While the classroom examples show work from the upper grades, the approach makes sense for any classroom situation. The author assumes that upper level math students have progressed from an overreliance on counting to the use of more efficient algorithms.*

Herman, J. L. (1992). What research tells us about good assessment. *Educational Leadership, 49,* 74–78. *The author reviews recent efforts at the state level to develop authentic assessment while being able to report accurate and reliable results to the public. Some large-scale assessment procedures have been developed and validated. More research needs to be done to show that the newer methods support quality education. Student performance on the newer assessments is generally dismally low. Perhaps classroom instructional strategies and exposure to the new complex concepts and skills need to be strengthened before students are expected to demonstrate mastery.*

Lambdin, D. V., & Walker, V. L. (1994). Planning for classroom portfolio assessment. *Arithmetic Teacher, 41,* 318–324. *The authors describe the pitfalls of their first attempts at portfolio assessment and how they refined their system to make it workable. They give valuable tips for getting started with portfolios, evaluating them, and using them to facilitate communication. These ideas may boost the confidence of a new user. The portfolio can be a wonderful addition to the math classroom.*

Owen, L. B. (1995). Listening to reflections: A classroom study. *Teaching Children Mathematics, 1,* 366–369. *The author shares a glimpse of questioning and listening in a second grade classroom. The teacher did not accept pat answers, such as "Because it was easy." She carefully elicited more reflection and understanding. The article reviews important research on how teachers should approach classroom interaction to promote Standard 2: Mathematics as Communication (NCTM, 1989).*

Stix, A. (1994) Pic-jour math: Pictorial journal writing in mathematics. *Arithmetic Teacher, 41,* 264–269. *The "pic-jour math" approach uses pictures, words, and numbers to help students express their ideas about math concepts. The examples in the article include the use of manipulatives to discover properties such as the relationship of the diameter to the circumference. An elaborate scoring system includes a way to rate pictures, words, and numbers as well as the central math ideas. A math journal has many valuable uses in today's classroom.*

References

Ann Arbor Public Schools (1993). *Alternative assessment: Evaluating student performance in elementary mathematics.* Palo Alto, CA: Dale Seymour Publications.

Bender, W. (1995). *Learning disabilities: Characteristics, identification, and teaching strategies* (2nd ed.). Needham Heights, MA: Allyn & Bacon.

Equals Minnesota Working Group on Assessment (1995). *Assessment tied to instruction: Make it happen and improve problem solving.* Paper presented at NCTM annual meeting, April 7, 1995.

Hart, D. (1994). *Authentic assessment: A handbook for educators.* Menlo Park, CA: Addison-Wesley.

Kamii, C. (Ed.) (1990). *Achievement testing in the early grades: The games grown-ups play.* Washington, DC: National Association for the Education of Young Children.

Knight, P. (1992). How I use portfolios in mathematics. *Educational Leadership, 49,* 71–72.

National Council of Teachers of Mathematics (1995). *Assessment standards for school mathematics.* Reston, VA: Author.

National Council of Teachers of Mathematics (1989). *Curriculum and evaluation standards for school mathematics.* Reston, VA: Author.

Schwartz, S. L., & Brown, A. B. (1995). Communicating with young children in mathematics: A unique challenge. *Teaching Children Mathematics, 1,* 350–353.

Stenmark, J. K., Thompson, V., & Cossey, R. (1986). *Family Math.* Berkeley: University of California.

13 Planning For Success: A Good Beginning

A COLLEGE CLASS of preservice teachers from the local university takes a field trip to visit the kindergarten classroom of a master teacher. The classroom is home to many creative learning centers. In one corner there is a large cage with a pet rabbit. Bird nests hang from the ceiling, within reach of young hands. Everywhere natural artifacts are artfully arranged. The prospective teachers wonder, "Will my classroom ever look as inviting as this room?"

In another school district, primary level teachers attend a workshop on mathematical problem solving. They are amazed when they watch videotapes showing how children think about word problems. They wonder, "Do my students have this potential locked inside?"

Both beginning and experienced teachers experience a sense of being overwhelmed when they face the challenge of change. The master teachers in the classroom and on videotape have spent many years perfecting their art. How does a person who wants to emulate these models begin? In this chapter we will explore some of the most common questions that teachers ask about implementing an appropriate mathematics curriculum.

How Do I Get Started?

There are three key ingredients to a successful beginning: a well-prepared environment, a developmentally appropriate math curriculum, and you.

The Well-Prepared Environment

Few teachers inherit a well-stocked, well-organized classroom with easy access to the outdoors. An effective environment has good traffic patterns, ventilation, room for movement, and lots of activity centers. For a detailed description of these centers and a model floor plan see Spodek and Saracho (1994).

A primary classroom has these elements plus an arrangement of children's desks (perhaps in fours), and tables and chairs for small group work. The math center consists of low shelves, or perhaps a cart, with well-labeled tubs, buckets, and boxes. Materials not in use may be stored out of reach. For example, some teachers ask the janitor to build a shelf above the coat rack.

Schwartz (1995) described many ways to prepare the classroom and to begin the new school year while incorporating mathematics into daily routines. Children like to label their own private space, whether it is a separate cubby or a storage box. In addition to the child's photo, each child may wish to create a personal design from precut geometric shapes. This design could carry over to other name tags, such as on the name strips used to chart daily attendance. The many attributes of these plane figures give students an opportunity to explore relationships such as angle matching, congruence, and symmetry.

One concern for new teachers is how to collect, organize, store, and distribute math materials. Teachers recycle many everyday objects from bottle caps to old jewelry. They ask families to contribute. They keep a wish list of major items, such as a baby scale, posted outside their classroom. Some teachers search second-hand stores and rummage sales. If parents can afford it, the teacher may request a donation of a new book, rather than a birthday treat, to celebrate a child's special day.

Commercially prepared materials are purchased as the budget allows. At times the parent organization will raise funds for manipulatives. Some materials, such as Unifix cubes, base-ten blocks, pattern blocks, and kindergarten blocks, are essential but expensive resources. These materials are virtually indestructible. The only disadvantage is that some items will disappear through neglect or when children inadvertently carry them home. Replacing equipment and manipulatives should be part of an ongoing budget.

Materials need to be safe, accessible, and in sturdy non-tip containers. Small objects such as buttons, shells, keys, or bread tags fit well in checkbook boxes. To secure the lid, it is possible to use elastic cord. (Directions: Poke a hole in the cover of the box. Thread the ends of the elastic through the hole and tie them to a paper clip. Cover the clip with duct tape.)

Many commercial products come packaged in buckets, or a teacher may use ice cream containers. Also, inexpensive plastic dish tubs work well and last indefinitely. Teachers label, color-code, and place a picture of the material, or a glue a sample of the object, on the front of each container.

Materials needed for large groups may be packaged in individual zipper plastic bags. When the time comes to use them, these bags are easy to distribute.

Rules guide children in their use of manipulatives. Here are some suggestions that may be modified as needed for each developmental age:

1. Pick up the container carefully. Walk slowly.
2. When you are done, put it back in the same place.
3. Leave other people's work alone.
4. Do not throw anything away.
5. If you want to keep an item, ask me.

Some teachers have suggested that when a child wants a particular item, such as a button or a piece of jewelry, it might be better to have the child tell you privately. Perhaps you have lots of shells and can give the child a shell instead. This approach acknowledges the child's need to collect objects of interest, while helping you maintain your collections. Fear of theft or loss of manipulatives is more myth than reality. Generally, children respond to rules in a safe, nurturing environment.

When children use manipulatives, their first reaction is to play with them. This is normal. They may wish to stack them, make designs or engage in other kinds of creative activities. The reflective teacher allows a certain amount of time for free choice, or non-structured use of the materials. As long as the basic rules are followed, children may do whatever they wish. At a certain point, the teacher lays the ground rules for using a certain material. For example, many part-part-whole activities require that designs use only two colors (Baratta-Lorton, 1976). This approach helps in writing number sentences that reflect the design. In this way, the materials become a hands-on way to illustrate a mathematical concept.

Some teachers report that children revert to play after an extended vacation from school. Free choice must be reinstated for a short time so learning can proceed. Eventually the materials cease to be toys and assume their rightful place in the curriculum.

A well-stocked classroom also needs computers, computer software, calculators, an overhead projector and screen, and a video monitor. Access to technology expands the kinds of math activities the teacher can use everyday.

In summary, a well-prepared environment means that the classroom has enough space, and is well organized and well stocked. Of the three key ingredients for a successful beginning, a well-prepared environment is probably the easiest to accomplish. Change involving the curriculum, or change involving a person's philosophy toward teaching, takes a much more sustained effort.

Developmentally Appropriate Math Curriculum

Curriculum involves choices and expresses what we value. The actual content strands come from many places, as illustrated by the NCTM Standards Guides (1989, 1991, and 1995). This textbook explains and gives examples of these strands and illustrates sample thematic units (see Chapter 14). Local school districts develop and publish curriculum guides by grade level. At times teachers rely on textbook publishers to provide a curriculum for their elementary math curriculum. An elementary math textbook can provide visual learning aids, sources for ideas, and one approach to curricular topics. However, it is the teacher who creates a climate and uses these resources wisely to promote real mathematical learning.

A teacher's education is never over. Teachers expand their sphere of knowledge by becoming lifelong learners. Teachers are professionals who attend seminars, conventions, workshops, and take classes to improve and update their understanding of children and mathematics.

Early childhood teachers learn how to plan for the year and for shorter periods of time. Thematic units may evolve from a curricular web approach (Piazza, Scott, and Carver, 1994). In curricular webbing, the teacher chooses a general theme, such as bears, the circus, or insects. The class and the teacher generate all the categories of interest surrounding the topic. From this discussion the teacher assesses the general level of interest and the prior background knowledge of the children. Thematic units contain a variety of activities, including strands in math. These units evolve into daily activities, perhaps limited only by the classroom schedule.

Primary teachers develop lesson plans based on the needs of the children and the local curriculum. A lesson plan differs from an activity in that it has a more formal educational outcome and a beginning, middle, and end. Time is both a friend and an enemy for most primary teachers. It is essential to allow enough time for students to absorb a math concept and make it their own. And there is a need to have time to practice in order to remember. Yet in each day there doesn't seem to be enough time to accomplish everything that was planned. Today's children spend many hours in school and child care settings, away from home. In the future there may be more continuity between formal and informal school math activities in these settings. For example, block building, checkers, and chess provide excellent informal math experiences when incorporated into after-school child care programs.

Teachers lead very busy lives. Planning, collecting materials, and organizing and labeling containers during the summer months or school breaks helps take some pressure away from the school year. Children enjoy a balance of active learning and quiet reflective self-paced work, such as puzzles, games, or pattern block activities. Preparing learning centers and independent work ahead of time makes teaching more enjoyable.

Your Philosophy and Attitudes

The teacher of mathematics plays a new role in orchestrating learning. One common expression is that the role has changed from "the sage on the stage to the guide on the side." Consider the following guidelines from Standard 5, *Professional Standards for Teaching Mathematics* (NCTM, 1991, p. 57): On the overall learning environment:

- Providing and structuring the time necessary to explore sound mathematics and grapple with significant ideas and problems
- Using the physical space and materials in ways that facilitate students' learning of mathematics
- Providing a context that encourages the development of mathematical skill and proficiency
- Respecting and valuing students' ideas, ways of thinking, and mathematical dispositions; and by consistently expecting and encouraging students to—
  - work independently or collaboratively to make sense of mathematics
  - take intellectual risks by raising questions and formulating conjectures
  - display a sense of mathematical competence by validating and supporting ideas with mathematical argument.

In much the same way, Standard 2 guides the way serious mathematical thinking occurs when there is genuine respect and thoughtful interest in each person's ideas. "The teacher of mathematics should create a learning environment that fosters the development of each student's mathematical power by—

- posing questions and tasks that elicit, engage, and challenge each student's thinking;
- listening carefully to students' ideas;
- asking students to clarify and justify their ideas orally and in writing;
- deciding what to pursue in depth from among the ideas that students bring up during a discussion;
- deciding when and how to attach mathematical notation and language to students' ideas;
- deciding when to provide information, when to clarify an issue, when to model, when to lead, and when to let a student struggle with a difficulty;
- monitoring students' participation in discussions and deciding when and how to encourage each student to participate"* (p. 35)

These standards help teachers to create classroom environment they may not have experienced as a child.

A *key assumption* is that the child plays an *active* role in learning. The child mediates the teacher's words, actions, and other stimuli such as social interaction and filters them through his or her own thinking and feelings. The child reconstructs knowledge, builds on knowledge, and elaborates on knowledge. The child comes to the classroom with a general willingness to learn. In that sense a child's learning is *unintentional*. The teacher has a purpose or *intent* to bring forth mathematical learning in a particular strand. To do this the teacher challenges the child to think about a problem and perhaps gain new insight or greater understanding. A delicate balance exists between a reasonable challenge and an overwhelming one (Steffe and Tzur, 1994). The teacher will find out quickly if the challenge is too easy, too difficult, or too boring by assessing the child's willingness to sustain interest.

Certain questions deserve thought:

- How much do I really believe in listening rather than talking?
- Do I know enough about mathematics to intentionally intervene to challenge my students? If not, how can I learn more and gain confidence in my abilities?
- What will I do if I feel pressure to revert back to an earlier tradition—from parents, next year's teacher, or the public?

Changing one's attitudes and sustaining that change is hard. Recent follow-up studies show that teachers who had intensive support in the form of a four-year plan involving workshops, mentors, and consultants, were able to achieve high levels of personal belief and classroom practice compatible with a cogni-

*Reprinted with permission from the *Professional Standards for Teaching Mathematics* (1991) by the National Council of Teachers of Mathematics.

tively guided math curriculum (Fennema, E., Carpenter, T. P., Franke, M. L., Levi, L., Jacobs, V. R., & Empson, S. B., in press). On the other hand, a study of 20 teachers who received a short summer workshop on cognitive problem solving, with no follow-up, showed a wide range in patterns of belief and classroom practice. After three or four years, half the group continued to use the new approach steadily, while the other half used it "only supplementary or occasionally" (Knapp and Peterson, 1995). Teachers need support and positive feedback from supervisors and the public as changes are made. A teacher may need to seek out a network of other professionals who want to travel the same path to reform.

How Can I Involve Parents in My Program?

Parents have a natural protective attitude about their child. They have seen many "educational reforms" come and go. They may recall disastrous effects and fallout from them. Perhaps they never understood the "new math" from several decades ago. They may harbor math anxiety from past experiences. Many people express a cautious mistrust about change.

Parents know that arithmetic is important. They use numbers and computation frequently. They need help to see that a problem solving curriculum uses numbers on a daily basis. It's not a question of choosing between one or the other. For parents who would like to see more worksheets, drills, and flashcards, a teacher may show them how to reinforce number sense using card games, dice, and activities from sources such as *Family Math* (Stenmark, Thompson, and Cossey, 1986).

Another suggestion might be to show parents how the new mathematics curriculum is more rigorous than the old one. Let parents review units and projects from middle school and high school. If students in the district score well on standardized tests, or bring home prizes in math meets, be sure to include this valuable supportive data. Most people fear what they don't know. Here are some additional ideas:

- Explain your program's philosophy and methods at open houses, in letters and notes, and at parent-teacher conferences.
- Make videos or slide presentations about life in your classroom.
- Start a lending library of children's books with math-related themes.
- Collect pamphlets and books written to help parents understand the curriculum.
- Be positive about the good things that the children are learning.

If there is some aspect of the math curriculum that troubles you, ask your supervisor or math specialist. It doesn't help to express negative feelings or confusion about the program to parents. They look to you for assurance that your early childhood curriculum is well thought out and offers their child an excellent education.

What Should I Do If My Students Have Had Background of Only Rote Math?

Inevitably students transfer into a school district who have had little exposure to a curriculum based on the NCTM Standards. And within a district, the curriculum is seldom perfectly aligned. Even when district administrators mandate change and provide ample in-service teacher retraining, some teachers continue to teach using traditional methods.

Students who have experienced rote learning may have serious deficiencies in such math strands as classifying, ordering, graphing, pattern, and problem solving. Perhaps they have developed math anxiety over their performance. They will adjust and thrive in a new curriculum as long as major areas of strengths and weaknesses are assessed and addressed in a timely fashion. They will need more time and opportunities to catch up on important developmental concepts. Teachers must stress that it is *not* the child's fault when the child is behind other children. Many of the recommendations often suggested for children of diverse backgrounds, or children with disabilities, apply when trying to reach these children.

How Can I Meet the Needs of Children from Diverse Backgrounds?

Teachers want to meet the learning and emotional needs of all children. Realistically, this goal is one of the biggest challenges in teaching. One study of experienced teachers, who were considered models of support and caring, found that very little individualization of instruction actually occurred. When teachers did modify their plans, they used small group interventions, such as cooperative learning, with the entire class. These regular education teachers were aware of modifications mandated by the Individual Educational Plans (IEPs) of the students with disabilities in their classes. However, there was a gap between a willingness to meet individual needs and actual classroom practice (Schumm, Vaughn, and Haager et. al., 1995). What implications are there for children who are at risk for a variety of reasons but do not have special education laws protecting their right to learn? One conclusion could be that a conscientious teacher must take this challenge seriously, and keep it in the forefront when planning.

Two areas are of major concern: providing for appropriate learning activities and assessing the child's progress. A variety of suggestions concerning assessment can be found in Chapter 12. This chapter concentrates on ways to modify classroom environments and to provide activities that increase the probability that all children have an opportunity to benefit from their educational experiences. These modifications include variety in grouping, variety in modes of learning, providing additional individual support, and bridging language barriers.

Variety in grouping includes flexible grouping (Tomlinson, 1995). At times during the year, the teacher will form small instructional groups based on ability. At other times, the whole class participates in an activity. Grouping depends on the particular topic and the needs of the students. No ability groups stay together indefinitely and become the sole means of receiving mathematics instruction.

Much conversation and informal learning occurs between partners or in small groups. Many young children need to learn the skills of sharing materials, listening, and cooperating. These attributes are important affective outcomes. Risk-taking behavior increase when the responsibility for a solution is shared. Co-operative learning (Johnson and Johnson, 1990) is a more formal method for organizing classroom groups. Research on co-operative learning clearly demonstrates academic gains and enhanced self-esteem for all ability levels.

Variety in modes of learning commonly refers to using a multisensory approach. Early childhood educators since the time of Montessori have incorporated active learning and hands-on experiences in all areas of the curriculum, including sight, sound, smell, and touch. Gardner and Hatch's (1989) approach for multiple intelligences reminds teachers that children may have certain gifts in many areas, such as music or movement (kinesthetic intelligence).

As children grow older and leave preschool and kindergarten classes for the primary grades, they do not lose their need for variety. It would appear that some teachers and parents associate rows of individual desks with a shift in modes of learning to listening, speaking, reading, and writing. This shift is detrimental to all, but especially to those children with difficulties or disabilities affecting language. At the very least, the classroom environment becomes extremely dull and boring.

Additional individual support may be provided by the teacher, an adult volunteer, a peer tutor, or an older student. Children in special education receive services from specialists. As more parents work, community volunteers, including retired teachers, may be an invaluable classroom addition. Many children benefit from one-on-one assistance (Jenkins and Mayhill, 1976). Roberts and Mather (1995) found that children with learning disabilities made academic progress when given a program of individualized instruction provided outside the mainstream.

Older children enjoy helping younger children at the computer or in a learning center. As classrooms include more children with diverse needs, a reflective teacher looks for ways to give children the special attention they need and deserve.

Bridging language barriers may mean that the teachers must learn enough conversational foreign language to communicate in an elementary fashion with non-native speakers of English. Phrase books, community volunteers, or classroom aides fluent in a particular language help the teacher communicate more effectively. If the child can read his original language, computer programs exist that translate one language into another. These programs, along with pictures and manipulatives, may help children make connections between the activities in the classroom and the child's ability to understand. The key is to make the extra effort and not to assume that young children will readily adapt and catch on to the intent of the teacher's math activities. Children want to fit in and often recede into the shadows of classroom life if left on their own. If these children are not behavior problems, it may be easy to overlook their real needs.

Finally, curricular activities that involve choice encourage children with diverse needs to make the best match between their interests and abilities and the learning environment. When faced with a wide range of opportunities, children make the best decisions about what activities are challenging yet feasible. The wider the menu of possibilities, the greater the probability that learning will occur for children at both ends of the developmental spectrum.

How Can I Use Technology to Enhance Learning?

Technology is an integral part of our everyday world. Many people think that technology will play a dramatic role in propelling our society into a new information age, preparing us to meet the challenges of the twenty-first century. Technology spans many continents and takes many forms. How should young children interact with technology? This section looks at the role of computers and calculators in the classroom.

Planning for Computer-Assisted Instruction

Parents and school boards welcome the addition of computers to the classroom environment. Unlike their misgivings about calculators, computers seem to signal that a school is keeping up with the times. As with any learning tool, this resource presents opportunities for wise use or misuse. Most professionals in early childhood education agree on three basic principles:

1. Technology should enhance active learning, the appropriate instructional model for young children. It does not replace active learning, but is integrated into the overall early childhood program.
2. Technology should enhance a problem-solving math curriculum. Computer programs that focus on narrow skills with much drill and practice or which overemphasize speed for its own sake, are often referred to as an "electronic workbook." Careful selection of computer software avoids this pitfall.
3. Technology has a language and a set of procedures that are unique to the media. Vocabulary concepts such as "keyboard, enter, load the disk, or connect the modem" are examples of the language. Children also learn to follow sequences, such as when they enter the symbols of a math problem into a calculator. Children not only learn to solve problems, but learn how to take control of these devices.

Most early childhood educators set aside one section of the classroom for a computer center. Each computer station has two chairs, as children often work in pairs, or with an older child who acts as a buddy. The teacher locates the center in a spot where an adult will be nearby. Teacher assistance may be needed so that the pair of children share and help one another. The goal is that both children have a chance to participate.

Campbell and Stewart (1993) suggested one practical way to organize the rotation system so everyone has a chance to visit the computer center. The teacher wrote each child's name on a separate index card. The teacher also purchased a pile of colored index cards and a key ring. Each pair of names was separated by a colored card, and all cards were punched and threaded on the ring. A quiet timer served as a reminder that time was up. As the children prepared to leave the center, they flipped up the next two cards. Over the course of a week all children participated in the center's activities.

Choosing Appropriate Software

Teachers and parents must preview a product and examine the accompanying documentation in order to determine whether the computer software is compatible with a child's current level of development. A child may be quick to learn how to activate the power source and load a disk. However, an adult's decision rests on whether the child shows real understanding of the concepts presented. Even in an active learning mode, such as creating a painting on the computer, Bowman and Beyer (1994) made the following observation:

> Children must understand the relationship between what is being represented and real ideas and objects. For instance, when a young child creates a picture using a computer, he must not only know how to make the computer respond, but also grasp the relationship the pictures created to real objects. (p. 20)

Reflective teachers listen, ask questions, and watch how children respond to educational software. If the material is too complex, it will not promote active learning.

Many writers have offered guidelines for choosing appropriate software. Here are some suggestions that may help:

1. Children are able to use the program independently. Frequent requests for help, or "What should I do?," mean that confusion reigns.
2. Children are able to control the program's pace and path.
3. Feedback is clear and comes quickly. Children stay interested. Errors can be corrected easily so the child may move on.
4. The graphics and sound appeal to young children. The material delights and engages the curiosity of young children.
5. Children experience success and feel empowered when they use the program.

Some excellent software programs are too complicated to approach on the screen immediately. Campbell and Stewart (1993) cited a case study of a second grade teacher who prepared her class to be successful with the program, Blocker and Finders. Preplanning involved using classroom simulations of the game board with wooden blocks, paper grids, and overhead transparencies. Once the class understood how to move on the board, the software could be used as part of the classroom computer center. Because the software encouraged logical reasoning, spatial interpretation, and data collection, her early efforts at preparing the group were well worth the effort. Additional titles of highly recommended or award winning software are listed in Appendix A. These computer programs have been integrated successfully into the curriculum found in many early childhood classrooms. They provide a good beginning for a comprehensive software collection.

Planning for Calculators

The National Council of Teachers of Mathematics (1989) wrote that "appropriate calculators should be available to all students at all times." Their analogy was that calculators and computers simplify work, much like word processing programs help writers. In addition, the calculator has the capacity to illustrate number patterns.

Specific calculator activities can be found in many chapters of this textbook. When planning for instruction, each student needs access to a machine with the following characteristics:

1. Easy-to-read numerals found directly on the keys
2. Easy-to-depress keys that move distinctly when depressed
3. A four-function calculator with the automatic constant for addition
4. Solar power

Children use calculators in everyday activities, such as playing shopkeeper. And they use them when computing long series of numbers or long division. It is hardly necessary to use a calculator to multiply 653×1000. Mental math, paper and pencil math, and calculators each have a place in the curriculum. Over the years, children learn which form of computation makes the most sense.

Summary

Planning for a successful beginning means paying close attention to the three key ingredients: a well-prepared environment, a developmentally appropriate math curriculum, and your new role. With perseverance, dedication, and creativity, each new school year will bring fresh ideas and new life to your classroom. As you refine your skills and learn from the children, the necessary keys to success will unfold. The process is never ending, but the journey is worth taking. Many wonderful teachers have gone before you. Now it's time to begin.

Activities and Study Questions

1. Choose a theme such as bears or bugs and develop a curriculum web with a small group of primary age students. Reproduce your web and be prepared to share it with the class.
2. Write a one-page essay describing your philosophy as you approach teaching mathematics. How does your philosophy differ from the way you were taught?
3. Visit a nearby early childhood classroom and make a sketch of the classroom's floor plan. Decide if you would make any changes and be prepared to describe your findings to the class.
4. Interview an early childhood professional about how classroom modifications were made for children with disabilities. Choose one child and write a short case study about a typical day in an integrated setting.
5. Preview one piece of early childhood math software and write a one-page review, based on the guidelines found in this chapter. Comment on whether the child would play an active or passive role when interacting with the software.

Further Reading

Chambers, D. L. (1995). Improving instruction by listening to children. *Teaching Children Mathematics,* 1, 378–380. *The author contrasts two teaching styles and discusses ways that the teacher can elicit information about the way children think by changing his or her style. Two classroom action research ideas are presented. These two ways of analyzing a day's lesson help teachers focus on the variety of strategies that children use to solve problems.*

Eisenhart, M., and Borko, H. (1993). *Designing classroom research: Themes, issues, and struggles* (Chapter 3, pp. 23–40). Boston: Allyn & Bacon. *One focus of this chapter centers on classroom research such as Cognitively Guided Instruction. The strengths and weaknesses of the research are reviewed, along with an extensive analysis of the roles that cognitive psychologists play in analyzing knowledge structures and metacognitive processes of teachers and students.*

Fennema, E., Franke, M. L., Carpenter, T. P., & Carey, D. (1993). Using children's mathematical knowledge in instruction. *American Educational Research Journal,* 30, 555–583. *The article traces the thinking and educational practice of "Ms. J" throughout a school year. Examples of actual classroom dialogue, activities, and organization give the reader a view into the life of one classroom. Ms. J. believed that understanding children's thinking was key to her success.*

Folkson, S. (1995). Who's behind the fence? Creating a rich learning environment with a nontraditional problem. *Teaching Children Mathematics,* 1, 382–385. *A classroom bulletin board becomes the focal point for problem solving. The problem posed concerned mysterious hidden animals and their legs sticking out from under the fence. Case histories of three kindergarten children illustrate how children solved the problem in different ways.*

Tomlinson, C. A. (1995). *How to differentiate instruction in mixed-ability classrooms.* Alexandria, VA: Association for Supervision and Curriculum Development. *The author describes several approaches that enable teachers to reach both "advanced" and "struggling" learners. Methods such as compacting, tiered assignments, and interest groups are described and highlighted in case studies.*

References

Baratta-Lorton, M. (1976). *Math their way.* Menlo Park, CA: Addison-Wesley.

Bowman, B. T., & Beyer, E. R. (1994). *Young children: Active learners in a technological age.* Washington, D.C.: National Association for the Education of Young Children.

Campbell, P. F., & Stewart, E. L. (1993). Calculators and computers. In R. L. Jensen (ed.), *Research ideas for the classroom: Early Childhood Mathematics* (pp. 251–268). New York: Macmillan.

Fennema, E., Carpenter, T. P., Franke, M. L., Levi, L., Jacobs, V. R., & Empson, S. B. (In press). Change in mathematics instruction and teachers' beliefs: A longitudinal study using children's thinking. *Journal for Research in Mathematics Education.*

Gardner, H., & Hatch, T. (1989). Multiple intelligences go to school. *Educational Leadership, 18,* (8), 4–10.

Jenkins, J. R., & Mayhall, W. F. (1976). Development and evaluation of a resource teacher program. *Exceptional Children, 43,* 21–29.

Johnson, D. W., & Johnson, R. T. (1990). Using co-operative learning in mathematics. In N. Davidson (ed.), *Co-operative learning in mathematics* (pp. 103–125). Menlo Park, CA: Addison-Wesley.

Knapp, N. F., & Peterson, P. L. (1995). Teacher's interpretations of "CGI" after four years: Meanings and practices. *Journal for Research in Mathematics Education, 26,* 40–65.

National Council of Teachers of Mathematics. (1989). *Curriculum and evaluation standards.* Reston, VA: Author.

National Council of Teachers of Mathematics. (1991). *Professional standards for teaching mathematics.* Reston, VA: Author.

National Council of Teachers of Mathematics. (1995). *Assessment standards for school mathematics.* Reston, VA: Author.

Piazza, J. A., Scott, M. M., Carver, E. C. (1994). Thematic webbing and the curriculum stands in the primary grades. *Arithmetic Teacher, 41,* 294–298.

Roberts, R., & Mather, N. (1995). The return of students with learning disabilities to regular classrooms: A sellout? *Learning Disabilities: Research & Practice, 10,* 46–58.

Schumm, J. S., Vaughn, S., Haager, D., McDowell, J., Rothlein, L., & Samuel, L. (1995). General education teacher planning: What can students with learning disabilities expect? *Exceptional Children, 61,* 335–352.

Schwartz, S. L. (1995). Planting mathematics in the classroom. *Teaching Children Mathematics, 2,* 42–46.

Spodek, B. & Saracho, O. N. (1994). *Right from the start: Teaching children ages three to eight.* Boston: Allyn & Bacon.

Steffe, L. P., & Tzur, R. (1994). Interaction and children's mathematics. *Journal of Research in Early Childhood Education, 8,* (2), 99–116.

Stenmark, J. K., Thompson, V., & Cossey, R. (1986). *Family Math.* Berkeley: University of California.

Tomlinson, C. A. (1995). *How to differentiate instruction in mixed-ability classrooms.* Alexandria, VA: Association for Supervision and Curriculum Development.

14 Thematic Units

This chapter takes a slightly different approach to the study of mathematics. Four thematic units outline ideas for activities of interest in a variety of curricular areas. The activities include many traditional ones found in the early childhood classroom, such as cooking, dramatic play, music, movement, and creative art. The units highlight math and use readily available children's literature to enhance language development. The unit, All About Bears, is suitable for very young children such as toddlers or preschoolers. The Circus unit and Insects and Spiders adapt easily to life in the kindergarten classroom. Peter Rabbit challenges first and second graders to explore emotions as well as gardening.

Thematic units have several advantages. They encourage the flow of ideas throughout the day. A thematic approach need not be rigid, where everyone must do the same thing on Monday and so on. It provides a beginning or launching pad for creativity. It encourages active learning, dramatic play, and curiosity about the natural world. Learning centers or activity centers enable the teacher to provide choices for children. There is a balance between child-initiated and teacher-guided learning.

Natural interconnections between curricular areas exist. The overlapping nature of thematic units helps children who need help or additional practice in language development. At the same time, units are often rich in ideas that challenge the most capable students. Finally, a theme is easy to convey to parents, who may wish to participate in activities at home. These sample units are a way to show how mathematics becomes a part of everyday life.

All About Bears (Preschool)

Stories about bears, and especially teddy bears, appeal to very young children. For many, a teddy bear is often a beloved companion. The fairy tale, *Goldilocks and the Three Bears*, brings suspense and delight to new generations every year. Familiar faces and familiar themes lend themselves to helping create a positive atmosphere for a child's first experiences at preschool.

Language Development
These words will help very young children learn about bears.

Kinds	Homes	Food	Movement
polar bear	ice	meat and plants	walk
brown bear	mountains	honey	run
black bear	forests		stand
grisly bear	the zoo, dens		swim
teddy bears	at home		

Colors		Positional Math Words	Sequencing Math Words
brown	red	over, around	first, last
black	yellow	in, out	middle
white	blue	under, over	
green			

Comparing Math Words	Measuring Math Words
big, little	lost, found
hot, cold	high, low
long, short	hard, soft
young, old	

Let's Find Out

1. What colors are bears?
2. Where do they live?
3. How does a bear move?
4. Where is a nice place to go for a picnic?
5. What stuffed animal is your favorite toy?

CREATIVE ART

Bear Rubbings
Materials: Cardboard cutouts of bears, art paper, crayons, glue, brushes, coffee grounds.

Procedure

1. Show the children how to put the cutouts under the art paper.
2. Rub the paper with crayons until bear appears.
3. Decorate by spreading glue on the bear and sprinkling it with coffee grounds.

SCIENCE

Porridge

Materials: Instant oatmeal, kitchen supplies, water, milk, sugar, bowls, thermometer, large classroom thermometer with easy-to-read red mercury colored tape.

Procedure

1. Measure the temperature of the coldwater before making

CREATIVE MOVEMENT

Bear Movements
Materials: A record with different tempos.

Procedure

1. Have the children practice moving like a bear: waking up from hibernation, stretching, walking on all fours, standing, swimming, and running.

DRAMATIC PLAY

Goldilocks and the Three Bears

Materials: Equipment in the housekeeping corner that can be used to retell the famous fairy tale. Bear caps made from fake fur.

Procedure

1. Read the story of *Goldilocks and the Three*

oatmeal. Mark the line with tape.
2. Put additional water in a bowl so the children can feel the temperature.
3. Cook the "porridge" in a microwave or oven. Talk about "hot" food. Measure the temperature again. Mark with another piece of tape.
4. Conduct a taste test. How many children like oatmeal? How many like it hot? How many like it cold? Graph the results.
5. Manipulate the large classroom thermometer to show hot and cold. Talk about foods that we like hot (hamburgers), and foods we like that are cold (ice cream).

Picnic Food Sort

Materials: Pictures of typical picnic foods. A space on the bulletin board or a large piece of cardboard.

Procedure

1. Sort the pictures into two groups: foods we like to eat when hot, and foods we like to eat when cold.
2. Leave the chart up and add to it as the class reads stories like *The Teddy Bear's Picnic* (Kennedy, 1992) and *It's the Bear* (Alborough, 1994).

Music

Sing along and act out the traditional songs:

Teddy Bear's Picnic

If you go down in the woods today
You're sure of a big surprise.
If you go down in the woods today
You'd better go in disguise;

Bears. Have the children retell each part.
2. Encourage the children to plan and act out the plot. They may wish to change the sequence, and add characters to their version.

For ev'ry Bear that ever there was
Will gather them for certain, because
Today's the day the Teddy Bears
Have their picnic.

Ev'ry Teddy Bear who's been good
is sure of a treat today.
There's lots of marvelous
Things to eat.
And lots of wonderful games to play
Beneath the trees where nobody sees
They'll hide and seek as long
As they please.

'Cause that's the way the Teddy Bears
Have their picnic.

If you go down in the woods today
You'd better not go alone
It's lovely down in the woods today
But safer to stay at home,

'Cause that's the way the Teddy Bears
Have their picnic.

The Bear Went Over the Mountain

The bear went over the mountain,
The bear went over the mountain,
The bear went over the mountain,
To see what he could see.

To see what he could see,
To see what he could see,
The bear went over the mountain,
To see what he could see.

The other side of the mountain,
The other side of the mountain,
The other side of the mountain,
Was all that he could see.

Was all that he could see,
Was all that he could see,
The other side of the mountain,
Was all that he could see.

COOKING

Bears in Bed
Materials: Bear cookie cutters, slices of cheese, white bread, a dull knife.

Procedure

1. Use a cookie cutter to cut out a bear from the cheese.
2. Make two rectangles from two pieces of bread using a dull knife. Make one smaller than the other.
3. Use the longer piece for a mattress, insert the bear, and "cover" with the sheet.
4. Enjoy a bear sandwich.

Variation: Bears can be cut from commercial refrigerator sugar cookie dough, baked, and decorated.

MATH ACTIVITIES

Numbers and Sets

Things in Threes

Materials: Sets of things scattered around the classroom. They need not be identical, for example, three different coffee mugs.

Procedure

1. Have the children search the classroom for sets of three objects.
2. Have each child tell about the set and count it for the group.
3. If needed, practice counting the objects in the story of *Goldilocks and the Three Bears.*

Matching/One-to-One Correspondence

Materials: Toy dishes and silverware, regular dishes and silverware, a picnic blanket or tablecloth, teddy bears brought from home, a special snack.

Procedure

1. Have the children set the table for their teddy bears with the small dishes and for themselves with the big dishes.
2. Talk about big and little.
3. Serve a special snack for the pretend picnic.

Sequencing Events

First–Last

Materials: Stories such as *Goldilocks and the Three Bears*, *The Three Little Kittens*, and *Three Billy Goat's Gruff*. Story cards if needed.

Procedure

1. Have the children retell the story in order, paying attention to the order of events.

2. Use picture cards of specific parts of the narrative if needed.

3. Stress the words: first and last.

Make Up a Story

Materials: The children's teddy bears. Extra bears for "adoption."

Procedure

1. Have the children bring a bear from home. Have extra bears available for those children who do not have one.

2. Let each child recall a specific event associated with the bear.

3. If a child cannot recall a story, let the child make up a story to share.

Shape—Parts and Wholes

Materials: Clay or play dough shaped into ovals (head and body), cylinders (arms and legs), and flattened spheres (ears and muzzle). A clay model of a bear.

Procedure

1. Let the children put together a clay bear, noting how the pieces fit on the model.

2. Talk about the various parts, and use the words "whole bear" to describe the animal.

Shape—Comparing Size

Make a Mountain

See directions in Chapter 10, Measurement.

Storytime: The following selections encourage listening, retelling, and dramatic play.

1. Alborough, J. (1992). *Where's my teddy?* Cambridge, MA: Candlewick Press. *A little boy loses his teddy bear in the forest. He finds a giant teddy bear that belongs to a giant real bear. The real bear has the boy's little teddy. They exchange bears and all is well.*

2. Alborough, J. (1994). *It's the bear.* Cambridge, MA: Candlewick Press. *In a sequel to* Where's My Teddy?, *the little boy and his mom go on a picnic. Mom forgets the dessert, so she leaves Eddy alone. The big bear returns and the adventure continues as the big bear has his own picnic. Eventually mom returns with a blueberry pie. The big bear grabs the pie and everyone scatters.*

3. Galdone, P. (1972). *The three bears.* New York: Clarion Books. *The traditional fairy tale of the three bears with a straight-forward narrative and illustrations.*

4. Huber, I. (1994). *Sleep tight, little bear.* New York: Abbeville Press. *A teddy bear tries to fall asleep in the forest homes of many animals. Finally he finds a child crying in a bed in a house. The bear crawls in, and both of them sleep soundly.*

5. Kennedy, J. (1992). *The teddy bear's picnic.* New York: Henry Holt & Company. *A beautifully illustrated storybook that uses the original lyrics of the famous song.*

6. Martin, B. (1983). *Brown bear, brown bear, what do you see?* New York: Henry Holt & Company. *The brown bear meets interesting creatures in a variety of colors. The verse rhymes so children can remember the sequence with practice.*

7. Taylor, G. (1995). *Bears at work: A book of bearable jobs.* San Francisco: Chronicle Books. *Each letter of the alphabet takes a turn at becoming a career, from an Adventurer* *to a Zoo Keeper. Some of the professions are easier for young children to grasp than others. The narrative will increase a child's exposure to the modern world.*

8. Tolhurst, M. (1990). *Somebody and the three Blairs.* New York: Orchard Books. *A modern reversal of the story of Goldilocks. A bear visits while the Blair family is out. The bear experiences many activities, such as finding some games. One is too noisy, one is too cold, and one game was just right. The bear makes quite a mess before the family comes home. A very entertaining story.*

9. Turkle, B. (1976). *Deep in the forest.* New York: Dutton Children's Books. *A picture book with no narrative. Three bears visit Goldilock's family home in the forest and go through the same adventure.*

10. Waddell, M. (1992). *Can't you sleep, little bear?* Cambridge, MA: Candlewick Press. *Big bear brings little bear three lanterns in progressively bigger sizes. But little bear cannot sleep because he is afraid of the dark. Finally big bear offers him the moon and the stars. Then little bear can sleep.*

11. Waddel, M. (1994). *When the teddy bears came.* Cambridge, MA: Candlewick Press. *A new baby in the house brings gifts of many teddy bears. Soon there are so many bears that Tom feels neglected. Mom senses the problem and gives Tom extra attention.*

The Circus (Preschool–Kindergarten)

The circus is a popular theme with young children. There are so many activities that enhance creativity and help children explore mathematical concepts. Small circuses tour many towns, so most children can attend at least once in their lifetime. The animal acts, the feats of daring, and the antics of clowns bring joy to people around the world.

Language Development

These categories of language concepts occur often in pictures, stories, and actual performances.

Animals	*People*	*Places*
bears	jugglers	tents (canvas)
elephants	clowns	rings
lions	high wire artists	
tigers	trapeze artists	
horses	master of ceremonies	
	animal trainer	

Objects/Events	*Positional Math*
circus wagons	up, down
parades	over, under
steam calliope	inside, outside
railroad cars	
large trucks	

Sequential Math	Comparing Math	Measuring Math
first, last	high, low	one cup
between	heavy, light	
	fast, slow	
	big (enormous), little	

Let's Find Out

1. What happens at the circus?
2. Where do the people live?
3. What do the animals eat?
4. How does the circus move from town to town?

CREATIVE ART

Clown Faces
Materials: Washable face paint, cold cream, leftover yarn in bright colors, mirrors.

Procedure

1. The children decorate their faces to transform themselves into clowns.
2. They use a pile of yarn loosely tied together and pinned on their head for a wig.
Variation: Decorate a doll's face or do a fingerpainting of a clown.

Thumbkin Prints at the Circus
Materials: The book, *Thumbprint Circus*, ink pad, paper, crayons.

Procedure

1. The child makes an ink print of a thumb. With the teacher's help, a face is drawn on Thumbkin.
2. The child imagines a place to hide Thumbkin and draws a picture around him.

CREATIVE MOVEMENT

Elephant Walk
Materials: Lyrics for "One Elephant."

Procedure

1. The children sit in a circle and sing:
One elephant went out to play,
Out on a spider's web one day,
He had such enormous fun,
He called for another elephant to come.
2. One child uses an arm as a trunk, and sways around the circle. The lyrics change to, *"Two elephants went out to play . . . ."*

Tightrope Walkers
Materials: A balance beam.

Procedure

1. Each child walks across the beam and tries to balance on one foot.
2. Children try to walk backwards.
3. Performance background music that has a slow beat,

3. The children share their secret hiding places for Thumbkin.

SCIENCE

Planting Peanuts
Materials: Unroasted peanuts, soil, stryrofoam cups.

Procedure

1. Plant one peanut in each cup. Water and place in sunny location.
2. Compare the results.

Wild/Domestic Animal Sort
Materials: Pictures of both kinds of animals (perhaps from National Geographic, and commercial sets).

Procedure

1. Sort the animals by these classifications.
2. Discuss why each animal belongs in that group. Are there any that could be in both groups?

Plant Foods Found
Above Ground/Below Ground
Materials: Pictures of vegetables from seed catalogs.

Procedure

1. Make a classroom chart with a line indicating soil level
2. Glue pictures of foods such as peanuts, beets, or potatoes below the line.
3. Glue pictures of foods such as tomatoes, corn, and peas above the soil line.

and a fast beat encourages a child to walk in various tempos.

THE CIRCUS PARADE

Materials: Homemade masks and costumes.

Procedure

1. The child dresses up and walks in the style of their animal or person. They carry props as needed. The teacher plays circus music, with calliope effects.

DRAMATIC PLAY

The Circus
Materials: Props, costumes, paper or "paper plate on a stick" masks, hula hoop rings.

Procedure

1. Let the children pretend to put on a circus.
2. Let the children act out their favorite circus story. Encourage them to invent new characters or add new plot lines to a story. [Note: Masks of any creature can be made by gluing eyes, ears, a nose, or other features on a paper plate and securing it to a large tongue depressor. These activities involve following directions and are not considered creative art for children. Children with better motor control may wish to help the teacher make circus masks.]

COOKING

Peanut Logs

Ingredients:

    1 cup of honey
    1 cup of creamy peanut butter
    1 cup of instant nonfat dry milk
    1 cup of raisins
    1 cup of graham cracker crumbs

Procedure

1. Mix honey, peanut butter, and dry milk.
2. Add raisins and mix well.
3. Add graham cracker crumbs.
4. Form logs and place on nonstick surface or wax paper.
5. Refrigerate 1 hour.
6. Math extension: Count how many logs were made before and after they were refrigerated. Did the number of logs stay the same? Why?

MATH ACTIVITIES

Number and Measurement

Peanut Perimeter

Materials: Peanuts in the shell, a large bowl, small tables.

Procedure

1. Children in groups of two decide how to line the edges of a small table. They pay close attention to staying by the edge and having peanuts touch.
2. After finishing the perimeter, the children remove the peanuts and count with the teacher. (It may take over 100 peanuts for some tables.)

Sequencing and Ordering (Time)

Mirette's Story

Materials: The book, *Mirette on the High Wire.*

Procedure

1.   Read the story of Mirette, and highlight the events in sequence.
        a. Mirette lives in the boarding house
        b. The retired high wire performer arrives
        c. Mirette learns to walk the high wire
        d. The performer decides to return to the stage
2.   Have the children act out and retell the story in sequence.

Sequencing and ordering (Size)

Animals on Parade

Materials: Stuffed circus animals in a variety of sizes.

Procedure

1. Have each child take a turn at putting the animals in order from smallest to largest. If the stuffed toys are not in proportion to the real animal, for example, a very small elephant, talk about what would happen in real life.

Space and Shape

Circus Tents

Materials: Old blankets, curtains, tables, chairs.

Procedure

1. The children construct a "circus tent" and discuss its use.
2. The teacher may wish to encourage the use of the concepts, inside and outside.
3. The children may want to guess how many children fit in a tent.

Patterning

Circus Animals and Circus People

Materials: Felt cutouts of various animals and clowns.

Procedure

1. The children create patterns on the flannel board by choosing two kinds of cutouts.
2. One child makes a pattern, while another child copies and/or extends it.

Measurement—Weight

How Much Does a Baby Elephant Weigh?

Materials: Pictures of things that are very heavy, like a baby elephant, and very light; poster board or bulletin board.

Procedure

1. Research the weight of a baby elephant. Compare it to the weight of a newborn person.
2. Make a more–less weight chart, with pictures of things that might weigh more or less than a baby elephant.

Part-Part-Whole—The Number 5

Mixed Nut Designs

Materials: Nuts in the shell, such as peanuts, almonds, walnuts, and pecans (any nuts that do not roll); a bowl; a large table or a rug.

Procedure

1. Make designs with two kinds of nuts, so that each design has five nuts.

2. Fill the whole table with designs, and tell the teacher about your combinations, for example, "This one has two pecans, and three peanuts. It looks like a star."

Story Problems

At the Circus: Add and Subtract

Materials: Children's books on the circus, a model of the 11 problem types (see Chapter 8).

Procedure

1. Have the children chose a favorite story.
2. The teacher writes story problems for the class using the storybook characters and the 11 problem types.
3. Present the problems to a small group of children. Have manipulatives available. Listen to how each child thinks about the problem.

Storytime: The following selections encourage listening, retelling, and dramatic play.

1. Booth, E. (1977). *At the circus.* Milwaukee: Raintree Books. *The author uses a circus setting to encourage counting, visual differences, and making up a story.*
2. DuBois, W. P. (1971). *Bear circus.* New York: Puffin Books. *The koala bears take seven years to use circus equipment and put together an act.*
3. Ehlert, L. (1992). *Circus.* New York: Harper Collins. *Colorful animals perform in an unusual circus.*
4. Ipcar, D. Z. (1970). *The marvelous merry-go-round.* New York: Doubleday. *After the circus comes to town, the wood carver decides to make magical figures for the carousel.*
5. Kennaway, A. (1991). *Little elephant's walk.* New York: Willa Perlman Books/Harper Collins. *A mother elephant and her baby take a walk on the plains of Africa. They meet the typical wild animals such as zebras and hippos. They also meet unusual natives such as the warthog, the mandrill, and the fruit bat. The author paints beautiful portraits of animal life.*
6. McCully, E. A. (1992). *Mirette on the high wire.* New York: G. P. Putnam & Sons. *Mirette lives in a boarding house in Paris over 100 years ago. A famous high-wire artist becomes a boarder and teaches her to balance on the wire. While helping Mirette, he overcomes his fear of falling and begins to perform again.*
7. Peppe, R. (1989). *Thumbprint circus.* New York: Delacourte Press. *Thumbkin is a little clown who wanted a job in the circus. He tries to help all the performers. Eventually he is shot out of a cannon and gets lost. Everyone looks for him, and he finally shows up in a tuba. The audience enjoys his show, and he gets a job.*
8. Petershan, M. F. (1950). *The circus baby.* New York: Macmillan. *Mother elephant tries to teach her baby how to eat like the circus folk. But the baby just can't manage a high chair and utensils. She decides that her baby is fine as he is.*
9. Riddell, C. (1988). *The trouble with elephants.* New York: J. B. Lippincott. *A magical story about all the trouble that happens when an elephant moves into a house and a neighborhood. Elephants are not very good at taking baths, going on picnics, or riding bicycles. But they are lovable just the same.*
10. Vincent, G. (1988). *Ernest and Celestine at the circus.* New York: Greenwillow Books. *Ernest finds his old costumes and transforms himself as a clown. He and Celestine put on a circus act in front of the crowd. Everyone has a good time.*

Insects and Spiders (Preschool–Kindergarten)

Another popular theme for young children is "insects and spiders." A number of ageless children's books, such as *The Very Hungry Caterpillar* (Carle, 1971) have become classics in preschool education. Children have a fascination for other living things, and bugs provide a plentiful source of investigation about the natural world.

Language Development

These categories of language concepts occur often in the study of insects and spiders.

Animal Helpers	*Animal Pests*	*Animal Predators*
most ants	carpenter ants	birds
most spiders	brown spiders	snakes
insects	black widow spiders	frogs
honey bees	tarantulas	toads
ladybugs	mosquitoes	
butterflies/moths	wasps, hornets	
grasshoppers	termites	
crickets	Garden/Crop Pests	
dragonflies	aphids	
	cucumber beetles	
	earwigs	
	Japanese beetles	

Body Parts

Insects	*Spiders*
six legs	eight legs
three parts (head, thorax, abdomen)	two parts
antennae or feelers (some)	Note: A spider is not an insect.
wings (some)	It is an arachnid.

Homes	*Sounds*	*Movement*
beehives	buzz	fly
ant hills	chirp	hop
spider webs		walk
bushes		crawl
water		swim
nests		
trees		
plants		

Safety tip: Do not try to capture a live bee or touch a spider. Either species may sting or bite.

Animal Roles

Ants	Some are nurses and look after the young.
	Some are soldiers who defend the hill.
	Some search for food and clear the hill.
Bees	The queen bee lays her eggs in the spring.
	During the summer the eggs hatch, producing worker bees.
	The worker bees gather nectar for honey and take care of the hive.

Comparing Math

young, old
near, far
fast, slow

Positional Math

inside, outside
in, out

Sequential Math

beginning, middle,
end

Time Words

morning, evening
day, night
spring, summer, fall

Shape Math

oval
tube

Number Math

2 and 3
6 and 8

Emotional Well-Being

A few preschool children develop an irrational phobia or fear of insects such as bees and/or spiders. If left untreated, this phobia can result in a lifetime of debilitating anxiety. For example, adults with this phobia will not enter a basement or enjoy the outdoors, in order to prevent a chance encounter.

Consult a mental health specialist on the latest techniques for desensitization and encourage parents to help their child overcome the phobia at a young age. Adults have a much more difficult time trying to regain a normal perspective.

Let's Find Out

1. How are bees different from ants?
2. What are antennae or feelers useful for?
3. Do insects make sounds? How? Why?
4. What colors do bees like?

CREATIVE ART

String Spider Web
Materials: Heavy string, shoe boxes, black and white paint.

Procedure

1. Paint the inside of a shoe box with black paint. Dip a string in white paint and drag across the bottom of the box.
2. The design should look like a spider web.

Clay Insects and Spiders
Materials: Clay, pipe cleaners, popcorn kernels. (Note: Do not use seeds, nuts, or balloons with children under five.)

Procedure

1. Mold each section of an insect (three parts) or two parts for a spider. Attach the pipe cleaner legs as needed. Use popcorn kernels for eyes.
2. Have the children tell about their animals.

CREATIVE MOVEMENT

Let's Pretend: Insects
Materials: None.

Procedure

1. Have the children take turns pretending to move like a bee, beetle.
Variation: Create teams and and have a relay race in which each person must move like a certain insect.

The Grouchy Ladybug: Faces
Materials: The children's book, *The Grouchy Ladybug.*

Procedure

1. Have the children change their facial expression as if they were a ladybug: happy, sleepy, scared, bored, sad.

Music, Finger Play, and Movement

Songs: "The Eensy Weensy Spider"
            "The Ants Go Marching"

Sing along to a recording and act out the motions.

Eensy Weensy Spider
The eensy weensy spider
Climbed up the water spout.
Down came the rain
And washed the spider out.

Out came the sun
And dried up all the rain,
And the eensy weensy spider
Climbed up the spout again.

The Ants Go Marching

The ants go marching one by one,
Hurrah, hurrah.
The ants go marching one by one,
Hurrah, hurrah,
The ants go marching one by one,
The little one stops to suck his thumb,
Any they all go marching down
Into ground to get out of the rain,
BOOM! BOOM! BOOM!

Two . . . tie his shoe . . .
Three . . . climb a tree . . .
Four . . . shut the door . . .
Five . . . take a dive . . .
Six . . . pick up sticks . . .
Seven . . . pray to heaven . . .
Eight . . . shut the gate . . .
Nine . . . check the time . . .
Ten . . . say "THE END"

SCIENCE

Close-up: Insects or Spiders

Materials: Homemade or commercial insect cage (with screen sides), grass, sticks, rocks, leaves, bottle cap for water, magnifying glass, pictures of spiders, grasshoppers, or beetles.

Procedure

1. Have the children study pictures of insects.
2. Let them use the magnifying glass to observe the creatures.
3. Release the animals as soon as possible.

Nature Walk

Materials: Magnifying glass, suitable outdoor habitat.

Procedure

1. Take an outdoor walk and look in the grass, under rocks, and in the bushes for insects and spiders.
2. If possible, use a magnifying glass to see them in detail.
3. Notice the colors of the various insects.

COOKING

Ants on a Log

Materials: Celery, peanut butter, raisins.

Procedure

1. The children fill the celery with peanut butter to make a log.
2. They place raisins on the log to make "ants."

Honey Balls

Materials: 1 cup peanut butter
1 cup powdered milk
½ cup honey
1 teaspoon vanilla
1 cup coconut flakes
½ cup raisins (optional)

Procedure

1. Mix the ingredients together and form balls. Roll in coconut and spread on wax paper.
2. Refrigerate one hour, and then eat.

Fine Motor

Insect Puzzles

There are many commercially produced puzzles of butterflies, ladybugs, and caterpillars (5–15 pieces). See a preschool educational catalog.

Visual Discrimination

Butterfly Match

Materials: Color pictures of various butterflies and moths—at least two identical pictures of each kind. (Note: Color pictures can be reproduced on certain photo copiers.)

Procedure

1. Have the children take turns sorting the pictures into matching sets.
2. Ask them to tell you about their favorite ones.

MATH ACTIVITIES

Number and Counting

Fruit and Food Match

Materials: The book, *The Very Hungry Caterpillar*. Real fruit and pictures of 10 treats. Numeral cards 1 to 10.

Procedure

1. Match the numeral card to the right number of objects.
2. Put them in order from 1 to 10.

Count by 10's to 100

Materials: Over 100 small plastic bugs, or large lima beans painted to look like bugs. (Note: For a bee, spray paint the beans yellow. Use an indelible black marker for designs. For a ladybug, use red paint and black marker.) Paper cutouts of leaves or hives.

Procedure

1. Practice counting groups of 10 bugs. Put each set in its own home.

Sequencing and Ordering (Time)

Around the Clock—The Very Grouchy Ladybug

Materials: The book, *The Very Grouchy Ladybug*. A large classroom clock. Pictures of the creature in the book. If available, a dozen small clocks.

Procedure

1. Read the story and retell the events in order, using a large classroom clock to illustrate the time of the encounter.
2. Match pictures of the creatures to the time of day, by making the time on a small clock. Put the animals and clocks in order.

Sequence and Ordering (Events)

Animals Talk to the Spider

Materials: The book, *The Very Busy Spider*. Pictures of the farm animals in the story. String for a web. A small toy bug.

Procedure

1. Read the story and retell the events, using string to make a bigger and bigger web.
2. Have the children recall what each animal wanted from the spider. Sequence pictures of the animals.
3. Put the toy bug in the web at the end of the retelling.

Sequence and Ordering (Size)

From Aphids to Whales

Materials: The book, *The Very Grouchy Ladybug*. Pictures of the animals in the story.

Procedure

1. Talk about how big each creature is. Find something in the classroom or building that might be the same size.
2. Put the pictures in sequence by size. Talk about other creatures that are very small or very large.

Space and Shape

The Beehive

Materials: Clay or play dough. Pictures of beehives.

Procedure

1. Have the children mold their own beehive. Look around for other objects that have similar shape.

The Spider Web

Materials: String, scissors, black construction paper. Pictures of spider webs.

Procedure

1. Cut string and form concentric circles. If possible, subdivide the web into sections, like the pieces of a pie, to simulate a real web.

Patterning

Q-Tip Butterfly Dot Painting

See directions for this activity in Chapter 5.

Part-Part-Whole (The Number 6)

Habitat Designs

Materials: Three-inch sections of twigs, small stones, dried leaves, the numeral card 6. Small plastic bugs (optional)

Procedure

1. Using two kinds of materials, create a design with six pieces.
2. Fill the table or rug with designs. Each design need not have the same two kinds of material. Hide a bug in each design. Put the numeral card 6 in front of the creations.
3. Tell the teacher about each design. For example: "I have four twigs and two leaves in this one. My bug is hiding under one leaf."

Story Problems

Insects and Spiders: Add and Subtract

Materials: Children's books on the subject, a model of the 11 problem types (see Chapter 8), small counters, base-ten blocks.

Procedure

1. Have the children choose a favorite story.
2. Write story problems for the class based on the 11 types.
3. Present the problems to a small group of children. Have manipulatives available. Listen to how each child thinks about the problem.

Storytime: The following selections encourage learning about the natural world.

1. Carle, E. (1977). *The grouchy ladybug.* New York: HarperCollins. *A grouchy ladybug meets many animals of progressively bigger size and wants to fight. He backs off until a whale slaps him back to reality. A clock tells the time from 6:00 AM to 6:00 PM.*
2. Carle, E. (1981). *The honey bees and the robber.* New York: Philomel Books. *Life in a bee hive is illustrated with motion. A bear tries to steal the honey. The bees attack and save the fruits of all their hard work.*
3. Carle, E. (1984). *The very busy spider.* New York: Philomel Books. *The spider ignores*

all the farm animals who want to play. She works diligently on her web. The rooster asks, "Want to catch a pesky fly?" And sure enough she does because she's done her work.

4. Carle, E. (1987). *The very hungry caterpillar.* New York: Philomel Books. *The hungry caterpillar goes through the days of the week eating more and more food. The numbers 1 to 10 are stressed with food illustrations. Then the caterpillar makes a cocoon and eventually turns into a beautiful butterfly.*

5. Carle, E. (1990). *The very quiet cricket.* New York: Philomel Books. *The baby cricket meets many insects that are able to make noises. He can't make a sound until he meets another cricket.*

6. Carle, E. (1995). *The very lonely firefly.* New York: Philomel Books. *A lonely firefly looks for a friend but finds a light bulb, a candle, a flashlight, a lantern, and lots of creatures. Finally he finds a large group of fireflies for company.*

7. Demuth, P. B. (1994). *Those amazing ants.* New York: Macmillan. *Life in an anthill is described and illustrated. The roles of each kind of ant show teamwork and amazing strength.*

8. Godkin, C. (1995). *What about ladybugs?* San Francisco: Sierra Club. *A gardener uses pesticides and scares away all the helpful bugs. When the garden declines, she orders a box of ladybugs in the mail. Soon things are back to normal.*

9. Hariton, A. (1995). *Butterfly story.* New York: Dutton Children's Books. *A detailed yet simple text and illustrations covering the life cycle of a butterfly in scientific detail.*

10. Kerk, D. (1994). *Miss Spider's tea party.* New York: Scholastic. *Bugs in groups of the numbers 1 to 9 arrive, but quickly depart before they become lunch for the lonely spider. She wants a guest for tea. Finally a moth encourages 11 guests to come, and they enjoy their tea. Twelve flowers adorn the table. This tale uses progressive numbers as well as a theme of belonging.*

11. Micucci, C. (1995). *Life and times of the honey bee.* New York: Ticknor and Fields Books. *An illustrated but brief encyclopedia on honey bees.*

12. Ryder, J. (1989). *Where butterflies grow.* New York: Lodeston Books. *A carefully illustrated story about the life cycle of a butterfly. Many details on cocoons and habitats are presented.*

13. Sundgaard, A. (1988). *The lamb and the butterfly.* New York: Orchard Books. *The butterfly is free to roam, while the lamb needs to stay with mother. Eventually the butterfly suffers a temporary setback in a storm, but decides to fly away when he recovers. The lamb stays close to her mother's side, realizing that a butterfly has different needs from sheep.*

14. Trapani, I. (1993). *The itsy bitsy spider.* Boston: Whispering Coyote Press. *The spider climbs up many things, like a tree, and keeps falling down. In the end she spins a web at the top and rests in the sun.*

Peter Rabbit (First and Second Grade)

The classic, *The Tale of Peter Rabbit,* captivates children around the world. While the story itself is suitable for very young children, the complexity of the narrative lends itself to the development of a thematic unit suitable for the early grades. Other rabbit stories, such as *The Runaway Bunny* (1977) and *The Velveteen Rabbit* (1985) express everyone's need for nurturing, love, and belonging. These ingredients for happiness and security are timeless and are of special importance to many of today's children.

Language Development

These categories of language concepts occur in *The Tale of Peter Rabbit.*

Creatures	*Places*	*Foods*	*Things*
Peter	a sand bank	brown bread	a basket
Flopsy	fir tree	currant buns	a sieve
Mopsy	fields	blackberries	a jacket
Cotton-tail	lane	lettuce	shoes
Mother	garden	French beans	watering can
Mr. McGregor	the gate	radishes	flower pot
sparrows	pond	parsley	a hoe
a white cat		cucumber	a wheelbarrow
goldfish		cabbages	a rake
		potatoes	plants in pots
		gooseberries	
		peas	
		onions	
		black currants	
		chamomile tea	

Positional Math	*Measurement Math*	*Space Math*	*Time*
underneath	inches/feet	rows	days
through the woods	meters	fencing	months
under	cups	cold frame	
on top of	pounds	netting	
into the can		door	
beyond		date	
inside/outside		shed	

Let's Find Out

1. Where do rabbits go in winter?

2. Are rabbits found around the world?

3. Why did Peter Rabbit have a hard time finding his way out of Mr. McGregor's garden?

4. Can we grow all of the crops in Mr. McGregor's garden in our climate?

5. How is chamomile tea made? What is it good for?

Creative Art

My Book of Presents

Materials: The book, *Mr. Rabbit and the Lovely Present* (Zolotow, 1962). Tempura paints in red, yellow, green, and blue; paper; brushes. Cleanup supplies. Black markers.

Procedure

1. Read the book and discuss various presents that come in each color.

2. Have the children decide on a gift in each color.

3. Paint a picture of the gift entirely in one color. Decorate with black marker.

4. Put together the four pages into a booklet. Staple them along with a cover, "My Book of Presents."

SCIENCE

Vegetable Dish Garden

Materials: Carrot and/or beet tops, a shallow saucer or dish, pebbles or sand, water, good light, ruler (centimeters).

Procedure

1. Cut off the top of the vegetables with about one inch of flesh.
2. Plant in the pebbles and water. Put in spot with good indirect sunlight.
3. The tops should sprout in 7 to 10 days.
4. Observe the root structure. Does it differ from carrot to beet?
5. Measure the height of the tops in centimeters.

Baby Bear Pumpkins

Materials: A garden plot, seeds for an easy to grow pumpkin variety such as Baby Bear (available from a number of seed catalogs), garden tools, scale, measuring tape.

Procedure

1. Plant the seeds when the soil is warm in early summer.
2. Have an interested volunteer tend the garden over the summer.
3. Pick the crop in October. The variety, Baby Bear, produces small but perfectly formed $1\frac{1}{2}$ to $2\frac{1}{2}$ pound fruits. (Note: These are not the mini-gourds found in produce sections.)
4. Weigh, measure, and order the produce by size.

Social Studies

People and Rabbits

Investigate your neighborhood and answer the following questions:

1. Does anyone you know have a pet rabbit? Why?
2. How do people you know cope with rabbits if they eat their tulips, young plants, or vegetables?
3. What folk remedies have people tried (e.g., human hair, moth balls)? Collect their ideas and give an oral report on your findings.

MATH ACTIVITIES

Space and Shape

Garden Diorama

Materials: The bottom section of a medium-size box, paints, clay, toothpicks, nylon netting, twigs, one-inch graph paper.

Procedure

1. Have each child or a team of two children design Mr. McGregor's garden on graph paper.
2. Make room for the following items: rows of vegetables, a tool shed, a pond, a door in a wall, netting, a garden gate.
3. Decorate the diorama according to the plan using paint, clay vegetable crops, nylon netting, toothpick poles, and twigs.
4. Have each team give an oral report on how they used their space.

Variation: Make a diorama of Peter Rabbit's home under the fir tree.

Patterning

Materials: Brass and non-brass buttons.

Procedure

1. Have the children make a pattern for Peter's coat using two kinds of buttons.
2. Ask them to tell about their pattern.

Classifying

Let's Eat

Materials: Garden catalog pictures of the vegetables in Mr. McGregor's garden mounted on cardboard.

Procedure

1. Have the children sort the pictures into three categories: "Can be eaten raw," "Can be eaten cooked," "Can be eaten both ways."
2. Let the children decide how they like their vegetables. If needed, conduct a taste test.

Measurement

Flower Pot Sizes

Materials: Tape measure, recording paper, measuring cup, dull knife, real plants in various sizes (optional), a five-pound bag of soil or sand, or small pebbles, if soil is not appropriate.

Procedure

1. Measure the circumference and diameter of various pots.
2. Estimate the number of cups of soil a pot will hold in cups and $\frac{1}{2}$ cups.
3. Measure the number of cups of soil, use a knife to even the top of the cup, and record the results. Try again on a bigger pot.
4. Transplant plants into slightly larger pots. Match the plant to the right pot (optional).
5. Talk about the relationship of pot size to the amount of soil. Some children may see a pattern.

Probability

Eggs in a Basket

Materials: 20 two-part plastic eggs, a bowl or basket, lima beans painted to represent fruit and vegetables: carrots, peas, radishes, onions, blackberries. A recording chart with the names of these choices.

Procedure

1. Hide one "vegetable or fruit" in each egg. Make the proportion of the 20 eggs uneven, such as 9 carrots, 5 peas, 3 radishes, 2 onions, and 1 blackberry.
2. Have the children work in groups of 4. One child picks 5 eggs and records the contents on the group chart. The eggs are reassembled, put back in the basket, and mixed.
3. Repeat the procedure with each child.
4. The group looks at the results of the experiment and decides which food is the most prevalent and which is the least prevalent in the basket.
5. Have the group explain their choices to the class.

Addition-Subtraction Problem Solving

Story Problems

Join-Result Unknown

Mr. McGregor had 8 rows of rashishes. He planted 4 more rows. How many rows of radishes does Mr. McGregor have now?
8 + 4 = ☐

Join-Result Unknown

Mr. McGregor picked 20 peas. Then he picked some more peas. When he was done he had 35 peas in his basket. How many more peas did he pick?
20 + ☐ = 35

Join-Start Unknown

Mr. McGregor planted some potatoes. Then he planted 3 more potatoes. Now he has 14 potato plants. How many potatoes did he plant to begin with?
☐ + 3 = 14

Separate-Result Unknown

Flopsy gathered 11 blackberries. She ate 6 of them. How many blackberries does Flopsy have left?
11 − 6 = ☐

Separate-Change Unknown

Mopsy gathered 7 blackberries. She ate some of them. She had 4 left. How many blackberries did Mopsy eat?
7 − ☐ = 4

Separate-Start Unknown

Cotton-tail had some blackberries. She ate 10 of them. Now she has 8 left. How many blackberries did Botton-tail have to begin with?
☐ − 10 = 8

Part-Part-Whole
Whole Unknown

Mrs. Rabbit had 3 girls and 1 boy. How many baby rabbits did she have?
$3 + 1 = \square$

Part-Part-Whole
Part Unknown

The old mouse had 4 beans and some peas. She had 5 vegetables in all? How many peas did she have?
$4 + \square = 5$ or
$5 - 4 = \square$

Compare
Differerence Unknown

Mr. McGregor had 9 rows of cabbages and 4 rows of potatoes. How many more rows of cabbages did he have?
$9 - 4 = \square$ or
$4 + \square = 9$

Compare
Quantity Unknown

Mr. McGregor had 6 rows of cucumbers. He had 4 more rows of lettuces than cucumbers. How many rows of lettuces did he have?
$6 + 4 = \square$

Compare
Referent Unknown

Mr. McGregor had 11 rows of French beans. He had 3 more rows of French beans than of cabbages. How many rows of cabbages did he have?
$11 - 3 = \square$ or
$\square + 3 = 11$

Storytime: Here are some classic books about rabbits that delight children everywhere.

1. Brown, M. W. (1991). *The runaway bunny.* New York: HarperCollins. *In this story a mother bunny and her baby bunny play a tale of hide and seek. The baby pretends to run away and becomes many imaginary objects. For example, the bunny becomes a rock but mother rescues the bunny by becoming a mountain climber. Or the bunny becomes a crocus and the mother arrives on the scene as a gardener. The moral of the story is that no matter how far the bunny strays, mother will always be there for him.*
2. Potter, B. (1993). *The tale of Peter Rabbit.* New York: Penguin Books. *This edition of the famous tale of Peter Rabbit is a small authorized reproduction of Beatrix Potter's original watercolors. It is an accurate reproduction of her 1902 tale. It would be suitable for reading with one child, as it is a very small book.*
3. Potter, B. (1988). *The tale of Peter Rabbit.* Saxonville, MA: Rabbit Ears Books. *This version of* The Tale of Peter Rabbit *is done with beautiful illustrations that fill a traditionally sized children's picture book. This text may be more appropriate for classroom use or for use with a small group of children who would like to see the pictures. The detail in the illustrations allows the audience to visualize the narrative in much more detail.*
4. Williams, M. (1985). *The velveteen rabbit.* New York: Random House. *A little boy loves his toy rabbit so much that it becomes "Real." The rabbit goes everywhere with the little boy and enjoys the summer. One time when the rabbit is outside he meets two real rabbits who tease him because he cannot jump or do the things that rabbits do. The little boy becomes very ill with scarlet fever and the Velveteen Rabbit must be burned. Before he is tossed in the fire a fairy comes and transforms the toy rabbit into a wild rab-*

bit. This story is well loved because of the way it conveys a sense of belonging and nurturing that is so important in everyone's life.

5. Zolotow, C. (1962). *Mr. Rabbit and the lovely present.* New York: Harper and Row. *In this tale a little girl visits a rabbit to find a very special gift for her mother's birthday. She mentions the colors that her mother loves, and the rabbit gives many suggestions for each color. Finally, the girl chooses a basket of fruit that represents the various colors that she wants to incorporate into her gift. She fills her basket with green pears, yellow bananas, red apples, and blue grapes. Mr. Rabbit has been a big help to the girl, and he is sure that her mother will have a wonderful birthday.*

Software Resources

Many of the following software titles have won awards of excellence, and come highly recommended by classroom teachers.

Hop to It

Company: Sunburst
Computer: Apple
Grade Level: K–3

A bunny hops back and forth to solve number sentences. The rabbit collects food along the way. Multiple solutions are possible.

Project Zoo

Company: National Geographic Society
Computer: Apple
Grade Level: 3–5

A multimedia courseware package that contains an entire teaching unit. Children use maps to explore a zoo and interpret data to guess mystery animals. They gather information, graph it, and learn what animals need to survive in a zoo. The final project involves working in teams to design a zoo.

Clowning Around

Company: Learning Technologies
Computer: Apple
Grade Level: K–3

Young children solve problems by remembering which clown pictures appeared in certain boxes. The format allows children to work independently.

Counting Parade

Company: Spinnaker
Computer: Apple
Grade Level: K–2

Children match numbers by depositing the right number of toucans in various palm trees. High-quality graphics and sound maintain interest throughout the program.

Patterns

Company: MECC
Computer: Apple
Grade Level: K–2

Children complete patterns consisting of objects and animated characters or sounds on four levels of difficulty. The program allows children to create their own patterns. The software program gives good feedback on errors.

Easy Street

Company: Mindplay
Computer: Apple
Grade Level: Pre K–2

Children visit stores and purchase items by counting out pennies. An optional sound feature enables the program to "talk" children through the activities.

Clock Works

Company: MECC
Computer: Apple, IBM
Grade Level: 1–3

This program offers a variety of activities with multiple difficulty levels that will have kids telling time quickly. Lessons include reading and setting clocks and converting time expressions with either Roman or Arabic faces. After mastering both analog and digital timekeeping, students can design their own clocks.

Counting Critters

Company: MECC
Computer: Apple
Grade Level: Preschool–K

Fun-filled lessons in numbers from 1 to 20. Children count animals on a safari, match numbers in a magic show, supply a pet store with puppies, and much more. The teacher can adjust the program for children with different keyboarding abilities.

Logo

Company: Logo Computer Systems
(Highgate Springs, VT 95460)
Computer: Apple
Grade Level: 3 and up

Logo Plus

Company: Terrapin Software
Computer: Apple
Grade Level: 2 and up

Children learn to move a cursor called a turtle by using commands. Drawings are made, and new commands are created. Logo mastery requires substantial time and effort on the part of both teachers and children if mathematical learning is to take place.

Balancing Bear

Company: Sunburst
Computer: Apple
Grade Level: K–4

A friendly bear encourages students to find combinations of numbered weights that will balance the beam or that will be greater than or less than a given weight. This software allows for a variety of levels of difficulty from Easy to Blockbuster, provides options for using words and/or symbols, and even allows teachers to challenge their students to dabble with mystery numbers and impossible problems. All in all, it adds up to an increased understanding of addition and inequalities.

The Pond

Company: Sunburst
Computer: Apple
Grade Level: 2–Adult

A frog leaps through a maze of lily pads. Can your students identify the pattern that leads to the magic lily pad? An enjoyable method for teaching students to organize information, uncover two-, three-, and four-step patterns, and describe the patterns mathematically.

Gertrude's Secret

Company: The Learning Company
Computer: Apple
Grade Level: K–3

This classic program develops logical thinking and is suitable for use with very young children. It is available as part of a bundle, with Mop Town Parade (math and reading) and Bumble Games (math).

Index